THE
Country Music
Lover's
GUIDE TO THE U.S.A.

Janet Byron

ST. MARTIN'S GRIFFIN
NEW YORK

IN MEMORY OF MY FATHER, JULES BYRON (1935–1992)

THE COUNTRY MUSIC LOVER'S GUIDE TO THE U.S.A. Copyright © 1996 by Janet Byron. All rights reserved. Printed in the United States of America. No part of this book may be used or reproduced in any manner whatsoever without written permission except in the case of brief quotations embodied in critical articles or reviews. For information, address St. Martin's Press, 175 Fifth Avenue, New York, NY 10010.

Book Design by Bonni Leon-Berman

All photos by Janet Byron except where noted.

Library of Congress Cataloging-in-Publication Data

Byron, Janet.
    The country music lover's guide to the U.S.A. / Janet Byron.
  —1st ed.
      p. cm.
   ISBN 0-312-14300-1
    1. Country music—Guidebooks.   2. United States—Guidebooks.
  3. Musical landmarks—United States.   I. Title.
  ML3524.B983   1996
  781.642'025'73—dc20   96-10605
                                         CIP
                                         MN

First St. Martin's Griffin Edition: July 1996

10 9 8 7 6 5 4 3 2 1

THE
Country Music
Lover's
GUIDE TO THE U.S.A.

Contents

Acknowledgments

A MILLION THANKS to editor Anne Savarese, Helen Packard, and everyone at St. Martin's Press; literary agent Philip Spitzer; Beth Weintraub, Paul Schor, Mollie Boero, and many other friends who encouraged me from the beginning; Anne Paine and Jazz, for their never-ending hospitality and companionship; and my mother, Elaine Byron, who is very excited about having an author in the family.

For their editorial assistance and advice, more thanks to Paul Schor, Elaine Byron, Scott Byron, Harriet Heyman, Margaret Dadian, Tim Wells, Jerilyn Watson, Tommy Goldsmith, Laura Bergheim, Dave Dunton, and George and Marianne Vescey.

Strangers are only friends you haven't met yet. My deep appreciation goes out to kind new friends met during my travels. In particular, Mary Wallace in Georgiana, Alabama, hometown of Hank Williams; Jimmy and Cleda Driftwood in Mountain View, Arkansas; Hal Miller and Rooster in Owensboro, Kentucky; and Ron Stein of Bubba's Bagel Nosh in Fort Worth, Texas.

Dozens of people around the country, too many to name, provided invaluable assistance in the form of information, interviews, tours, directions, advice, and insights, as well as warm welcomes to their attractions, shows, and towns. Thanks to all.

Introduction

During nearly three years of working on this book, the question most often asked of me was, "Do you like country music?"

I guess I'm not the stereotypical country fan, if there is such a thing. I grew up in a suburb of New York City and currently live in Washington, D.C. I'm a journalist by trade, and have spent most of my career writing about a variety of other issues.

Early on, my parents transferred their love of travel to me. When my brothers and I were kids we would all pile into the family station wagon and drive places, always a little farther afield. Between semesters of graduate school in California, I drove back and forth across the country six or seven times, taking the backroads as much as possible. In 1990, I took a southern route to spend the summer as an intern for the Nashville *Tennessean,* and fell in love with that city. In 1991, I visited my fiftieth state, Vermont. On those long drives across deserts, mountains, cornfields, and plains, I listened to country music. (There's *always* a country station!)

I knew that besides being the most devoted, energetic, and passionate fans, country music lovers will go anywhere, and often build vacations around their favorite stars. In writing this book, my goal was to tell travelers about out-of-the-way places, such as the cabin where Loretta Lynn grew up in Paintsville, Kentucky, or the Hank Williams Museum in Georgiana, Alabama, and to offer guidance on popular destinations like Nashville, Branson, and Pigeon Forge.

This is the first travel guide for country music lovers that covers the entire United States, and a few spots in Canada. I have defined "country music" broadly to include bluegrass, cowboy song and poetry, folk, Western swing, Cajun, rockabilly, and more. Numerous attractions, large and small, are listed, including theme parks, memorials, halls of fame, museums, stars' hometowns, and historical sites.

In towns and cities across America, country music shows, jamborees, and "little Oprys" take place regularly on weekend evenings or nightly. Very often, little Oprys serve as training grounds for up-and-coming stars, or showcase multitalented local folks. Many are run by families (the Salt River Opry in Hannibal, Missouri, features nine members of the Eber family!) and provide inexpensive entertainment in a pleasant environment with no alcohol or smoking. I have also featured several tourist towns that offer a cluster of country music shows, such as Nashville, Indiana; Hot Springs, Arkansas; and Custer, South Dakota.

Hundreds of music festivals take place annually in the United States and Canada. I have not attempted to catalogue them, but do point out festivals wherever possible. The magazine *Dirty Linen* (P.O. Box 66600, Baltimore, MD 21239; (410) 583-7973) lists numerous folk and country festivals, while *Bluegrass Unlimited* (P.O. Box 111, Broad Run, VA 22014; (800) 258-4727) catalogues bluegrass events.

Now, back to that initial question.

Yes, I love country music! I love all kinds: traditional, New Traditional, bluegrass, newgrass, folk, old timey, Western Swing, Western Beat, honky tonk, singing cowboys, country blues, and contemporary country. Over the years, I have been particularly inspired by the music of Hank Williams, Jimmie Rodgers, Lucinda Williams, Ernest Tubb, Alison Krauss, Kevin Welch, Jim Lauderdale, Emmylou Harris, Johnny Cash, and Loretta Lynn. I listened to Robert Earl Keen's *Gringo Honeymoon* more than two hundred times while working on this book.

During the past decade, my love for country music has taken me over more than 15,000 miles of road to many exciting country music attractions and shows. I am eager to hear how you enjoyed places described here, to correct mistakes, and learn about new destinations. Please contact me c/o *The Country Music Lover's Guide to the U.S.A.*, St. Martin's Press, 175 Fifth Avenue, New York, NY 10010. I hope that this book guides you to some wonderful adventures!

—Janet Byron

AUTHOR'S NOTE

Attractions are listed by state, generally from north to south and east to west within the state. Directions are provided from the nearest interstate or highway. "I-10" is U.S. Interstate 10; "Hwy. 10" is U.S. Highway 10; "Rt. 10" represents state route or road 10. Where no specific street address is listed, the town is so small that there is none: If you find the town, you can't miss the attraction. I strongly recommend getting off the interstate whenever possible. The backroads are much more interesting, and fun.

I've made every effort to make sure that the information is correct, but keep in mind that things change. Museums close; prices go up or down; hours are expanded or limited; theaters are bought and sold. Please protect yourself, and your vacation, by calling ahead before traveling long distances.

Alabama

Fort Payne
GREETINGS FROM THE SOCK CAPITAL OF THE WORLD

A member of Alabama, the most successful country group of all time, once quipped that band members decided to take a shot at stardom because "it sure beat working the swing shift in a sock factory."

The boys' hometown of Fort Payne, Alabama, "Sock Capital of the World," does make a mess of socks; more than 150 factories produce millions every year. As if that weren't enough, Fort Payne (pop. 14,000) holds the record for baking the "World's Largest Cake": 128,238 pounds, 8 ounces.

But when Alabama burst onto the country scene in 1980, they did more to put Fort Payne on the map than lots of socks or a really big cake ever could. Tens of thousands of fans pour into Fort Payne every summer for Alabama's **June Jam,** a weeklong festival ending with a star-studded concert. And throughout the year, thousands visit **Alabama's Fan Club Headquarters and Museum.**

Fort Payne is located in the hilly northeast corner of Alabama. First cousins Randy Owen and Teddy Gentry started singing at Lookout Mountain Holiness Church, while their distant cousin Jeff Cook began performing in grade school. Drummer Mark Herndon, a military brat from the Northeast, was recruited later on.

The band, then known as Wild Country, left town in 1973 for a bar called the Bowery in Myrtle Beach, South Carolina. They played six nights a week for tips, honing their skills and three-part harmonies. After paying their dues for a decade, they were discovered at a Nashville showcase in 1979 and signed by RCA in 1980.

The rest is history. Alabama instantly shot to the top of the charts, and has since sold more than 45 million recordings. On August 3, 1985, Alabama broke a record held by Sonny James with their seventeenth consecutive number-one hit, "40-Hour Week (for a Livin')." They sent four more songs to the top of the charts for a total of twenty-one in a row. They were named Entertainers of the Year eight times by the Country Music Association and the Academy of Country Music. (ACM even created an "Artist of the Decade" category for them at the end of the eighties.) Well into the nineties, Alabama was still charting hits with such likable songs as "Pass It On Down" and "Cheap Seats."

Instead of building their mansions in the Nashville suburbs or Hollywood hills, the boys quickly returned to Fort Payne (Herndon settled down in Myrtle Beach). All four have busy second careers as Fort Payne boosters, devoting countless hours toward promoting and improving the town. The first June Jam was staged here for fans in 1981.

Since then, June Jam has raised millions of dollars for local charitable causes. At the same time, the Fort Payne community has responded with spirit, supplying thousands of volunteers.

June Jam has grown into a ten-day event in early June, capped by a huge concert on the forty-acre field behind Fort Payne High School. In addition to local acts, some of the biggest stars in country music perform. Pre-concert charity events include Randy Owen's Celebrity Golf Tournament, the Jeff Cook Celebrity Bass Tournament, and a popular VIP Softball Game. A "Salute to Alabama" parade, talent search, beauty pageant, and crafts festival are held during Jam Week. Concert tickets $30; (205) 845-9300.

If you're in Fort Payne, spend a few hours at the Alabama Fan Club and Museum, or a whole day satisfying the need for all things Alabama. The museum features displays and memorabilia for each of the band members. Song lyrics are displayed on large glass panels, and dozens of awards and photographs line the walls.

In a twenty-minute film narrated by Lorianne Crook, Owen eats sorghum and butter on buttermilk biscuits at his granny's house; Gentry gives a tour of the DeKalb County Library (built by Alabama) and introduces his paw-paw (Burt Eller), who raised him. The fan club and gift shop displays scrapbooks with current photos and newspaper clippings and every kind of Alabama souvenir imaginable.

Alabama is genuinely loved in Fort Payne, not just for their talent and charitable works but because they're still a bunch of great guys. "They just come and go like anyone," says Mary, who has worked for more than a decade at Alabama headquarters. "People here know them and they're just a part of the town."

At the gift-shop counter, ask for a free map with directions to local sites, including:

- Owen's "Feels So Right" homestead
- Cook's castle (built with stone quarried locally)
- Gentry's house, up the road from Owen's
- Burt's Barn (Paw-Paw died in 1995)
- Little River Canyon National Preserve, the canyon in the song "Pass It On Down"

Downtown points of interest include the 1891 Fort Payne Depot and the Fort Payne Opera House, built in 1889. The **DeKalb County Southern Mountain Festival** over Labor Day weekend usually includes a fiddlers' convention, arts and crafts, and a fishing derby; (205) 845-3957.

GETTING THERE: Fort Payne is about 50 miles southwest of Chattanooga, Tennessee. Alabama's Fan Club is open Monday through Saturday, 8 A.M. to 4 P.M., and Sundays, noon to 4 P.M. Closed Easter, Thanksgiving, Christmas, and New Year's Day. Museum admission $3 for adults, $1.50 for children. Allow an hour. Take I-59/Exit 222 to Hwy. 11 five miles through town. 101 Glen Blvd. SW; (205) 845-1646.

For information on Fort Payne area and June Jam Week events, call (205) 845-2741.

Athens

TENNESSEE VALLEY OLD-TIME FIDDLERS' CONVENTION

The Tennessee Valley Old-Time Fiddlers' Convention the first full weekend in October is the flagship of mid-South fiddlers' conventions and has sparked renewed interest in authentic old-time music. This two-day festival includes more than fifteen competition categories in music and dancing, crafts, and concessions at Athens State College campus, west of Huntsville. Take I-65/Exit 351 to Hwy. 72 west; (205) 233-8205.

Tuscumbia

STARS DO FALL ON ALABAMA

Rhythm and blues, country, rock and roll, and gospel are a vital part of Alabama's cultural history. To honor and preserve its rich musical heritage, Alabama established the nonprofit **Alabama Music Hall of Fame and Museum** in 1985. In 1990, the Museum opened its doors in Tuscumbia, in the northwest corner of the state. The location is no accident. The quad-cities of Tuscumbia, Muscle Shoals, Florence, and Sheffield make up the Muscle Shoals area, home of the world-famous "Muscle Shoals Sound" and a legendary rhythm-and-blues recording industry. The scene took off after Percy Sledge, a local hospital orderly, recorded "When a Man Loves a Woman" in 1965. Subsequently, Aretha Franklin, Arthur Alexander, Willie Nelson, Paul Simon, Hank Williams, Jr., Wilson Pickett, Larry Gatlin, Delbert McClinton, and the Rolling Stones recorded here.

The museum is housed in an unattractive warehouse-style building along a Tuscumbia highway. Don't be put off, though. Inside, there's a spacious $2.5 million museum that tells the fascinating story of Alabama's musical past in an educational and entertaining style.

The museum starts off with a "walk of stars," followed by the Hall of Fame. Exhibits include Elvis's original contract with Sun Records, a tour bus used by the band Alabama, wax figures, stage costumes, and memorabilia accompanied by video and text. Several interactive displays allow visitors to sample the sounds. Standing in the center of a huge guitar, you can hear country songs like "D-I-V-O-R-C-E," "Your Cheatin' Heart," and "Next to You, Next to Me." When completed, the complex will include the Alabama Research Library on Southern Music and a 1,200-seat auditorium.

Annual events include the **Harvest Jam**, a large concert the second Saturday in September, and induction banquets in odd-numbered years in mid-January.

The Muscle Shoals area offers several other attractions, including Helen Keller's birthplace in Tuscumbia, (205) 383-4066; and bluesman W. C. Handy's birthplace in Florence, (205) 766-6434.

Tennessee River Fiddlers' Convention in Florence's McFarland Park usually takes place the first weekend in May, with music and dance competitions, a crafts fair, and a concert; (205) 760-6416.

GETTING THERE: Tuscumbia is about 125 miles northwest of Birmingham. The Alabama Music Hall of Fame and Museum is open Monday through Saturday, 9 A.M. to 5 P.M., and Sunday, 1 to 5 P.M. Admission $6. Allow two hours. Hwy. 72 west; (800) 239-AMHF or (205) 381-4417.

Montgomery
MEMORIES OF HANK

Hank Williams certainly made an impression during his thirty years on earth, catapulting to stardom on the *Grand Ole Opry* in 1949, recording timeless compositions like "I'm So Lonesome I Could Cry" and "Your Cheatin' Heart," living hard, and dying young on New Year's Day in 1953.

For the people in Georgiana, where Hank was born, and Montgomery, where he came of age and was laid to rest, the memories are more personal. No one in this part of Alabama asks whether you mean "Junior" or "Senior" when you mention Hank Williams and everyone you meet who's older than fifty has a story.

"My husband Bill went to Hank's funeral," says the manager of a hotel downtown.

"My sister's first husband played in a band with Hank," a docent in a museum offers. "The place they played was rough, and I had to sneak out because my father wouldn't let me go there."

A man selling peaches by the interstate says he worked at the Montgomery mortuary that dressed Hank's body in 1953, and that Hank's mother and ex-wife Audrey fought like alley cats.

"I remember seeing Hank downtown on Saturdays," says Harold Sellers, owner of a truck stop in Georgiana. "He'd be leaning against one of those pillars at the station, and he would slide around them to keep from talking to anybody. He was a lonely person."

Talking to people who remember Hank is one of the highlights of visiting the southern Alabama communities where he grew up. Hank's boyhood home is open to the public in Georgiana (*see page 11*). In 1937, Hank's mother Lillian moved the family from Greenville to Montgomery, the state capital. Hank was fourteen years old, a sickly but cocky kid who formed his own band called Hank and Hezzy and began singing on local radio stations.

The following are suggested stops on a "Hank Tour" of Montgomery. Stop by the **Visitors' Center,** 401 Madison Ave., to pick up free city maps.

* Hank won a talent show at the **Empire Theatre** (Montgomery and Molton Streets) in 1938 with a song he wrote called "WPA Blues." The movie house is closed, but a historical marker in front labels Williams the "Alabama Troubadour." (The flip side of this marker commemorates the spot where civil-rights pioneer Rosa Parks sparked the Montgomery bus boycott in 1955.)

* Thousands of people crowded into Montgomery's old **Municipal Auditorium** (North Perry and Madison) for Hank's funeral on January 4, 1953, including Ernest Tubb, Roy Acuff, Bill Monroe, and Webb Pierce. More than 20,000 mourners crowded the streets outside. Hank had performed here many times.

* Hank Williams, Jr., placed a **Hank Williams Statue** in the plaza across the street from the municipal auditorium in 1991. The life-size bronze statue shows Hank playing his guitar and wearing his famous "musical note" suit. (Lister Hill Plaza, North Perry St. and Madison Ave.)

The Hank Williams Memorial stands in Montgomery's Oakwood Cemetery Annex.

* Hank's mother once operated a **boardinghouse** in downtown Montgomery at 114 S. Perry St. A parking garage is on the site now.

* The **Alabama Department of Archives and History** has a small Hank Williams display on the third floor with a portrait, stage costume, and guitar. The exhibit quotes Williams's collaborator

Fred Rose: "Music, women, and drinking were the three strong-
est influences in Hank's life." The archives are located on Alabama's Capitol Hill; admission is free. Open 8 A.M. to 5 P.M.,
Monday through Friday, and 9 A.M. to 5 P.M. Saturdays, 624
Washington Ave.; (334) 242-4363.

* Hank's final resting place is in **Oakwood Cemetery Annex,** on a
hill overlooking the city. The elaborate **Hank Williams Memorial** features tall twin marble monuments to "Hank and Audrey"
standing in an Astroturf-lined enclosure. (Remember that Hank
was married to Billie Jean Jones Eshilman, not Audrey, when he
died!) Hank's marker is engraved with "Praise the Lord, I Saw
the Light" and hit song titles. A footstone with a cowboy hat
remembers Hank's gospel-singing alter ego, Luke the Drifter.

Poems are engraved on the backs of the monuments, including
one from Audrey to Hank which begins, "There are no words in
the dictionary that can express my love for you," and others from
Hank Jr. and his half sister Lycrecia to Audrey. Hank's mother is
buried just outside the enclosure under a simple stone that reads
"Mother." Open daily. Follow the signs from the Annex entrance
at 1304 Upper Wetumpka Rd.

The Hank Williams, Sr., International Fan Club hosts a **birthday
celebration** on the weekend closest to September 17. A concert and
memorial service are held in Montgomery on Friday night and Saturday morning, and the party continues in Georgiana on Saturday
and Sunday.

Montgomery is a gracious, clean city of about 200,000 people,
finally rebounding from the turbulence of the fifties and sixties.
It's a charming place to visit, with numerous attractions, including
a modern barrier-free zoo, the state capitol, historic sites, civil-
rights memorials, art and science museums, and performing arts
venues. (You have to love a city that prints its slogan "Hey Y'All!!"
on T-shirts.) The **Montgomery Visitors' Center,** in an 1850s mansion, supplies free maps and brochures. 401 Madison Ave.; (334)
262-0013.

Next door, **Old Alabama Town** is a living history museum of central Alabama life during the nineteenth century, with three blocks of
homes and period buildings. An **acoustic country jam session** takes

place here on the second Saturday of each month. Open daily, except major holidays. Call for hours. 310 N. Hull St.; (334) 240-4500.

GETTING THERE: Montgomery is in central Alabama at I-65 and I-85, 95 miles south of Birmingham and 160 miles southwest of Atlanta, Georgia. Call (334) 240-9455 or 262-0013.

Georgiana
HANK WILLIAMS'S BOYHOOD HOME AND MUSEUM

When I met Mary Wallace at the Hank Williams, Sr., International Fan Club booth during Fan Fair, she urged me to visit Hank Williams's Boyhood Home and Museum in Georgiana. "Come and sit on the porch and we'll rock, and I'll tell you stories about Hank," she promised. "We're going to put Georgiana on the map."

Mary Wallace, founder of the Hank Williams, Sr., International Fan Club, gives tours of Hank Williams's Boyhood Home and Museum, which features a handmade Hank Williams quilt.

A native of Georgiana, Wallace is a spunky, persuasive woman who's also the self-proclaimed "Number-One Female Fan of Hank Williams." "My parents embedded the love of Hank in me," she explains. "I remember when I heard 'Hey, Good Lookin' ' I would jump up and run to the radio and listen. I thought he was singing to me."

The house and museum were opened to the public in 1993, due to tireless efforts of Wallace, a corps of devoted fans, and Georgiana officials.

The day the city bought Williams's former home at 127 Rose St. in 1991, Wallace had the idea for the fan club. It now has nearly 1,000 members. "The purpose is to get artifacts for the museum and promote the memory of Hank," says Wallace, who runs the club from Georgiana.

Club president Beecher "Junior" O'Quinn could be called the "Number-One Male Fan of Hank Williams." O'Quinn says one of his goals is to "bring out the good stuff Hank did" and refute Williams's image as a "hard-drinking SOB."

"He did drink, but he wasn't a seven-days-a-week drunk," O'Quinn says. "The fact is, the man was a genius, probably the greatest singer and songwriter of all time."

Young Hiram Williams (he took the name "Hank" later) was seven when his house across town burned to the ground in 1930. A prominent citizen offered the seven-room Rose Street place to the Williams family, who stayed five years rent-free. Georgiana spent a year restoring the house to the way it was back then.

Now a wooden Indian out front welcomes visitors and there are white rockers and a swing on the front porch. Inside, the house is full of genuine treasures donated by fans or secured by Wallace: Hank's first recordings on the Sterling label, "Calling You" and "Never Again Will I Knock On Your Door"; custom-made curtains printed with the lyrics to "Your Cheatin' Heart"; the bench young Hiram stood on to sing beside his mother at Mt. Olive Baptist Church; and Hank's shoeshine box. Also on display are many rare photographs, album covers, and sheet music.

One day a woman from Oklahoma named Betty Robinson showed up with an incredible 44-panel Hank Williams quilt. The project took her a year. "If you do not know the story of Hank Williams, you can read it on this quilt," Wallace says.

Thigpen's Log Cabin, an Alabama roadhouse where Hank played, was moved behind the museum to **Hank Williams Park.** It is used as a stage for two annual festivals, **Hank Williams Day** the first Friday night and Saturday in June, and **Hank Williams's Birthday Celebration** around September 17. Jett Williams, Hank's daughter, often performs with members of her father's band, the Drifting Cowboys.

Mt. Olive, where Hank was born, is a few miles away. From Georgiana, take I-65 south to Mt. Olive/Garland exit to Rte. 7 (Hank Williams Memorial Drive). **Mt. Olive Baptist Church**, where Hank first sang, is on the left, a small white building to the left of the main church. Farther down the road, the spot where the Williams's original log home stood can be viewed from the road. It's on the right, to the left of a red barn with two white horses painted on the front.

Mary Wallace, this is for you. Here's hoping millions of Hank fans have no trouble finding Georgiana on the map.

GETTING THERE: Georgiana is about 60 miles south of Montgomery. The museum is open daily in the summer, 10 A.M. to 5 P.M. Closed Monday and Tuesday in the winter, but appointments can be made. Admission $3. Allow one hour. Take I-65/Exit 114 to Rte. 106 east. Look for signs. 127 Rose St.; (334) 376-2555.

Contact the Hank Williams, Sr., International Fan Club at P.O. Box 280, Georgiana, AL 36033.

Alaska

Fairbanks
ATHABASCAN OLD-TIME FIDDLING FESTIVAL

The four-day Athabascan Old-Time Fiddling Festival in Fairbanks features dozens of Athabascan and Eskimo fiddlers, singers, and dancers. Held annually since 1983 on the second weekend in November, this festival is a testament to the far-reaching appeal of traditional music. Many of the musicians are skilled Native hunters and fishermen by trade, who must fly into Fairbanks during the off season to perform. Events include dances, performances all day and well into the night, and a banquet. Contact the Athabascan Fiddlers Association, 409 4th Ave., Fairbanks, AK 99704; (907) 452-8479 or 452-1825.

Arizona

Valentine
COUNTRY DANCING ON ROUTE 66

On a barren stretch of historic Route 66 in northwest Arizona, a small beer joint called **Country Dancing** offers live music every Saturday night. Country Dancing is run by Darlyn and Mervin Dwiggins and their son, Moe. During the summer, roping contests take place every few weeks in the Valentine Arena behind the bar, followed by a potluck supper.

While in mid-May and early October, the Dwigginses host their **Country Music Jamboree,** a free weekend of picking and singing. Saturday night is an old-fashioned potluck supper, followed by a cowboy breakfast for $5 on Sunday morning. "We have a ball," Darlyn Dwiggins says. RVs and tents are welcome for dry camping (restrooms are available inside the bar).

While in Seligman, don't miss **Delgadillo's Snow Cap,** the goofiest and most colorful ice cream and burger joint on Route 66. Juan Delgadillo will do his best to embarrass and crack you up with "the treatment," his famous routine of cornball humor and practical jokes; (520) 422-3291.

The old-fashioned barbershop next door is run by Juan's brother, Angel Delgadillo. The shop displays Rte. 66 memorabilia, sells souvenirs, and gives haircuts.

GETTING THERE: Valentine is between Seligman and Kingman in northwest Arizona. Country Dancing is open from 10 A.M. to 1 A.M. Take I-40/Exit 123 to Rte. 66 west to Milepost 83; (520) 769-2627.

Prescott

ARIZONA JAMBOREE

Prescott twice served as Arizona's pre-statehood territorial capital. The resort town is known for its Victorian homes and Whiskey Row, a city block once lined with saloons. *Arizona Jamboree* is presented on weekend evenings June through September, Thanksgiving weekend, and in December. This two-hour variety show features country music and comedy. Tickets $9.50. Prescott College—Elks Theatre, Cortez and Gurley Streets; (520) 445-1160.

Prescott's **Frontier Days Celebration and Rodeo** during Fourth of July week is said to be the nation's first public rodeo, begun in 1888. **Prescott Bluegrass Festival** takes place in June or July.

GETTING THERE: Prescott is 95 miles north of Phoenix. Take I-40 to Hwy. 89, or I-17 to Rte. 69. Contact the Prescott Chamber of Commerce; (800) 266-7534 or (520) 445-2000.

Phoenix Area

WILD WEST TOWNS AND MUSIC SHOWS

Red River Opry in Tempe is Arizona's premier country-music show, presented year-round in a 1,000-seat, state-of-the-art venue southwest of Phoenix. Three different shows are offered: *Spirit of America,* a fast-paced variety show with a mix of country, gospel, bluegrass, pop, and nostalgia; *Legends of Country Music,* paying tribute to classic singers like Hank Williams, George Jones, and Tammy Wynette; and the seasonal *Christmas Jubilee.* Tickets $14.50 per show. Take 202 Freeway. 730 Mill Ave.; (800) 466-OPRY or (602) 829-OPRY.

In Mesa, 20 miles east of Tempe, **Rockin' R Ranch** is a working family-owned ranch with a Wild West town, staged shoot-outs, and a petting zoo. The Rockin' R Wranglers present Western stage shows most nights at the Chuckwagon Dinner Theatre and Cowboy Steakhouse. Call for schedules. Take I-10 or I-17 to Hwy 60/360 east (Superstition Freeway), right on Power, then right on Baseline; (602) 832-1539.

In Scottsdale, **Rawhide** calls itself "The West's Most Western

Town." Visitors take stagecoach rides through an 1880s town full of good guys and bad guys, shoot-outs, crooked card dealers, and raucous saloons. Amusements include panning for gold, a shooting gallery, rodeos, and burro rides. The Rawhide Steakhouse serves full dinners with a Wild West show. Guests can also take chuckwagon rides into the desert for a meal and entertainment. Festivals, rodeos, and dances take place throughout the year. Call for schedules and reservations. Take I-17 to Bell Rd. east to Rawhide. 23023 N. Scottsdale Rd.; (602) 502-1880.

Tucson
BEST OF THE OLD WEST

Attractions in Tucson, a city in southeast Arizona, include wildlife, history and art museums, historic sites, parks, and botanical gardens. Since 1971, the Camp family has offered hearty chuckwagon suppers accompanied by songs and stories of the Old West on their turn-of-the-century **Triple C Ranch.** The show takes place in a rustic building at the foot of the Tucson Mountains. Open nightly, December through April. (The Triple C Wranglers perform at the Bar J in Jackson Hole, Wyoming, Memorial Day through Labor Day.) Reservations required. Admission $13. 8900 West Bopp Rd.; (800) 446-1798 or (520) 883-2333.

Old Tucson Studios is an 1860s town built for the 1939 movie *Arizona.* More than 300 films, TV episodes, and commercials were filmed here, including the movie *Young Guns.* A major fire severely damaged the studios in 1995; the park is being rebuilt and is expected to reopen to the public in late 1996. Amusements include musical reviews, gunfights, stagecoach rides, and a mine. Call for information. Take I-19 to Rt. 86 west (Ajo Way); (520) 883-0100.

GETTING THERE: Tucson is 120 miles southeast of Phoenix at I-10 and I-19. Contact the Visitors Bureau; (800) 638-8350 or (520) 624-1817.

Willcox

REX ALLEN ARIZONA COWBOY MUSEUM AND FESTIVAL

Rex Allen, the last of Hollywood's singing cowboys, originally tried his luck on the rodeo circuit but quickly realized that playing the guitar was more fun and a lot safer. He got his start on the WLS Barn Dance in Chicago and went on to star in nineteen movies for Republic Pictures between 1950 and 1954.

Known as the "Arizona Cowboy," Allen spent thirty-five years recording for Decca, and had hits with songs like "Streets of Laredo" and "Tiny Bubbles." He is also known for his Purina and Tony Lama commercials, the television series *Frontier Doctor,* and narration for Walt Disney nature films and 150 cartoon-character voices.

The Rex Allen Arizona Cowboy Museum in Willcox, just two blocks from where Allen was born and raised, chronicles his career with memorabilia, posters, and photos. Housed in an 1890s adobe building, the museum includes the Willcox Cowboy Hall of Fame, which pays tribute to the region's real ranchers.

Willcox staged its first **Rex Allen Days** in 1951. In the early seventies, Allen handed the reins to his son, Rex Allen, Jr., a singer who starred on The Nashville Network's *Statler Brothers Show* and now hosts its successful spin-off, *Yesteryear.* (The younger Allen gave his first singing performance at the Willcox Theatre during Rex Allen Days.) The four-day festival, held the first full weekend in October, includes a Rex Allen concert, parade, rodeo, country fair, and more.

GETTING THERE: Willcox is 85 miles east of Tucson on I-10. The museum is open 10 A.M. to 4 P.M. daily. Admission $2. Allow an hour. Take I-10/Exit 340. Turn right on Bus. I-10, then left at the light, and left again to 155 N. Railroad Ave.; (520) 384-4583.

Arkansas

Arkansas Ozarks

Mammoth Spring
INSPIRATION FOR THE *GRAND OLE OPRY*

A few years after World War I, a young reporter for the Memphis *Commercial Appeal* named George D. Hay was sent to Mammoth Spring to cover the funeral of a war hero. As Hay related the story, a farmer invited him to a "hoedown" in a cabin up a muddy road.

"He and two other musicians furnished the early rhythm," Hay wrote years later. "About twenty people came. There was a coal-oil lamp in one corner of the cabin and another one in the 'kitty corner.' No one in the world has ever had more fun than those Ozark mountaineers did that night.

"It stuck with me until the idea became the *Grand Ole Opry* seven or eight years later."

Hay moved to Chicago, where he became a radio announcer and started the *WLS Barn Dance,* then became WSM's station director in Nashville. On November 28, 1925, he went on the air calling himself "The Solemn Old Judge" and launched the *WSM Barn Dance,* which he later renamed the *Grand Ole Opry.*

Mammoth Spring displays a huge "Inspiration for the *Grand Ole Opry*" sign at the entrances to town on Rte. 9 and Hwy. 63, and celebrates **Solemn Old Judge Days** over Labor Day weekend. The festival usually includes a historical play about Hay, fiddle and dance contests, and a headline country concert.

Mammoth Spring Country Music Association expected to open its new building in 1996. Dances with live bands are planned for Saturday nights, as well as additional weekly concerts, events, and festivals. The building is on Hwy. 63, about ¼ mile south of Rte. 9. Call (501) 625-3988 for schedules.

One of the world's largest natural springs is in **Mammoth Spring**

State Park, which includes a visitors' center with exhibits, a short walking trail, a railroad museum, and picnic facilities. Hwy. 63 and Rte. 9; (501) 625-7364.

Mammoth Spring's **Main Street,** on Rte. 9, has several restaurants and stores selling antiques and collectibles. In 1912, outlaw Ben Jones was gunned down here while trying to rob a bank. A historical marker and some bizarre photographs of the scene, with citizens milling around the body, are displayed across from City Hall.

GETTING THERE: Mammoth Spring is on the Missouri border at Thayer, about 110 miles east of Branson, Missouri. Take Hwy. 63 or Rte. 289. Contact the Mammoth Spring Chamber of Commerce; (501) 625-3312 or 625-3378.

Salem
MAKING OZARK MUSIC

Two free country, folk, and bluegrass shows are offered year-round on Saturday nights in Salem, a small town in north-central Arkansas. The Salem Country Music Association puts on the **Saturday Night Jamboree,** featuring the local band Southfork Express and guest performers. There's plenty of room for dancing at Southfork Music Hall, a half-mile east of Rte. 9 on Hwy. 62.

Ozark Mountain Music Makers, organized in 1964, is a nonprofit organization that offers all bands, musicians, and singers a standing invitation to perform onstage. Jig-dancing is encouraged at the 500-seat Music Barn, one mile east of Rte. 9 on Hwy. 62.

GETTING THERE: Salem is 20 miles west of Mammoth Spring and 10 miles south of the Missouri border. Take Hwy. 62 or Rte. 9. For information, contact the Salem Chamber of Commerce; (501) 895-3478.

Mountain View

2 MILES AHEAD, 50 YEARS BEHIND

A cartoon in Mountain View's tourist office shows Snuffy Smith riding a donkey toward a sign that reads, "Mountain View—2 miles ahead, 50 years behind." A small town (pop. 2,439) in the heart of Arkansas' Ozark Mountains, Mountain View is a sort of Brigadoon, where folk music lovers can take a giant step back in time.

Here in the "Folk Music Capital of the World," **Ozark Folk Center State Park** does not allow music written after 1940 to be played at its concerts. Twice a week at the **Jimmy Driftwood Barn,** the legendary octogenarian folk singer and his friends gather to sing Stephen Foster and Jimmie Rodgers songs. Every night, pickers and singers meet at the Stone County Courthouse Square for impromptu acoustic jams.

To be sure, tourism is booming, due to increased traffic headed toward Branson, Missouri. Locals say you can't count the number of motels and restaurants on one hand anymore. There are even several modern **music shows** in town, including Cash's White River Hoedown and Leatherwoods Music Show. Additional area attractions include Blanchard Springs Caverns and Buffalo National River, trail rides, and a go-cart park. (*See full entries for these attractions in the following pages.*)

Yet Mountain View will never be like Branson, because too many locals like the town just the way it is. Instead of trying to give tourists what they want, newcomers are eased into the Mountain View way.

Stone County Courthouse Square is the center of the town's social life. "Howdy Folks. Welcome to Mountain View," reads the hand-lettered sign in front of Aunt Minnie's Little Yellow House. "You folks from 'off' slow it down and enjoy yourself. Come on in and visit with me, and browse around."

In front of **Signal Hill Music Shop** at Howard Ave. and Washington St., folks linger over ice-cream cones and lemonade, catching up with old friends or new acquaintances. As the sun goes down, they set up chairs and listen to jamming musicians. Mellow men thoughtfully whittle down long sticks of cedar, as piles of shavings slowly grow around them.

Across the square, the **Hearthstone Bakery,** housed in a 1918 hotel, serves homemade breads, pastries, and desserts. **Wildflower Bed and Breakfast** is upstairs (closed January and February). Washington and Peabody Streets; (800) 591-4879 or (501) 269-4383.

There are several RV parks and campgrounds within walking distance of the square, and additional motels, inns, and bed-and-breakfasts scattered around town. Mountain View's restaurants include Southern-style eateries, a pizza parlor, burger shacks, and national chains. **Woods' Pharmacy** has an old-fashioned soda fountain with lunch specials. Main Street, one block west of the Courthouse Square; (501) 269-8304.

Shops sell locally made crafts, dulcimers, quilts, hand-crafted rocking chairs, ironworks, and antiques. **Mellon's Country Store,** in a turn-of-the-century barn with a forty-foot windmill out front, sells "something for everyone" including cured hams, musical instruments, antiques, RC cola, and Moon Pies. The Mellon Patch shop produces thousands of unique wood whistles and toys. Hwy. 5-9-14 north; (800) 882-3170 or (501) 269-4005.

The Ozark Mountains are the largest highlands between the Appalachian and Rocky Mountain ranges, covering 60,000 square miles in Arkansas, Missouri, and Oklahoma. **Blanchard Springs Caverns,** fifteen miles north of Mountain View on Hwy. 14 north, is an awesome cave and recreation area; (501) 757-2211.

Forty-five miles north of town, the **Buffalo National River** was declared America's first national river in 1972. Free-flowing and wild, it runs 132 miles from Buffalo City to Boxley, through dramatic sandstone and limestone bluffs, waterfalls, and forests. From Mountain View, the closest river access is at Buffalo Point. Take Rt. 14 north; (501) 449-4311.

Going strong in its fourth decade, the **Arkansas Folk Festival** takes place the third weekend in April. The festival includes regional performers, crafts, folk-dancing, and food, at various locations including the Courthouse Square, Jimmy Driftwood Barn, and Ozark Folk Center.

The **Annual Bean Fest and Great Arkansas Championship Outhouse Race** is held the last Saturday in October, on the square. Free pinto beans are served from huge kettles. Entertainment includes teams pushing functional outhouses in competition, a "tall tale"–telling contest, and lots of live folk music.

GETTING THERE: Mountain View is 100 miles north of Little Rock and 125 miles southeast of Branson, Missouri. Take Hwy. 5-9-14 or Rte. 66. Mountain View Chamber of Commerce is in Courthouse Square. (Hwy. 14 and 66), Howard Ave. and Washington St.; (501) 269-8068.

ENTERTAINMENT IN MOUNTAIN VIEW

In addition to casual jamming around the Stone County Courthouse, Mountain View offers numerous opportunities to hear great music. On Saturday nights from June through August, free programs are presented on a stage at the south side of the courthouse.

On Friday and Sunday nights year-round, members of the **Rackensack Folklore Society** take the stage at the **Jimmy Driftwood Barn and Folk Music Hall of Fame.** The loose-knit society was founded by Driftwood in 1962 with talented local people devoted to the preservation of traditional folk and old-time country music.

The Jimmy Driftwood Barn has a small stage and seats 300 in church pews; it was built in conjunction with the University of Central Arkansas (Driftwood's alma mater) and the Ozark Heritage Institute. The walls are lined with photos of Rackensack Society members and paintings of Driftwood. A row of "TN STUD" license plates commemorates one of Driftwood's most successful compositions. A small record shop sells his tapes, songbooks, and T-shirts.

The atmosphere during shows is casual, with guests drifting in and out during the evening. Singers and players do several songs each, accompanied by an acoustic guitar or two. Driftwood, in his eighties, sits with Cleda by the side of the stage, joining in now and then or letting out a "yahoo" when he hears something he likes. If he's up to it, he might play a few songs on his grandfather's guitar. The free show begins at 7:30 P.M. and ends two or three hours later with the group singing of "Will the Circle Be Unbroken." Two miles north on Hwy. 5-9-14; (501) 269-8042.

Rhythm & Brews Coffee House books local and regional bands and offers an open microphone to amateur and professional musicians. Gourmet coffee, sandwiches, salads, cheese plates, and cobblers, cakes, and pies are served. Open Monday through Friday for lunch;

Friday and Saturday for dinner and music. 112 East Main St.; (501) 269-5200.

Mountain View's music show season is April through October, with varying schedules at different theaters and special shows for Thanksgiving and Christmas. Tickets $8 to $10. Call venues for days, times, and prices.

Cash's White River Hoedown, Mountain View's original music show, stars "Aunt Minnie Miles" (a.k.a. Pat Cash) as a hilarious country comedy character. The variety show features big-band music, rock and roll, bluegrass, contemporary country, and clogging. Hwy. 5-9-14 north; (800) 759-6474 or (501) 269-4161.

Two different shows are presented at Brickshy's Showboat Theatre and restaurant, on the White River about five miles north of Mountain View. The *Leatherwoods Music Show* is a fast-paced acoustic variety show starring bluegrass fiddler Roger Fountain and Tara Sky, a champion clawhammer banjo player. The River Rats do an electrified country show featuring comedy by Don Jones, known onstage as "Brickyshy" (as in "one brick shy of a full load"). Hwy. 5-9-14 north at Allison; (800) 794-2226 or (501) 585-2205.

Ozark Folk Center State Park, the Ozark Mountains were originally settled by poor Appalachians heading westward for a better life. Unfortunately, things weren't much easier here.

"When you learn how to eke out a living in a place like Arkansas, you're tough," says Moon Mullins, a guitar

Performers at the Ozark Folk Center Theater preserve the traditional music of the region. (Arkansas Department of Parks and Tourism/ Ozark Folk Center)

player and emcee for performances at Ozark Folk Center State Park. "People relieved themselves of the drudgery of the work week by kicking up their heels and blowing on a jug. That's what the music was for." Musical traditions in the Ozarks are quite similar to those in Appalachia, and as deeply ingrained in the culture.

Folk singer Jimmy Driftwood was instrumental in obtaining federal funding for the folk center, the first facility of its kind in the United States. "We took twenty old country musicians to Washington and met with [Arkansas congressman] Wilbur Mills," Driftwood explains. "They played for the Senate in the morning and the House in the afternoon, and just about brought the place down." Originally looking for about $45,000 to build the center, Driftwood and company went home with more than $2 million.

The park, dedicated to the preservation and perpetuation of Ozark mountain music and culture, opened in 1973. It also serves the purpose of employing regional people and promoting tourism.

The center employs more than 100 talented local people to sing traditional ballads, dance lively jigs, saw out fiddle tunes, and show off fancy thumb-picking. They present short programs daily in an open-air pavilion, as well as a full-length show every night in the 1,000-seat **Ozark Folk Center Theater.** The unusual, round auditorium is large but not impersonal. Visitors often waltz or clog onstage behind the performers.

"We're trying to preserve the music in the Ozarks area, from 1940 on back, the way it was before it was diluted," Mullins says. That means Jimmie Rodgers, the Carter Family, Woody Guthrie, and Stephen Foster are in; Hank Williams, Pete Seeger, Bob Dylan, and Joan Baez are out.

A visitor might wonder, why 1940?

"In 1941, Ernest Tubb recorded a song called 'Walking the Floors Over You' with an electric guitar," Mullins explains. "I think it's great. I love it," he adds quickly, so as not to disparage Tubb. "But there's still folks with real heart who need to hear the older stuff."

The center also offers craft demonstrations daily in nineteenth-century skills such as printing, quilting, weaving, lye soap making, tintype photography, and blacksmithing. Bob LeFever carves beautiful wood psalteries, dulcimers, and other traditional instruments here. Craftspeople work out of small modern air-conditioned structures scattered in a small park with a fragrant herb garden.

The complex includes an archive, library, gift shop, the Iron Skillet restaurant, and Dry Creek Lodge. A full schedule of workshops, youth activities, special celebrations, and festivals are offered, including the **Arkansas Folk Festival** the third weekend in April, and the **Arkansas Old-Time Fiddler Championship** the last Saturday in September.

GETTING THERE: Open daily 10 A.M. to 5 P.M. April through October, with special events for Thanksgiving and Christmas. Admission $7 for crafts only, $7 evening show only. Combination tickets and family discounts are available. Spur 382 off Hwy. 5; (800) 264-FOLK or (501) 269-3851.

Jimmy Driftwood

B A R D   O F   T H E   O Z A R K S

Perhaps no one has done more to lure outsiders to the Arkansas Ozark Mountains than Jimmy Driftwood, the Grammy award–winning folk singer who abandoned a lucrative career to fight tough battles at home.

Driftwood and his wife, Cleda, live in Timbo, a hamlet about ten miles west of Mountain View. Both are natives of the Ozarks. Their modest stone-and-wood ranch house, on 1,000 acres, is decorated with relics: old farm implements and shotguns, butter churns and mauls, and a sidesaddle ridden by Jimmy's grandmother. Two Grammys stand on the mantle above the fireplace (the third is broken), and his grandfather's guitar rests in a place of honor on a rocking chair.

Approaching his ninetieth birthday, Driftwood (his real name is James Morris) is in excellent health and spirits, resplendent in his trademark red shirt and black Western hat. He has written more than 1,000 songs so far and is still composing, although "not as many as before." His current project is an album of songs about Appalachia.

For more than three decades. Driftwood worked as a teacher

Jimmy Driftwood shows off his grandfather's guitar.

and school administrator nearby in Snowball, Arkansas. (Cleda was one of his students.) All the while he was writing songs and playing his grandfather's guitar at regional folk festivals. "My family was rich in these songs, which they had brought from the Appalachians and from England," Driftwood explains.

The revival of interest in American folk music brought Driftwood to a Nashville recording studio for the first time when he was fifty-one years old. In 1958, he cut an album of folk songs with Chet Atkins, which included an original composition about the time Andrew Jackson fought the British down in New Orleans, written forty years earlier for his sixth-grade American-history class.

Johnny Horton heard "The Ballad of New Orleans," and recorded a countrified version. The song was a sensation in 1959, hitting number one on the country and pop charts. (Driftwood's version went to number 24 the same year, his only charted song.)

In 1959, six of Driftwood's folk songs were on the *Billboard* charts at one time, including Eddy Arnold's version of "Tennessee Stud," Hawkshaw Hawkins's "Soldier's Joy," and Johnnie and Jack's "Sailor Man." He joined the *Grand Ole Opry,* and was the first folk musician to play Carnegie Hall.

Yet by the early sixties, Driftwood had tired of the Nashville treadmill. Homesick for his beloved Ozarks, he returned and worked tirelessly to lift the area out of its isolation and chronic poverty by nurturing its greatest natural resources: the culture and the land.

Driftwood had a three-part plan for bringing tourists to the Ozarks: build the Ozark Folk Center, develop Blanchard Springs Caverns as an attraction, and preserve the free-flowing Buffalo River. To win over skeptical locals and intransigent politicians, he often performed songs written especially for the occasion. Visitors to Blanchard Springs Caverns hear Driftwood's sugary voice singing, "Father Time, Mother Nature . . ." on the introductory film. His song about the beautiful Buffalo River triumphantly describes "Uncle Sam's blue ribbon" as "Arkansas' gift to the nations / America's gift to the world."

"We'd say, 'Damn anyone who wants to dam the river!' " he remembers. "We felt that surely there was one river in this mighty United States that could be a national river." As chairman of the Arkansas Parks, Recreation and Travel Commission, he proudly signed the final papers transferring the river to the National Park Service in 1972.

While largely forgotten by the country music establishment, he's a hero back home in Mountain View, where he presides over free acoustic folk shows twice a week at the Jimmy Driftwood Barn (*see page 22*). (When an out-of-town writer and her traveling companion dropped in, Jimmy and Cleda insisted that they come out to the ranch the following morning for a breakfast of eggs, ham, biscuits, fresh-stewed peaches and cinnamon rolls.) Driftwood, a natural storyteller, entertains his guests with colorful yarns and anecdotes. "I want to tell you a little story you won't soon forget," he'll say.

When asked about his grandfather's guitar, Driftwood starts at the beginning: "Well (my ancestors) came out here in covered wagons . . ."

Highway 65 from Buffalo River to Branson

Highway 65 is the preferred route to Branson, Missouri, from central Arkansas. The highway winds through beautiful mountain and lake territory, prime for trout fishing, bird-watching, hunting, canoeing, and water sports. In addition to the 132-mile Buffalo River, attractions along the way include cave tours, craft galleries, rock shops, and flea markets. The **Kenda Drive-In** on Highway 65 in Marshall is one of the only remaining open-air movie theaters in the Ozarks; (501) 448-2393.

The **Searcy County Museum** in Marshall has a permanent exhibit on native son Elton Britt, who received country music's first gold record for his patriotic 1942 song, "There's a Star-Spangled Banner Waving Somewhere." The local history museum, in the 1907 Searcy County jailhouse, includes historic artifacts and genealogical information. Open Monday, Wednesday, and Friday, 9 A.M. to 4 P.M., and by appointment. (Additional days and hours are planned.) Just off Marshall Square, at Hwy. 65 and Rte. 27; (501) 448-5786 or 448-2722.

In Leslie, at Highway 65 and Route 66, the **Ozark Heritage Art Center** displays and sells the work of local artists. Upstairs, a small free museum tells the history of Searcy County. Housed in Leslie's old gymnasium, the fully renovated center includes a professional 400-seat theater which presents dramas and occasional music concerts. Open 10 A.M. to 4 P.M. Monday through Saturday. Oak St.; (501) 447-2500.

Leslie (pop. 481) was once a boomtown with the "World's Largest Whiskey-Barrel Factory." After the plant closed, the town gained notoriety as the "Whittling Capital of America." A few of Leslie's old-time whittlers still hang around downtown, practicing the craft one champion described as "making nothing out of something." Shops sell antiques, books, and ice-cream sodas. **Serenity Farm Bread,** a natural organic bakery, makes sourdough loaves in a wood-fired brick oven. Main St. and Rte. 66; (501) 447-2211.

The popular **Leslie Homecoming,** held annually for more than forty years, features old-time singing, a parade, rodeo, dance, and talent competition the third weekend in June. Contact the Searcy County Chamber of Commerce; (501) 448-5788.

Annual festivals in Harrison include the Arkansas Fiddlers' Convention the third weekend in March; Crooked Creek Crawdad Days the weekend after Mother's Day; and Northwest Arkansas Bluegrass Festival the third weekend in August. Contact the Harrison Chamber of Commerce; (800) 880-6265 or (501) 741-2659.

Eureka Springs

LITTLE SWITZERLAND OF AMERICA

An hour south of Branson, Missouri, Eureka Springs is a refreshing change of pace, a fairy-tale community (pop. 1,900) where tourists stroll along winding alleyways, discover charming little shops, and enjoy live music shows. What a pleasure to visit a progressive resort town where the tourist board urges guests to leave their cars behind and "rediscover the pleasures of walking"!

"This town is laid back," says Dave Drennon, owner and host of the *Pine Mountain Jamboree* (*see page 31*). "We enjoy the quality of life here."

Locals call their city "Eureka," which means "I have found it!" A boomtown during the 1880s, Eureka was once a famous spa and health resort known worldwide as the "Little Switzerland of America." The area's cool spring waters were believed to have restorative and healing powers.

Today, it's an artists' colony and popular travel destination. The entire city is on the National Register of Historic Places. The downtown is carved into hillsides, with art galleries, cafes, boutiques, antique stores, and specialty shops. Here and there, cold springs emerge from underground in little parks with flowers and benches.

The best way to explore Eureka Springs is to park at the Chamber of Commerce or a lot downtown, and set out on foot. When you get tired, hop on one of the inexpensive city trolleys. There are six color-coded routes covering the whole town; maps are widely available. The cost is $1 per trip or $3 for an all-day pass. The trolleys run roughly 9 A.M. to 7 P.M., April through October; (501) 253-8737.

Eureka offers dozens of attractions, including quirky museums, botanical gardens, scenic train rides, Victorian home tours, lake cruises, caverns, and outdoor recreation.

Miles Musical Museum is an outstanding collection of hundreds of mechanical musical instruments and machines, including vintage nickelodeons, carnival and band organs, player pianos, circus calliopes, and music boxes. Floyd Miles bought his wife, Martha, her first player piano in 1955; the collection grew so fast that he needed to open a museum by 1960. During an hour-long guided tour, visitors listen to dozens of wonderful instruments.

Miles, who died in 1995 at age 88, also collected other people's odd collections, which are on display: button paintings; historical scenes carved in Ozark onyx; strange stringed instruments, including a cello made out of matchsticks; collections of envelopes, coins, stamps, and shells; barber's tools and whiskey decanters; a department store's Christmas displays; moving dioramas of Mother Goose fairy tales from the 1904 World's Fair; and a huge miniature animated circus, hand-crafted by a Kansas couple over a 25-year period. The Miles Musical Museum is an enthralling, eclectic American museum that should not be missed. Open May through October, 9 A.M. to 4 P.M. daily. Closed Thursday. Hwy. 62 west; (501) 253-8961.

The *Great Passion Play* is an elaborate dramatization of the last days of Jesus Christ performed by a cast of hundreds, in an outdoor 4,000-seat amphitheater on a mountaintop. The 67-foot **Christ of the Ozarks** statue is on the grounds, as well as a Bible museum, sacred-arts center, restaurants, turn-of-the-century church, and a ten-foot section of the Berlin Wall. The **New Holy Land** is a theme park with reproductions of biblical scenes. Call for current hours and times. Take Hwy. 62 east to Statue Rd.; (800) 882-PLAY or (501) 253-9200.

Accommodations are available in dozens of bed-and-breakfasts, cabins, cottages, hotels, and motels. There are campgrounds and RV parks near downtown and a few miles away at Lake Leatherwood, Beaver Lake, and the White River. Many romantic inns cater to couples, making Eureka a popular wedding and honeymoon destination.

The **Crescent Hotel,** built in 1886, is an aging beauty on a mountaintop with guest rooms, a restaurant, and sports bar. The fourth-floor public observation deck has terrific views of the Ozarks and the Christ of the Ozarks statue. Hwy. 62B; (800) 342-9766 or (501) 253-9766.

At the **Palace Hotel and Bath House,** built in 1901, "taking the waters" means classic mineral baths, eucalyptus steam cabinets, and massages. 135 Spring St.; (501) 253-7474.

Dozens of **special events** take place year-round in Eureka, including the four-day Ozark Folk Festival, with concerts and acoustic music workshops in late September.

GETTING THERE: Eureka Springs is at Hwy. 62 and Rte. 23, in northwest Arkansas near the Missouri border. Contact the Chamber of Commerce; (501) 253-8737.

DINING IN EUREKA SPRINGS

Eureka has a surprising number of fine restaurants and steak houses, as well as numerous ethnic eateries serving Greek, Chinese, Italian, French, and German fare. For authentic American, try **Bubba's Barbecue,** which slow-cooks its meats over hot hickory coals to juicy perfection. A colorful, fun joint in a blue-and-white shack, Bubba's is riotously decorated with pig knickknacks, colorful posters, and pictures clipped from glossy magazines. 60 Kingshighway (Hwy. 62 west); (501) 253-7706.

At the **Pound Sisters Dinner Theater,** Bonnie, Linda, Loree, and Audry alternately sing, take orders, play their instruments, work the grill, dance, and harmonize beautifully. Wearing headset microphones, the bouncy and sweet sisters expertly run their restaurant while belting out originals songs, country standards, and gospel numbers. "You've got half your mind thinking about the song and half about the food," Bonnie Pound explains.

A no-frills, country-cooking establishment, the restaurant serves sandwiches, burgers, and dinner platters of fried chicken, catfish, and steak. Mom Jane Pound makes the breakfast biscuits. Open 7 A.M. to 2 P.M. and 5 P.M. to 8 P.M. daily. Reservations are recommended on Friday and Saturday nights. Hours limited in winter; call first. Hwy. 62 east; (501) 253-7933.

LIVE ENTERTAINMENT IN EUREKA SPRINGS

Eureka Springs' live entertainment season runs from mid-March through late October, with some performances in November and December. Tickets generally cost between $10 and $13 per person. Call ahead for schedules.

Of the family music shows I've seen so far, *Pine Mountain Jamboree* is my favorite. The Drennon family has achieved the perfect balance of first-rate singing and musicianship, genuinely funny comedy, and down-home Ozarks hospitality. The variety show is professional but not too slick. You really get to know—and like—the small, multitalented cast.

The Drennons have been performing in the Ozarks since 1967. Deanna (Dee) Presley, of Branson's musical Presley family, and her husband Dave Drennon appeared on the Presleys' show before opening their own theater in 1975. Dave Drennon is the emcee and straight man for the hilarious comedy character "Hargus." Their son Mike has played drums on the show since he was three years old. Daughter Mindee retired from the stage at age two, and runs the theater with her mother. Mindee's husband, James Prosser, a featured singer, is a handsome young man with star quality and a recording contract.

After seeing *Pine Mountain Jamboree,* you'll understand why it's Arkansas' oldest and most-attended country-music show. The comfortable theater is in a shopping village with crafts, restaurants, ice cream, and carriage rides. The Jamboree is presented daily, except Sundays. Hwy. 62 east; (501) 253-9156.

Eureka Springs' other popular variety show is **Ozark Mountain Hoe-Down,** going strong since the early 1980s. This show features a talented cast performing country, western swing, and pop, with lots of comedy and a high-spirited Elvis imitator. The Norris Twins, guests on television's *Hee Haw,* do a matinee show. Open daily, except Tuesdays. Hwy. 62 east; (501) 253-7725.

The **Gem of the Ozarks Theater** features Donnie Sneed and his Double Diamond Band. A singer, champion yodeler, and veteran country and gospel performer, Sneed presents a variety music show with a little comedy. (Sneed is a member of the *Arizona* Country Music Hall of Fame, not *the* Country Music Hall of Fame as his ads claim.) Memorabilia and awards from the Texas-based Gospel Music Museum are displayed in the lobby. Open daily, with regular matinees. Hwy. 62 east; (501) 253-6011.

May through October, **Red Bud Valley Chuckwagon** takes guests on a wagon ride to a mountain cook-shack on Wolf Ridge, for a filling campfire dinner followed by Western music and dancing. Rock House Rd., off Hwy. 62 east; (501) 253-2000 or -9028.

West Fork
LITTLE O' OPREY

Founded in 1989, the **Little O' Oprey** in West Fork is a nonprofit organization dedicated to "furthering the evolution of the music and the artists of the entire Ozark Mountain region for the benefit of all," director Dan Wiethop says. The authentic old-time Opry show, presented Saturday nights year-round at 7 P.M., features unrehearsed acoustic country and bluegrass music presented by a rotating 100-member cast of talented Ozark artists. The showcase is performed from a renovated eighteenth-century building and is broadcast live over a dozen regional radio stations.

GETTING THERE: West Fork is about 10 miles south of Fayetteville in northwest Arkansas. The Oprey is across from West Fork City Hall. Take Hwy. 71 to Rte. 170; (501) 839-2992 or (501) 846-2111.

Central Arkansas

Hot Springs
TAKING THE WATERS

Singer Patsy Montana was born in Hot Springs, and so was President Clinton. But the city doesn't need to rely on celebrities to attract tourists. Hot Springs, about fifty miles west of Little Rock, is a lovely resort town where it is possible to "take the waters" in stately turn-of-the-century bathhouses and modern spas, and see several fine country music shows.

For hundreds of years, visitors came to experience the healing and restorative powers of the 143°F waters of Hot Springs Creek. President Andrew Jackson declared Hot Springs a federal reserve in 1832; the entire downtown eventually became part of the National Park System.

To keep it clean, Hot Springs Creek was channeled under what is now Central Avenue, and a row of grand bathhouses were built. By the 1950s the public had lost interest in bathhouses and many fell into disrepair. During the 1980s, local citizens and the Park Service got together to restore several bathhouses and Hot Springs to its former glory.

The **Museum of Hot Springs** tells the city's colorful history with films, historic items, and photos. 201 Central Ave.; (501) 624-5545. **Magic Springs Theme Park** offers rides, games, music shows, and concerts. 1701 Grand Ave.; (501) 624-5411.

From downtown, which has dozens of tasteful art galleries, shops, and restaurants, you can hike right into forests of oak, pine, and hickory. A 216-foot **observation tower** atop Hot Springs Mountain can be reached by car or foot; (501) 623-6035. The surrounding lakes, streams, and mountains provide opportunities for fishing and outdoor recreation.

The country music shows in Hot Springs are family-run, and are open year-round except January with varying schedules. Tickets are in the $10 range.

Tom and Kelley Wilkins opened their 300-seat theater in downtown Hot Springs in 1988. Tom is emcee for the ***Bath House Show***

and plays several comedic roles, including "Buford Presley" and "Soul Man," while Kelley and daughters Katie and Marcie sing. A full cast of performers and musicians present a variety show based on nostalgia from the thirties through the seventies. 701 Central Ave.; (501) 623-1415.

The Music Mountain Jamboree hosts a family-run show in a 700-seat theater complex.

Just up the street in Hot Springs' oldest venue, the renovated **Central Country Music Theater** showcases the Chattertons, a group whose charted songs include "Sugar-N-Spice" and "Oo-Wee." The show features country standards, guest singers, and comedy. 1008 Central Ave.; (501) 624-2268.

The Mullinex Family's **Music Mountain Jamboree** takes place outside Hot Springs in a seven-acre complex with a modern 700-seat theater, mini-golf, go-carts, and a restaurant. The show, Hot Springs' oldest, stars three generations of Mullinexes performing country, bluegrass, pop, gospel, and patriotic music. Ted Mullinex, an Arkansas state representative for many years, plays a comedy character called "Homestead." 2720 Albert Pike; (501) 767-3841.

The Hot Springs visitors' center can provide a brochure with a driving tour of President Clinton's youth, including his boyhood homes, schools, and church, as well as his favorite movie theater, and the site of his senior banquet and prom. Clinton's hamburger hangout was the Polar Bar, now **Bailey's Dairy Treat,** 510 Park Ave. The president's favorite barbecue joint was **McClard's Bar-B-Q,** established in 1928. McClard's has a national reputation for pork ribs. As the story goes, Alex and Gladys McClard, then in the motel business, got their sauce recipe from a down-and-out traveler who couldn't pay his bill. The sauce was so good that they turned the motel into a restaurant. At its present location since 1942, McClard's is a neat, simple place with Formica counters and red leather booths. The sauce, pungent and complex, is terrific. So are the tamales, beans, and barbecue. 505 Albert Pike; (501) 624-9586.

GETTING THERE: Hot Springs is 55 miles west of Little Rock, at Hwys. 70 and 270, and Rte. 7. Contact Hot Springs Promotion Commission; (800) SPA-CITY or (501) 321-2277.

Pine Ridge
JOT-EM DOWN STORE AND LUM AND ABNER MUSEUM

When Chester "Chet" Lauck and Norris "Tuffy" Goff were growing up in Mena, a small town in west-central Arkansas, they would team up to entertain at school and civic functions. On April 26, 1931, the pair drove to Hot Springs to try out their old country storekeepers routine on the radio. Their hilarious characters, Lum Edwards and

Kathryn Strucker (left) runs the Jot-Em Down Store and Lum and Abner Museum in Pine Ridge.

Abner Peabody, were an instant smash. The *Lum and Abner* radio show quickly became a national radio phenomenon rivaling the *Grand Ole Opry* in popularity. Lauck and Goff once received more than a million fan letters in one week!

Lauck and Goff's inspiration for the Jot-Em Down Store was Dick Huddleston's general store in rural Waters, a hamlet near Mena which they called "Pine Ridge." Huddleston and other locals, expertly parodied by Lauck and Goff, became minor celebrities.

"As soon as Lum and Abner started talking about Pine Ridge, Dick Huddleston realized he had a good thing," says Kathryn Stucker, who runs the Jot-Em Down Store and Lum and Abner Museum in Pine Ridge. "He started selling souvenirs as soon as the program got started." In 1936, the town's name was officially changed to Pine Ridge in an elaborate ceremony at the state capitol in Little Rock.

Stucker and her husband Lon now manage Huddleston's store and are curators of the museum. Equal parts local history and Lum and Abner memorabilia, the museum has a room full of farm implements and tools, another with household items and school registers going back to the 1880s, and a third with movie posters, photos of residents featured on the show, and dusty items from the old store. The old Waters–Pine Ridge "phone book" is still scrawled on the wall by the original register. It isn't hard to imagine the fellers chewing the fat here, gabbing on the phone, gossiping, and ignoring customers while they had their little arguments and (mis)adventures.

The store sells show tapes for $2.50, memorabilia, locally made crafts, and the same souvenirs Huddleston hawked, such as corncob pipes, postcards, and back-scratchers.

Lauck and Goff went on to make seven Lum and Abner movies in Hollywood, but Pine Ridge stayed about the same. The town's population is currently eighteen souls, just a tad fewer than lived here in the 1930s. The road to Pine Ridge wasn't paved until the fifties. The nearest stoplight is a hundred miles away, and there are only two stop signs in the whole county.

The Lum and Abner show has enjoyed a modest revival in recent years, and is being rebroadcast on a number of radio stations around the country. The Lum and Abner Society was founded in 1983, with the blessing of Chester Lauck, Jr. (Lauck and Goff died in 1980 and 1978, respectively.) Their national convention, **Lum and Abner Days,** takes place in Mena the fourth weekend in June.

GETTING THERE: From Hot Springs, take Hwy. 270 west to Rte. 88 west. Admission to the Jot 'Em Down Store is free; museum admission 50¢. Open March through November 15, Tuesday to Saturday, 9 A.M. to 5 P.M., and Sunday, noon to 5 P.M. During the winter, call for an appointment; (501) 326-4442.

Timberlands of the South

The timberlands area of southwest Arkansas, from Pine Bluff to the Louisiana border to Texarkana, is thick with piney woods, lakes, and oil fields.

Johnny Cash was born near Kingsland in Cleveland County, southwest of Pine Bluff at Hwy. 79 and Rte. 97. A sign in Cash's honor is posted at the entrance to town. Seven miles northeast in Rison, **Pioneer Village** displays the Man in Black's "bicentennial suit," worn during a series of concerts in 1976. Hwy. 79 and Rte. 35; (501) 325-6536.

In downtown Magnolia, the *KVMA Columbia County Hayride* is performed by comedian Otis Fudpucker and Union Station Band on the third Saturday of every month. Magnolia is at Hwys. 79 and 82. 406 W. Union St.; (501) 234-6010.

Southwest Arkansas' premier country-music show is the **Ashdown Jamboree,** presented by the Tommy Cornelius family every Saturday night at 8 P.M. The show features local and regional acts, and the Ashdown Jamboree Band. Ashdown is 15 miles north of Texarkana off Hwy. 71. 356 Keller; (501) 898-6242.

California

San Francisco Bay Area

SULLY RODDY—THE QUEEN OF ECLECTIC COUNTRY RADIO

Sully Roddy's radio show, **All Kinds of Country,** kicks off at 7 P.M. on Saturday and Sunday nights on KNEW Radio (910 AM) with Bob Wills's "Stay All Night" and prances off into the metaphorical sunset at midnight with Roy Rogers's "Happy Trails." Sandwiched in between, Sully plays an intelligent mix of old-time country, bluegrass, blues, western swing, Cajun and zydeco, local bands, current hits, and alternative country.

During any hour of the show, you could hear Jim Reeves, Los Lobos, the Grateful Dead, Bill Monroe, Laurie Lewis, Tammy Wynette, Garth Brooks, Elvis Presley, or Dire Straits. Sully opens listeners' minds to an uncommonly broad range of what is widely known as "country music," especially if they've been exposed exclusively to commercial, mainstream radio stations. The clever sets are interspersed with Sully's hilarious "Tales from the Tabloids," ticket giveaways, the local concert calendar, and live studio visits by performers. If only the rest of country programming could be this diverse and imaginative!

California Festivals

For information on upcoming California bluegrass festivals, call *California Bluegrass* magazine, (209) 293-1559. The publication lists events around the state. For a free copy, write: P.O. Box 9, Wilseyville, CA 95257.

The California Bluegrass Association's four-day Grass Valley **Father's Day Weekend Bluegrass Music Festival** is the state's premier bluegrass event. National and regional bands perform all day, while pickers jam among the pine trees at Nevada County Fairgrounds. Grass Valley is about sixty-five miles north of Sacramento in the Sierra Nevada foothills. Take 1-80 to Rte. 49 or 20; (209) 293-1559 or (707) 762-8735.

The **Shasta Serenade** bluegrass festival takes place Columbus Day weekend at the Shasta County Fairgrounds in Anderson, south of Redding, with national bands and camping. Take 1-5 to Rte. 273; (800) 707-2681.

National Entertainment Network produces several three-day **bluegrass festivals** in San Jose, including Fallgrass Veterans Day weekend and Wintergrass in March. Call for details; (800) 746-TUNE.

Michael Martin Murphey brings his three-day **WestFest** to Mammoth Ski Area, in the Sierra Nevadas east of Yosemite National Park, in mid-August. Mammoth is 165 miles south of Reno on Hwy. 395; (800) 228-4947. (*See also:* Colorado—Copper Mountain.)

For three days in late January, the **Colorado River Country Music Festival** in Blythe, on the Nevada border, features contests, competitions, and live entertainment. Take I-10; (800) 443-5513 or 445-0541 (CA only).

Country Music Television's **StarFest** in Los Angeles is a fan-driven event in early spring with three days of live entertainment, vendors, and songwriting contest. More than forty headline acts perform at the Fairplex Park of the Los Angeles County Fair and Exposition Center in Pomona. Take I-10; (310) 358-0900.

Colt's End of the Trail Cowboy Shootout and Wild West Jubilee in Norco is a four-day extravaganza with live entertainment, a Wild West show, film festival, cowboy poetry, chuckwagon cookoffs, and Western gear venders. The highlight is the nation's largest cowboy action shooting contest, with more than 400 competitors in 1880s garb. The festival takes place in late April at Raahauge's Ranch, about 30 miles east of Los Angeles. Call for directions; (714) 998-0209.

The two-day **Visalia Spring Round-Up** in mid-April features cowboy poetry and music. "Almost any Round-Up I have attended has been exceptionally enjoyable, warm, friendly, and relaxed," says Lani Hernandez of the Visalia Cowboy Cultural Committee. "Just a good time for everyone involved." Visalia is in the San Joaquin Valley, about 40 miles south of Fresno. The festival is at College of the Sequoias. Take Hwy. 99 to Hwy. 198 east. 915 S. Mooney Blvd.; (209) 627-0287.

Bakersfield
COUNTRY MUSIC CAPITAL OF CALIFORNIA

Buck Owens was born in Texas and raised in Arizona, but his home is in Bakersfield, the "Country Music Capital of California." Bakersfield is an oil, gas, and cotton center in the flat San Joaquin Valley north of Los Angeles.

As a young honky-tonk singer, Owens performed at a Bakersfield bar called The Blackboard for seven years and drove to Capitol Records in Hollywood to play guitar on Wanda Jackson and Jean Shepard records. Signing with Capitol himself, he went on to record more than thirty number-one songs. Many Americans know Owens from his years as a regular on *Hee Haw*.

Before Dwight Yoakam lured Owens out of retirement for a reprise of his hit song, "Streets of Bakersfield," Owens focused his energies on **Buck Owens Productions.** The complex houses Owens' radio and television stations. Informal thirty-minute tours can be arranged. If Owens is in his office, he might step out and say hello. Call for an appointment. 3223 Sillect Ave; (805) 326-1011. **Buck Owens's Crystal Palace,** a combination museum, theater, restaurant, and dance club, is in the works for downtown Bakersfield and is expected to open in late 1996.

The legendary Merle Haggard, a member of the Country Music Hall of Fame, was born and raised in Bakersfield. Haggard's antiauthoritarian streak ran a mile wide; he served time at San Quentin prison during the 1950s and sat in the audience when Johnny Cash performed there. The **Kern County Museum** displays a small collection of Haggard memorabilia, as well as items from other purveyors of the Bakersfield Sound including Spade Cooley, who lived in Kern County before his 1961 murder trial. The museum features fifty historic buildings, and an indoor display of more than 250,000 objects. Open 8 A.M. to 5 P.M. weekdays; 10 A.M. to 5 P.M. Saturdays; and noon to 5 P.M. Sundays. Take Hwy. 99 to Rte. 204 east. 3801 Chester Ave.; (805) 861-2132.

GETTING THERE: Bakersfield is 110 miles north of Los Angeles. Take I-5 to Rte. 58 east, or Hwy. 99. Contact the Bakersfield Visitors' Bureau; (805) 861-2367.

California Honky-Tonkin'

Southern California's country scene has its roots in the great Dust Bowl migrations, when cars and trucks full of folks from Oklahoma, Texas, Arkansas, and Missouri poured into the Golden State looking for a better life.

The honky-tonks that thrived in the forties and fifties were gritty bars where homesick Midwesterners and Southerners could drown their troubles in cheap beer and dance to the sounds of the Maddox Brothers and Rose, Buck Owens, Jean Shepard, and Spade Cooley. In the sixties and seventies, Merle Haggard, Emmylou Harris, Bobby Bare, Hoyt Axton, and Dwight Yoakam did the honky-tonk rounds.

The eighties were hard on California's **country club scene,** but today you can still two-step till two A.M. at a number of joints. Any time you're in California and have the urge to dance, call the **Country and Western Dance Information Hotline,** (800) 427-8101. Leave your name, number, and location, and they'll let you know where it's happening.

Los Angeles Area
KINGS OF THE COWBOYS

The flip side of the hard-edged southern California honky-tonk scene was Hollywood, where singing cowboys always wore white hats and caught the bad guys in the end. The studios cranked out hundreds of B Westerns during the thirties, forties, and fifties, which both glamorized and distorted the true American West.

Gene Autry, an Oklahoman, was the reigning King of the Cowboys during the thirties and forties, starring in more than 90 films. In 1988, Autry fulfilled a lifelong dream with the opening of the **Gene Autry Western Heritage Museum** in Los Angeles' Griffith Park. Rather than highlight his own achievements, Autry chose to provide a world-class showcase for America's rich Western heritage. Seven permanent galleries and two changing exhibits, designed with creative input from Walt Disney Imagineering, present conflicting versions of the real and mythical West.

The museum shows how the American Dream, the environment, frontier life, weaponry, cowboys, Native Americans, and Hollywood shaped the West and how it is perceived. The tour ends with a multimedia film and special-effects show. A full program of movies, lectures, discussion groups, and classes is offered year-round. A statue in the courtyard commemorates Autry's theme song, "Back in the Saddle Again." (*See also:* Oklahoma—Gene Autry.)

Admission $7.50 adults, $3 children. Open 10 A.M. to 5 P.M., Tuesday through Sunday (and select Monday holidays). Closed Thanksgiving and Christmas. Take I-5 or Ventura Freeway (134) to the Victory Blvd. or Zoo Drive exit and follow signs. 4700 Western Heritage Way; (213) 667-2000.

Another Oklahoman who ended up in Hollywood was **Will Rogers,** the beloved cowboy philosopher of the early twentieth century. (Autry reportedly was inspired to pursue his singing career after a chance meeting with Rogers.) Rogers wasn't a singer himself (although he was game, and would sing on occasion), but he could do amazing things with a lariat. His early vaudeville act centered on humorous comments about news of the day, interspersed with impressive trick roping.

In 1919, Samuel Goldwyn lured Rogers to Hollywood, where he started making movies. During the twenties, he bought a ranch above Sunset Boulevard in Pacific Palisades, and built a 31-room house for his wife, Betty, and their three children. After Rogers's death in 1935, the 186-acre ranch property became **Will Rogers State Park.** Admission includes a tour of the house, an audio tour of the grounds, documentary, and access to hiking trails. The ranch has commanding views of western Los Angeles and the Pacific Ocean.

Open 8 A.M. to 5 P.M. daily. Admission $5 per car. Take I-405 to Sunset Blvd west, to Will Rogers State Road; (310) 454-8212. (*See also:* Oklahoma—Claremore.)

Roy Rogers (known then as Leonard Slye) replaced Gene Autry as the King of the Cowboys in 1938, after Autry walked off a movie set. It was, as they say in Hollywood, Rogers's "big break." Rogers made more than 35 films for Republic Pictures before his successful switch to television. Rogers is also the only living founder of the original Sons of the Pioneers, formed in the early thirties with Bob Nolan and Tim Spencer.

After visiting the Will Rogers Memorial in Claremore, Oklahoma, Rogers vowed he would never throw anything away so that he could have his own museum someday. The nonprofit **Roy Rogers and Dale Evans Museum** opened in the mid-seventies in Victorville, on the southern edge of the Mojave Desert about 100 miles east of Los Angeles.

More than 30,000 square feet are filled with items collected by Rogers and his leading lady Dale Evans, from mementos of his boyhood in Portsmouth, Ohio, to his fabulous gun collection, Rose Parade saddle, family memorabilia, and numerous hunting trophies. In 1996, the museum was completely renovated, redesigned, and expanded, with new items now on display. Videos and films are shown in two small theaters.

When Trigger died in 1965, Rogers had his beloved horse stuffed and mounted in the reared-up position, perhaps the museum's most popular exhibit. Trigger was known as the "smartest horse in the movies"; he was housebroken and knew nearly seventy tricks, forty on word cue.

The highlight for most visitors is meeting the King of the Cowboys himself. In his eighties, Rogers greets fans most mornings when he's able. A major $45 million for-profit development called **RogersDale,** a retail and entertainment complex, is scheduled for completion in late 1997. (*See also:* Ohio—Portsmouth.)

Open 9 A.M. to 5 P.M. daily. Admission $5 adults, $2 children. Take I-15 to Roy Rogers Dr. 15650 Seneca Dr.; (619) 243-4547.

Hollywood
COUNTRY STAR RESTAURANT

Visitors enter the Country Star Restaurant through a jukebox forty-two feet high. (Ron Wolfson)

Country Star Restaurant is a high-concept theme restaurant, like the Hard Rock Cafe multiplied by ten. Billed as the "ultimate high-tech country-music experience," Country Star has a hundred television monitors (even in the restroom!), ten audio-CD listening posts, and interactive kiosks where Reba McEntire, Vince Gill, Wynonna Judd, and Lorianne Crook and Charlie Chase talk to you at the touch of a screen. Dwight Yoakam and Buck Owens have side-by-side stars on the Walk of Fame out front.

Located at Universal Studios, Country Star is huge—14,000 square feet—with a 42-foot jukebox as an entryway. Memorabilia is displayed in cases, and there's a stage for live music performances and karaoke.

Country Star serves large portions of "American Country Comfort Food." (The chef was recently inducted into the International Chili Society Hall of Fame.) The menu includes all-meat/no-bean chili, pork and beef ribs, chicken-fried steak, sandwiches, salads, and desserts. Meals cost between $6 and $10. (Look for Country Star Restaurants in Las Vegas, Nevada, and Atlanta, Georgia, in 1996.)

GETTING THERE: Country Star is at the entrance to Universal Studios in Hollywood, north of Los Angeles. Open 11:30 A.M. to midnight during the winter season, and 11 A.M. to 1 A.M. in summer. Take 101 or 134 Freeway to Lankershim Blvd.; (818) 762-3939.

Colorado

Golden

BUFFALO BILL MEMORIAL MUSEUM

The story of William "Buffalo Bill" Cody, America's most famous frontier personality, is the stuff of Western legend. At age fifteen, Cody broke a Pony Express record with a 24-hour ride of 322 miles. During the Civil War, he fought in the Kansas cavalry. As a buffalo hunter for the Kansas Pacific Railroad, he allegedly shot 4,289 buffalo in eight months (for food, not sport), earning the nickname "Buffalo Bill." Cody received the National Medal of Honor for his bravery as a scout in government battles with the Native Americans, including the Custer Massacre. Americans learned of his exploits from more than 700 dime novels.

Cody launched the *Wild West and Congress of Rough Riders* show in 1883, with much fanfare in Omaha, Nebraska. In his trademark Stetson, buckskin coat, and handlebar mustache, he cultivated his image as the romantic "knight-errant of the frontier." Annie Oakley and Chief Sitting Bull were featured, as were corps of fancy riders from Russia, Germany, France, Mexico, and the Middle and Far East. At its height, the traveling extravaganza featured 200 performers, 250 horses, and herds of elk, deer, and buffalo. If not for a small herd

Cody saved for his Wild West show, the American buffalo might have gone the way of the carrier pigeon.

Cody perpetuated myths about cowboys and American Indians that endure today. For example, in order to eliminate intertribal squabbles, he employed only Oglala Sioux for his show. Subsequently, it was the culture of the Sioux, with its feathered headdresses, peace pipes, and tepees, which became the prominent stereotype for all Native American tribes. At the same time, he promoted the Indian way of life and redefined them as proud and honorable people with a culture worthy of respect. "I can put a pair of boots, a big hat, and a red shirt on any man and call him cowboy," Cody said. "But I cannot dress anyone up and call him Indian."

Cody died while visiting his sister in Denver on January 10, 1917. He never lived in Denver, but often took friends up to Lookout Mountain for the day. His grave was dug after the snow melted, and he was buried here on June 3, 1917. However, even Cody's resting place was controversial. Years later, the people of Cody, Wyoming, hatched an unsuccessful plot to steal the body and bring it up north. "William F. Cody wanted to be buried in Wyoming. It was in his will," says Michael Martin Murphey, a Western singer and Buffalo Bill scholar.

Johnny Baker, a trick shooter who was like a son to Cody, tried to keep the show going after his death but failed. Baker opened a museum next to the tomb in 1921, which his family ran until 1954 when it was turned over to the city of Denver.

The large, professional museum explores Buffalo Bill's multifaceted life and his enduring impact on American culture. The story is told with a movie, extensive dioramas of Cody's life, a chronological time line, rare film footage, personal artifacts, family mementos, and colorful Wild West posters. A stuffed Buffalo is on display, as well as exhibits on Native Americans, Western fine arts, antique firearms, and women of the West.

An observation deck adjacent to the museum provides spectacular views of Denver. On the Sunday closest to June 3, **Buffalo Bill's Burial Procession** is reenacted at the museum, followed by a festival with live music, an antique car show, and buffalo burgers. Several special events are held throughout the year, including the **Buffalo Bill Days Celebration** in mid-July.

Herds of buffalo and elk can be viewed about 5 miles from the museum in **Gennessee Mountain Park** near I-40. A special tunnel allows the buffalo to roam under the highway.

GETTING THERE: Golden is about 15 miles west of downtown Denver. The Buffalo Bill Memorial Museum is open daily 9 A.M. to 5 P.M. May through October; 9 A.M. to 4 P.M. the rest of the year (closed Mondays and Christmas Day). Allow two hours. Admission $2 adults, $1 children. Take I-70/Exit 256 and follow the signs; (303) 526-0747 or -0744.

Copper Mountain
MICHAEL MARTIN MURPHEY'S WESTFEST

Michael Martin Murphey's WestFest comes to Colorado's Copper Mountain, in the Rocky Mountains west of Denver, every year on Labor Day weekend. Since the first WestFest took place here in 1986, Murphey has staged several dozen of the extravaganzas around the country, in locations including Mammoth, California; Amarillo, Texas; Deadwood, South Dakota; Stillwater, Oklahoma; and Chicago, Illinois.

WestFest is modeled after Buffalo Bill Cody's Wild West shows of the late nineteenth century. "The main thing WestFest shares with Cody is the sense of brotherhood, of bringing down barriers and showcasing other cultures," Murphey says. "Cody hated the word 'show.' You'll never see a poster that has that word. He considered himself a cultural exhibitionist. It was an early form of what's called 'edutainment' today."

A native Texan, Murphey has released 23 albums over twenty-five years, all with cowboy songs. His hits include "Wildfire," "Cowboy Logic," and "Geronimo's Cadillac."

The festivals offer a traditional Indian Village, a cowboy camp with campfire singing, a 1840s-era mountain-man village, a rodeo arena, a wildlife corral, a chuckwagon circle, hundreds of Western art and craft exhibitors, and plenty of gear such as tack, saddles, and boots.

The heart and soul of WestFest, Murphey is everywhere, roaming the grounds on his horse, telling stories, and singing. "WestFest is a

Michael Martin Murphey presides over WestFest. (Wildfire Productions)

three-ring circus," he says. "I walk around the grounds and I can't believe what's going on." Before each WestFest, Murphey leads a three-day trail ride in the wilderness.

For the main stage, Murphey says he books headline country stars who "like the West and fit in," in addition to cowboy poets and traditional Western singers. Asleep at the Wheel, Merle Haggard, Mary Chapin Carpenter, and David Ball often perform at WestFest.

Murphey hopes to repeat the successes of his guru Buffalo Bill Cody around the country. At a time when the American West was suffused with white-male machismo and braggadocio, he explains, Cody exposed people to Native American, European, and Asian cultures, black and Mexican cowboys, expert women riders, and target shooters such as Annie Oakley. "Cody was known as the best marksman in the world. For him to have the guts and humility to hire a little girl who was a better shot than him was incredible. That just wasn't done."

GETTING THERE: Copper Mountain is 80 miles west of Denver. WestFest tickets, which include all activities and concerts, are $15–$20. Children, $3. Take I-70/Exit 195; (800)458-8386, ext. 7885, or (970)968-2318.

For general information about WestFest dates and locations around the country, call (505) 751-3425.

Denver
BLACK AMERICAN WEST MUSEUM AND HERITAGE CENTER

The motto of the Black American West Museum and Heritage Center is "We Tell It Like It Was." For example, it's a little-known fact that a third of the cowboys in the Wild West were black; that black families went West in covered wagons and set up self-sufficient towns; or that the all-black 10th Cavalry Division took San Juan Hill with Teddy Roosevelt during the Spanish-American War.

The museum is located in Denver's Five Points neighborhood, the historical center of the city's African-American community. The goal is to fill in the blanks in the untold story of black Western pioneers. Historical artifacts, memorabilia, photographs, and documents are displayed in the Justina Ford House, the historic home of a pioneering black woman doctor. In front, the first star on the **Black Cowboys Walk of Fame** went to Bill Picket, a turn-of-the-century bulldogger.

GETTING THERE: Open 10 A.M. to 5 P.M. weekdays; noon to 5 P.M. weekends. Closed Easter, Thanksgiving, Christmas, and New Year's Day. Allow an hour. Admission $3. Take I-25 to Colfax Ave. east. Turn left on Downing St. The museum is on the left. 3091 California St.; (303) 292-2566.

Telluride
PLANET BLUEGRASS FESTIVALS

Planet Bluegrass hosts three major bluegrass and folk festivals in Colorado every summer, which are as much about communing with nature in the clean Rocky Mountains as they are about music. "It's time to start packin' your bags because if you like great acoustic music outdoors in spectacularly beautiful places, well, you're coming with us," the colorful Planet Bluegrass brochure chirps. "Yes, all ye festivarians, it's time to take flight."

The nation's finest bluegrass, "newgrass," and folk performers come back to Planet Bluegrass year after year. Nanci Griffith, Shawn Colvin, Sam Bush, Tim and Mollie O'Brien, Mary Chapin Carpenter, Bela Fleck, and Alison Krauss are all regulars.

The legendary four-day **Telluride Bluegrass Festival,** in its third decade, takes place in a dramatic canyon in mid-June. Plan far in advance; attendance is limited to 10,000 per day and sellouts are common. Telluride is about 115 miles north of Durango. Take Hwy. 160 to Rte. 145 north.

Planet Bluegrass' two other productions are on the opposite end of the state in Lyons, north of Denver. Bill Monroe helped start the **RockyGrass/Rocky Mountain Bluegrass Festival** in the early seventies. This traditional festival, in early August, features three days of nonstop music and camping in "Bluegrass Hollow" by the St. Vrain River.

Two weeks later, the **Folks Festival** showcases the nation's finest practitioners of "the song," with headline concerts, singer/songwriter showcases, family activities, and campfire sing-alongs. Lyons is about 60 miles north of Denver and 15 miles north of Boulder, at Hwy. 36 and Rte. 66.

GETTING THERE: Plan ahead for Planet Bluegrass Festivals. For information and tickets, call (800) 624-2422 or (303) 449-6007.

Colorado Chuckwagons and Western Shows

Colorado's country-music shows come with chuckwagon suppers, covered wagon rides, and entertainment by real live buckaroos, with rugged mountains as the backdrop. Tickets (meal and entertainment) cost about $13, and reservations are required.

At the **Lazy B Ranch** in Estes Park, on the edge of Rocky Mountain

National Park, chuckwagon meals of sliced beef, peaches, and biscuits are served on tin plates. After supper, the Lazy B Wranglers perform in a rustic 1,600-seat hall. The ranch also offers trail rides, a collection of 400 Jim Beam bottles, and a preshow movie called *Western Odyssey*. Open June through Labor Day. Estes Park is 60 miles north of Denver. Take Hwy. 66 to Hwy. 34 east. Turn left at Sombrero Stables; (800) 228-2116 or (970) 586-5371.

More than 150,000 guests visit the **Flying W Ranch** in Colorado Springs every year for chuckwagon suppers and a Western show under the stars. The Flying W is a working horse-and-cattle ranch, with a Western town of a dozen restored buildings. The chuckwagon is open mid-May through September. During the off-season (except January and February), shows are offered in the Winter Steak House. Colorado Springs is 60 miles south of Denver. Take I-25 to Garden of the Gods Rd. 3330 Chuckwagon Rd.; (800) 232-FLYW or (719) 598-4000.

CHUCKWAGONS OF THE WEST

Throughout the West, a number of ranches offer cowboy-style dining accompanied by Western music, singing, and comedy. These shows are a true bargain, priced at around $13 for a big meal and show. The Flying W Ranch in Colorado Springs, founded by Russ and Marian Wolfe in 1953, is the oldest in the country. Over the years, a number of employees have gone on to open their own places: Bar D in Durango, Colorado; Lazy B in Estes Park, Colorado; Bar J in Jackson Hole, Wyoming; Circle B in Rapid City, South Dakota; Triple C in Tucson, Arizona; Rockin' R in Mesa, Arizona; and the Flying J in Ruidoso, New Mexico (see listings in state chapters).

These outfits make up Chuckwagons of the West Association, which take turns hosting a jamboree every fall. Call the Flying W for information; (800) 232-FLYW or (719) 598-4000.

Durango, in the Four Corners region of southwest Colorado, is home of **Bar D Chuckwagon Suppers.** This Western meal is served outdoors among tall pines, with entertainment by the Bar D Wranglers. The ranch's Western town includes a chapel, train, blacksmith, and leatherworks. Open nightly Memorial Day weekend through Labor Day. Take Hwy. 550 to 8080 Country Rd. 250 (north); (970) 247-5753.

West of Durango, **Dolores River Line Camp** presents a ranch-style meal and Western show by the Trailhands. The site is an original 1877 homestead with a museum in an old barn. Early-birds can fish in the Dolores River. Take Hwy. 160 to Rte. 145 north (at Cortez); (970) 882-4158.

District of Columbia

Bluegrass in the Nation's Capital

When in the Washington, D.C., area, turn on **WAMU (88.5 FM),** a public radio station with more than thirty-five hours of bluegrass, old-time, and classic country programming every week.

All the bluegrass and country that commercial stations don't play is broadcast weekdays from 3 to 6 P.M., Saturdays from noon to 6 P.M., and Sundays from midnight until 5 P.M. *Grand Ole Opry* announcer Eddie Stubbs spins classic country and honky-tonk on Sundays from 2 to 5 P.M. Call WAMU's **Bluegrass Bulletin Board** for regional festival and concert listings; (800) 525-8338 or (202) 885-1234.

Georgetown
MUSIC CITY ROADHOUSE

Music City Roadhouse doesn't quite fit in in Georgetown, a few steps away from the trendy stores, cosmopolitan eateries, and loud sports bars. When asked why the funky Southern restaurant and bar is located here, co-owner Larry Work doesn't miss a beat. " 'Cause we're crazy," he says.

Work and his partners may be a little crazy, but they sure know how to make hassled city folks feel at home. One of Music City Roadhouse's mottoes is "Anybody Caught Eatin' Chicken with a Knife and Fork Will Be Thrown Out." The other is "Conserve Water—Drink More Beer."

The Roadhouse is a handsome two-level joint overlooking the historic C&O Canal, halfway between Georgetown's main drag (M Street) and the Potomac River. It's got exposed brick walls, rough-hewn beams, linoleum-topped tables, and mismatched chairs. The walls are covered with old license plates, business cards, photos of country stars, and things like a *Grand Ole Opry* stage costume worn by one of the Stony Mountain Cloggers and a pair of Tanya Tucker's jeans. (If you bring in an old hat or cap, the waitress will hang it up and give you a free draft beer or dessert.)

Anything goes, whether it's enjoying an intimate meal with twenty of your closest friends, bellying up to the bar for a microbrewed beer, or filling up on bottomless family-style trays of fried chicken and mashed potatoes. For dinner or lunch, choose from catfish, pot roast, or spare ribs, with sides of greens, slaw, sweet potatoes, and vegetables. "We grew up in the South. This is the kind of food we were raised on," Work says.

The real treat is the old-fashioned **Sunday gospel brunch** with funky music provided by Brother Luke Sanders and the Sensational Stars. While you wait, the waitress brings out warm loaves of moist banana bread and cold balls of butter. Then the platters arrive, piled high with blueberry pancakes, scrambled eggs, crispy fried chicken, and home fries, accompanied by sausage, bacon, and cheese grits. Then there are the buttermilk biscuits, homemade blueberry jam, and rich sawmill gravy. The pièce de résistance is the baked peaches, swimming in a sweet sauce surrounded by pecans. Eat all you want for about $12.95.

"A lot of our customers are people who grew up in the South, or people living around here who want something different," Work says.

The **C&O Canal** offers fun and educational boat tours through the locks, leaving near the restaurant, April through mid-September. Call (202) 653-5190.

GETTING THERE: Washington, D.C. is between Maryland and Virginia on I-95. Take Metro to the Foggy Bottom stop and walk west on Pennsylvania Ave., which becomes M St. (about ten blocks). Free parking is available for customers. 1050 30th St. N.W.; (202) 337-4444.

Florida

White Springs
STEPHEN FOSTER STATE FOLK CULTURE CENTER

Stephen Foster apparently never saw the Suwannee River, but he immortalized it nonetheless in his timeless composition, "Old Folks at Home" ("Way down upon the Swannee River . . ."). America's Troubadour wrote more than 200 classic songs during the nineteenth century, including "Oh! Susannah" and "Camptown Races." Florida adopted "Old Folks at Home" as its state song in 1935.

Stephen Foster State Folk Culture Center in White Springs honors Foster with a small museum, and serves as a gathering place for Florida folk crafts, music, and culture. The park is located on the banks of the Suwannee River, which originates in Georgia's Okefenokee Swamp and flows 250 miles to the Gulf of Mexico. Activities include craft demonstrations, boating on the Suwannee, and daily carillon concerts from the Foster Tower.

Special events take place year-round, including the two-day **Jeannie Auditions and Ball** the first weekend in October. Now in its fifth decade, the event selects an outstanding female vocalist to serve as Jeannie ("with the light brown hair"). Entrants wear authentic 1850s ballgowns. The **Florida Folk Festival** is held over Memorial Day weekend with songs, music, dance, and storytelling.

(*See also:* Kentucky—Bardstown.)

GETTING THERE: White Springs is in north-central Florida, about 30 miles south of the Georgia border. Open 8 A.M. to sundown daily. Admission $3.25 per car. Take I-10/Exit 43 to Hwy. 41 north or I-75/ Exit 84 to Rte. 136; (904) 397-2733.

Live Oak
SPIRIT OF THE SUWANNEE RIVER PARK

Farther down the Suwannee River in Live Oak, the three-day **Suwannee River Country Music Jam** draw tens of thousands of people in October. The festival, held at Spirit of Suwannee River Park, features headline acts, camping, and hiking on 580 acres of riverside parkland. Bluegrass and gospel concerts are presented year-round, as well as Saturday-evening jamming in the Pickin' Shed. Live Oak is midway between Jacksonville and Tallahassee, 15 miles west of the Stephen Foster Folk Culture Center (*see page 54*). Take I-10/Exit 40 to Hwy. 129 north; (904) 364-1683.

Panama City Beach
THE OCEAN OPRY

Panama City Beach is a popular resort town on the Gulf of Mexico with sandy white beaches and clear blue waters. Scuba-diving, snorkeling, and golf are popular activities, while fishing piers extend far into the Gulf.

The *Ocean Opry Show* in Panama City Beach presents country-music variety shows year-round in a 1,000-seat theater, with special appearances by stars from Nashville. Schedules vary, with nightly performances in the summer and fewer performances in the off-season. Tickets $14.95. Two miles west of Hathaway Bridge on Hwy. 98A (Front Beach Rd.); (904) 234-5464.

GETTING THERE: Panama City Beach is on the Gulf of Mexico in western Florida. Take I-10 to Hwy. 231 south. Contact the Visitors' Bureau; (800) PC-BEACH.

Georgia

Young Harris
THE REACH OF SONG

The Reach of Song is Georgia's official historic drama, about the state's deep-rooted Appalachian mountain music. The performance, with fiddling, buck-dancing, and singing, takes place in a 900-seat air-conditioned theater at Young Harris College. Shows are Tuesday through Saturday evenings late June through August; a Southern meal can be purchased beforehand. Tickets $10–12.

GETTING THERE: Young Harris is in the Blue Ridge Mountains of northeast Georgia, below the North Carolina border. Hwy. 76; (800) 262-SONG or (706) 896-3388.

Macon
GEORGIA MUSIC HALL OF FAME

Since 1979, Georgia has been inducting new members into the Georgia Music Hall of Fame. The 42,000-square-foot Georgia Music Hall of Fame will open to the public in downtown Macon, a small city in the center of the state, during the summer of 1996.

Among more than sixty members of the Hall of Fame are country music's Fiddlin' John Carson, the Lewis Family, Alan Jackson, and Ray Stevens, as well as Georgia natives who have made vital contributions to rock and roll (R.E.M., Little Richard), rhythm and blues (James Brown, Otis Redding, Ma Rainey), gospel (Amy Grant), jazz (Lena Horne, Johnny Mercer), and other genres.

The $6.5 million, three-floor museum re-creates a Georgia village, with theaters, parks, outdoor stages, and nightclubs. Visitors walk down a typical street, wandering in and out of places like the Skillet Licker Cafe, Rock-n-Roll Record Shop, Songwriters Alley, and Gospel Chapel. Exhibits include multimedia audio-visual displays with memorabilia, photographs, music, and oral histories. A movie theater allows guests to pick videos. The second floor houses a library and archive, while the top floor is used for conferences and banquets.

GETTING THERE: Macon is 80 miles south of Atlanta. The museum is downtown at I-75 and I-16/Exit 4, Martin Luther King and Walnut Sts. Call for hours and events; (912) 738-0017.

For area information, contact Macon Visitors' Bureau; (800) 768-3401.

Tifton
GEORGIA AGRIRAMA AND *WIREGRASS OPRY*

The Georgia Agrirama in Tifton is a 95-acre outdoor living history museum depicting an 1890s town, forest industries complex, and farmsteading communities. There are three dozen authentic structures, as well as barnyard animals, cane grinding, cotton ginning, and a working smokehouse. The **Folk Life and Fiddlers' Jamboree** takes place here in late April. Next door to the Agrirama Country Store, the *Wiregrass Opry* offers open-air performances of bluegrass, country, and clogging on the first Saturday night of every month, May through September. Tickets $4. (Due to the Olympics in Atlanta, schedule may vary in 1996.)

GETTING THERE: Tifton is in south-central Georgia. The Agrirama is open 9 A.M. to 5 P.M. Tuesday through Saturday; 12:30 to 5 P.M. Sundays. Closed Thanksgiving, Christmas Day and three days prior, and New Year's Day. Tickets $8. Take I-75/Exit 20; (912) 386-3344.

Georgia Festivals

America's first family of bluegrass gospel music hosts the **Lewis Family Homecoming and Bluegrass Festival** in their hometown of Lincolnton the first weekend in May. The three-day event takes place at Elijah Clark State Park in central-east Georgia across the South Carolina border. In addition to bluegrass stars and local bands, the 447-acre park has RV hookups, camping, a white-sand lake beach, miniature golf, and a playground. Take I-20/Exit 59 to Hwy. 78 north, to Rte. 43, to Hwy. 378 east; (706) 864-7203 or 359-3458.

In its third decade, the **Dahlonega Bluegrass Festival** features the best bands in the business for three days at Blackburn Park and campgrounds the third weekend in June. Dahlonega is in northeast Georgia in the southern Blue Ridge Mountains. Take Hwy. 19 to Old Hwy. 9E. Burnt Stand Rd.; (706) 864-7203.

Northeast of Atlanta, the two-day **Fiddlin' Fish Arts and Crafts Festival** at Lake Lanier Islands in late May includes a carnival, fresh fish and seafood, lakeside camping, a fiddle-off for $2,500 in prizes, and headline concerts. Take I-985/Exit 2 and follow the signs; (800) 840-LAKE or (770) 932-7200.

Dillards Music Park in Rome hosts bluegrass festivals year-round, including Thanksgiving and New Year's weekends, and in late March, mid-April, mid-July, and late October. The park has RV hookups, covered sheds for jamming, concessions, and arts and crafts. Rome is between Atlanta and Chattanooga, Tennessee. Take I-75 to Hwy. 411 west. At Rome, take Old Calhoun Rd. north; (706) 291-0216.

The Atlantic Ocean resort town Jekyll Island hosts the **Country Music by the Sea** festival the first Saturday in June, with performances on the beach. Jekyll Island is on Georgia's southeast coast. Take I-95/Exit 6 to Rte. 520 east; (800) 841-6586 or (912) 635-3636.

Idaho

Weiser
NATIONAL OLDTIME FIDDLERS' CONTEST AND HALL OF FAME

Fiddling contests have been held in Weiser since the 1890s, when westward migrants on the Oregon Trail brought the instrument to this beautiful region of western Idaho. The National Oldtime Fiddlers' Contest, begun in the early fifties, is held the third full week in June and draws more than 20,000 people annually.

Contests for $15,000 in prize money take place day and night at Weiser High School (West Seventh and Indianhead Rd.), while events such as live entertainment, dancing, jam sessions, craft fairs, food concessions, a golf tournament, and a carnival are held around the city. The Saturday fiddle parade is the largest in the state with more than 125 entries.

The National Oldtime Fiddlers' Hall of Fame, which displays instruments and photographs of musicians, can be viewed year-round at the Weiser Chamber of Commerce, 8 East Idaho St.

Weiser is about 70 miles south of **Hells Canyon National Recreation Area,** a park with the deepest gorge in North America (7,993 feet) and more than 600,000 acres of prime wilderness for fishing, hunting, boating, and camping; (509) 758-0616.

GETTING THERE: Weiser is on the Oregon border, northwest of Boise. Take I-84 to Hwy. 95 north. For contest tickets and information, call (800) 437-1280 or (208) 549-0452.

Illinois

Chicago
CHICAGO COUNTRY MUSIC FESTIVAL

The Windy City's premier country-music event, the Chicago Country Music Festival, draws 250,000 people every year. It's held in Grant Park on the first weekend of the ten-day **Taste of Chicago** festival, which features dozens of food booths, sports, contests, and concessions. National, regional, and local country artists play all day and into the night on two stages. The free festival is usually at the end of June. Grant Park is on the lakefront at Jackson and Columbus; (312) 744-3315.

Taylorville
NASHVILLE NORTH U.S.A.

Major Nashville recording artists are booked every weekend at Nashville North U.S.A., a theater 25 miles southeast of Springfield that brings country music's best to the Midwest. Paula Marohl and the Northern Lights Band open all shows. "Guests really like to come here for the family orientation," says Marohl, who also owns the theater. The state-of-the-art, 1,100-seat venue does not allow alcohol or smoking. Tickets $15 to $22; no seat is more than 25 yards from center stage. Take I-55/Exit 82 to Rte. 104 east; (217) 287-2103.

Indiana

Indianapolis
INDIANA COUNTRY MUSIC EXPO

This unique three-day event, begun in 1995 by mega–country stations WFMS (95.5-FM) and The Bear (104.5-FM), combines a country-music fan fair with an industry trade show. The Indiana Country Music Expo features a headline concert, new-artist showcases, Western wear fashion shows, meet-and-greets with up-and-coming stars, exhibit booths, line-dancing lessons, and "how-to" seminars on getting into the music business and starting a fan club. It's held annually in late March/early April at the Indiana State Fair Grounds in Indianapolis. Tickets $5. Call for more information. 1202 E. 38th St.

The stations also host **several major country-music festivals** every year: the Indy 500 Mini-Marathon Concert in May, July Jam on Independence Day at Indianapolis' Pan Am Plaza, Free Stage at the Indiana State Fair in August, and Fan Jam (Indiana's largest music festival) in late September. Contact the stations; (317) 842-9550.

Nashville
THE OTHER NASHVILLE

It's pure coincidence that Nashville, Indiana, has the same name as Nashville, Tennessee. But the fact remains that Nashville, Indiana, happens to be a great town for country music and live entertainment.

Located in rustic Brown County, Nashville is a charming Midwestern resort town with a proud history of nurturing and inspiring artists, writers, and musicians. There are 3,500 theater seats in and around Nashville, from major regional venues like the Little Nashville Opry to the tiny Melchior Marionette Theatre (*see page 63*). Bill Monroe's Festival Park is just up the road, while Bloomington, with its own thriving entertainment scene, is 25 miles west.

Downtown, more than 350 specialty shops are interspersed with
Victorian mansions, Greek Revival homes, handsome stone buildings, and rough-hewn log cabins. It's a pleasure to amble up and
down the narrow streets and alleys, wandering in and out of little
shops selling antiques, original art, handmade crafts, quilts, gourmet
coffee, flowers, ice cream, collectibles, woodwork, sandwiches,
books, clothing, candles, brooms, socks, and bird feeders.

The core shopping area has no fast-food or chain stores, no neon
signs, and no outlet malls. Unwilling to sell its soul to court tourists,
Nashville has taken the high road and emphasized the characteristics
that make it special. "We want to make sure that the attitude of the
town doesn't get destroyed," says Mary Fredrickson of the Brown
County Visitors' Bureau. "We're very careful to keep it unique."

More than 2.5 million people come here annually, yet visitors still
feel like they've discovered a secret getaway. There are horse-drawn
carriage rides, charming inns, bed-and-breakfasts, house tours, and
several fine restaurants.

Besides shopping and entertainment, additional attractions include the **John Dillinger Historical Wax Museum.** Claiming to
have ninety percent of "all Dillinger material known to exist," the
museum displays the trousers Dillinger died in and the gun that
killed him, as well as 25 wax figures. Call for hours. Admission $3.
90 W. Washington St.; (812) 988-1933.

Other attractions include the **Brown County Historical Museum,**
open on weekends from 1 to 5 P.M., May through October (Old School
Lane, just east of the Brown County Courthouse; (812) 988-6647), and
the 16,000-acre **Brown County State Park,** a few miles from Nashville
(Rte. 46 east; (812) 988-6406).

Musicians often perform for free on the streets, from a small stage
in front of the Brown County Art Barn, and at the Daily Grind coffeehouse on weekends. Nashville's entertainment season generally
runs from March through November, with some shows in February
and around Christmas. Call for schedules and prices.

The **Pine Box Theatre** is run by an exceptionally high-spirited couple named Bob and Romilda Hamontre. When they fell in love back
in the 1950s, Romilda gave up a promising career in musical theater;
Bob promised Romilda her own theater someday. Fast-forward to the
nineties, when the Hamontres were running a print shop across the

street from the Old Bond Funeral Home in Nashville. When the funeral home died in 1992, Bob converted it into a theater called, naturally, the Pine Box.

The Hamontres describe their unique style of cabaret show "Broadway in reverse." "We take existing music and write a script around it," Bob explains. Shows are performed by "Those Good-Time Gals and Guys," an energetic group led by Romilda. The gals just *love* to entertain. They dance, they act, they sing their hearts out every single night. The guys are a terrific pianist and percussionist, and Bob gamely playing all the male roles.

The troupe performs nine original shows every year. Each includes seventy to eighty songs, with a focus on close harmony, popular music, country, and gospel. "We have never repeated a song, ever," Romilda brags.

Seeing a show at the Pine Box Theater is guaranteed fun, because Those Good-Time Gals and Guys overflow with good humor, verve, and enthusiasm. "Sometime during the evening we're going to play something everyone likes," Romilda says. "Country fans don't think they'll like it, but they always do." Reservations recommended. One block from downtown, 168 S. Jefferson St.; (812) 988-6827.

Also downtown, the intimate **Nashville Follies Musical Theater** presents a series of variety shows featuring country music, dancing, and comedy. 63 East Washington St.; (800) 449-SHOW or (812) 988-9007.

The Brown County Playhouse is the home of Indiana's oldest professional summer-stock theater, operated in conjunction with Indiana University's Department of Theatre and Drama in Bloomington. A full season of dramas, mysteries, and musical comedies are presented annually in an intimate 400-seat theater. S. Van Buren St.; (812) 988-8230.

The **Melchior Marionette Theatre** is a comedy cabaret on strings with hand-crafted puppets in a small outdoor alcove a few doors from the Brown County Playhouse. The 20-minute shows are presented at 1 and 3 P.M., July through October. West side of S. Van Buren St.; (800) 849-4853.

Headline acts from Loretta Lynn to Pam Tillis are booked on Saturday nights at the 2,000-seat **Little Nashville Opry,** a major regional country-music venue one mile from Nashville. The popular *Friday Night Opry* is a variety show with the Little Nashville Express band

and guests. Special events include talent shows and gospel concerts. Hwy. 46 west; (812) 988-2235.

The Lloyd Wood Show is presented in the comfortable Country Time Music Hall at Ski World a few miles west of Nashville. An Indiana native, Wood fronted the house band at the Little Nashville Opry for many years before striking out on his own. Affable and funny, he's got a strong voice in the traditional style of George Strait, and a gift for country star impersonations.

Wood is especially fond of classic country songs by George Jones, Faron Young, and Willie Nelson, but his two-and-a-half-hour show also features bluegrass, country rock, Western Swing, and a few originals on weekend nights. From Nashville, take Rte. 46 west 4.5 miles to Ski World; (812) 988-0717.

GETTING THERE: Nashville is at Rtes. 135 and 46, about 25 miles east of Bloomington and 15 miles west of Columbus. Take I-65/Exit 68 to Rte. 46 west. The Visitors' Bureau is at the corner of Main and Van Buren Sts.; (800) 753-3255 or (812) 988-7303.

Bean Blossom
BILL MONROE'S BLUEGRASS HAVEN

When Bill Monroe first played the *Grand Ole Opry* in 1939, the story goes, he was hired on the spot. His bosses told him that the only way he could leave was if he fired himself. Monroe's hard-driving style of traditional music got its name from his band, the Blue Grass Boys. He was inducted into the Country Music Hall of Fame in 1970. Well into his eighties, Monroe continued to perform constantly, on the *Opry* stage and at bluegrass festivals.

It's no surprise, then, that the "Father of Bluegrass Music" would be responsible for the longest continuously running bluegrass festival in history. For more than 30 years, he has staged the **Bean Blossom Bluegrass Festival,** a four-day gathering on the third weekend in June. Bluegrass fans from all over the country and world pour into **Bill and James Monroe's Festival Park and Campground** for the star-studded event, as well as his three-day **Bluegrass Hall of Fame Festival and Uncle Pen Day** the second weekend in September. The 55-acre park is in Bean Blossom five miles north of Nashville, Indiana. The rusting hull of "The Bluegrass Express," an old pickup truck, sits at the entrance to the festival grounds. The stage is at the bottom of a wooded dell. There's a fishing lake and hiking trails, and plenty of room for primitive camping and RVs in adjoining fields. The 5,000-square-foot **Bill Monroe Country Star Museum and Bluegrass Hall of Fame** opened in 1992. It features Bill's Circle, a display of his awards and early stage clothing; Monroe family items; a photo gallery of band members going back to the 1930s; memorabilia donated by Dolly Parton, Johnny Cash, Loretta Lynn, George Jones, and others; and Monroe's Hall of Fame, with pictures and short sketches of a dozen bluegrass greats. In addition, Monroe restored a cabin originally owned by his uncle Pendleton Vandiver, an early mentor and musical inspiration, and placed it next to the museum. Out front, the **Walkway of Stars** honors Charlie Monroe, Ricky Skaggs, Elvis Presley, the Oak Ridge Boys, and dozens of Monroe's heroes.

(*See also:* Kentucky—Rosine, Owensboro.)

GETTING THERE: Bean Blossom is about 25 miles east of Bloomington. Museum and campground are open end of May through October. Tuesday through Saturday, 9 A.M. to 5 P.M. Admission $4. Allow an hour. Take I-65/Exit 68 to Rte. 46 west, to Rte. 135 north. 5163 State Rd. 135; (812) 988-6422, (812) 988-0333, or (615) 868-3333.

Corydon
LEE KING'S JAMBOREE

About 15 miles west of Louisville, Kentucky, southern Indiana's *Corydon Jamboree* serves up country and gospel music every Saturday night in a 400-seat theater. The show features owner Lee King's house band and a different special guest each week. "We get everyone from six-week-old babies to ninety-year-old grandmas," King says. "It's family entertainment." Showtime is 7:30 P.M. and tickets cost $4.50 for adults, $2.50 for ages six through twelve. Take I-65/Exit 105. Go south on Rte. 135 and bear left onto N. Capitol Ave. Turn right onto Hurst Lane and follow the signs; (502) 422-3122 or (812) 969-2049. (*See also:* Kentucky—Louisville Area.)

Iowa

Walnut
TRADITIONAL COUNTRY MUSIC IN THE HEARTLAND

Since 1976, the **National Traditional Country Music Association** has worked to preserve and promote "real" country music, acoustic old-time sounds from a slower, less complicated time. Based in Walnut, President Bob Everhart and the NTCMA have been quite enterprising in achieving their goals.

The association publishes a sixty-page bimonthly newsletter for members, and produces regular programs on Iowa public television and radio. Every year over Labor Day, 50,000 people pour into Avoca, Iowa, for the **National Old-Time Country Music Contest and Festival.** Held at the Pottawatamie County Fair Grounds, 6 miles west of Walnut, the festival presents seven full days of acoustic music on seven stages. Take I-80/Exit 40 to Hwy. 59 south.

In 1986, NTCMA purchased the 1899 **Walnut Country Opera House** for $3,000. Now fully restored, the theater in downtown Walnut houses a performance center, the **Pioneer Musical Instrument Museum,** the **Mid-America Old-Time Fiddlers Hall of Fame,** and the **Mid-America Old-Time Country Music Hall of Fame.** The displays are open Memorial Day to Labor Day, and by appointment. Traditional country-music shows are booked regularly. Central and Pearl Sts.

The organization acquired a second theater in Anita, 35 miles east of Walnut. After a renovation is complete, the **Oak Tree Theatre** plans to present old-time country music, films, and food.

Walnut is known as Iowa's **Antique City**. There are eighteen antique shops and malls, four bed-and-breakfasts, and several restaurants in town (but no stoplight!). The Walnut Visitors' Center downtown provides free maps and coffee.

GETTING THERE: Walnut is 85 miles west of Des Moines, 1 mile south of I-80/Exit 46. Contact the Visitors' Bureau, 607 Highland St.; (712) 784-2100.

For information about NTCMA events and projects, write P.O. Box 438, Walnut, IA 51577; (712) 784-3001.

Clear Lake

SURF BALLROOM

Shortly after a performance before 1,500 people at Clear Lake's Surf Ballroom on February 2, 1959, Buddy Holly, Ritchie Valens, and J.P. "The Big Bopper" Richardson took off in a small charter plane for Moorhead, Minnesota. The plane crashed shortly after takeoff, killing the performers and their pilot, Roger Peterson. (There was no room on the plane for Waylon Jennings, then a member of Holly's band, the Crickets.)

Built in 1933, the Surf Ballroom still holds concerts, and big-band and polka dances. The hall, with music memorabilia commemorating "The Day the Music Died," welcomes visitors year-round. Open 9 A.M. to 5 P.M. weekdays, noon to 1 A.M. Saturdays, and by appointment. 460 North Shore Dr.; (515) 357-6151.

The three-day **Buddy Holly Tribute** festival takes place on the weekend closest to February 2, drawing fans from around the world.

(*See also:* Texas—Lubbock; New Mexico—Clovis.)

GETTING THERE: Clear Lake is in north-central Iowa. Take I-35/Exit 193. Contact the Clear Lake Chamber of Commerce; (515) 357-2159.

Kansas

Kansas Music Shows

Singer Chely Wright's mother, Cheri Smith, bought the Blue Moon Theater in Blue Mound, about 90 miles south of Kansas City several years ago. Her **Flint Hills Opry** is a variety show with country, gospel, and comedy on Saturday nights year-round. (The Flint Hills are tall grasslands stretching from Nebraska to Oklahoma.) Take Hwy. 69 south to Rte. 52 west. On Main Street; (913) 756-2464.

In Council Grove, 50 miles southwest of Topeka, the **Trailside Jamboree Country Music Show** offers a live family variety show with the BJ4 Band on Thursday evenings, once a month at the Ritz Theatre. Tickets $5.50. Take I-335/Exit 147 to Hwy. 56 west. Call for current dates. 212 W. Main St.; (800) 732-9211.

Winfield
WALNUT VALLEY FESTIVAL

Bob and Kendra Redford's Walnut Valley Festival has been bringing together acoustic musicians for rigorous competition and camaraderie since 1972. Contests include the National Flat-Picking Guitar Championship, as well as showdowns in autoharp, finger-picking, old-time fiddle, hammer and mountain dulcimer, and bluegrass banjo. The four-day festival takes place the third full weekend in September, with entertainment by national and regional bands, crafts, a songwriters' showcase, a spirited campsite-decorating contest, and lots of jamming. Winfield is in south-central Kansas, about 50 miles southeast of Wichita. Take I-35 to Hwy. 160 east; (316) 221-3250.

Kentucky

East Kentucky Appalachians— The Country Music Highway

Kentucky has been working hard to promote development and tourism in its historically poor, mountainous eastern region. In addition to its natural beauty, the state hopes to take advantage of one of the area's greatest assets: the many popular country superstars born here. A recent innovation is the Country Music Highway, Highway 23, which runs from Portsmouth, Ohio, in the north, along the Ohio River to the Big Sandy, and down through Pike County to the Virginia border.

The hometowns of Patty Loveless (Elkhorn City), Dwight Yoakam (Betsy Lane), Tom T. Hall (Olive Hill), the Judds (Ashland), Billy Ray Cyrus (Flatwoods), and many other bluegrass and country artists are along the way. The plan is for every county to have signs honoring local stars. Already, streets and plazas have been renamed by the towns. Attractions include Loretta Lynn's homeplace in Van Lear, the Keith Whitley Fan Club in Sandy Hook, the Kentucky Opry in Prestonsburg, and several music shows and festivals.

Some of the towns are right on the Country Music Highway, while others are reached by rural two-lane routes. These drives through the rural east Kentucky Appalachians are intrinsically enjoyable, if you give yourself enough time to take it all in. The roads (ones that haven't been bypassed by new four-lane highways) wind slowly through the mountains and along rushing creeks, making hairpin turns over and through lush green hollows. Several well-run state parks provide access to stunning forests, lakes, caves, and natural bridges.

Bungalows, trailers, and barns dot the sloping hillsides and rolling fields of bluegrass and pine woods. Small coal mines, ironworks, and rail lines, working and abandoned, appear from time to time. Most towns are quiet and isolated, a bit stuck in time, with few modern conveniences. Huge new mega-malls at the edges of the larger highways, while economically important, seem monstrously out of place in this terrain.

The following attractions are generally listed from north to south on the Country Music Highway, with a few detours east and west.

GETTING THERE: For information about state parks, contact the Kentucky Department of Parks; (800) 255-PARK or (502) 564-2172. A free booklet listing attractions, historical sites, parks, festivals, and accommodations in the Kentucky Appalachians is available from the Kentucky Department of Travel; (800) 225-8747.

Flatwoods
ACHY BREAKY MAN

Billy Ray Cyrus grew up in Flatwoods (pop. 10,000) at the northern end of the Country Music Highway. **The Art Department,** a local graphic-design and silk-screening shop, publishes a brochure of local points of interest and is "your official Billy Ray Cyrus center" in Flatwoods. The store sells BRC-licensed merchandise.

The brochure lists Russell High School, from which Cyrus graduated in 1979, the Faith Christian Assembly church that he attended, and Flatwoods Fire Department, where he liked to hang out. At **L&J Tops-O-Kreem,** you can sit in Billy Ray's booth and ask for his standing order, a foot-long hot dog with sauce and thin vanilla milkshake.

"The next time you travel this way, stop by," the brochure urges. "We love company and know how to make you feel welcome." There is a "Home of Billy Ray Cyrus" sign on top of Wheeler Hill off Highway 23. A BRC **Fan-O-Rama** takes place in Flatwoods most summers; call for current information.

(Cyrus used to play at the **Ragtime Lounge** in Huntington, West Virginia, across the Ohio River from Ashland; (304) 429-5030.)

GETTING THERE: Flatwoods is 5 miles north of Ashland. Take I-64/Exit 191 to Hwy. 23 north. The Billy Ray Cyrus brochure is available from the Ashland Visitors' Bureau (*see page 71*) or The Art Department, (606) 836-7033.

Ashland
AT HOME WITH THE JUDDS

The Judds, the harmonizing mother-daughter duet from Ashland in Greenup County, were hugely successful before Naomi Judd's chronic hepatitis forced them to disband in the early 1990s. Wynonna Judd has launched a successful solo career. Naomi's younger daughter, Ashley Judd, is a critically acclaimed actress.

Ashland, the largest city in eastern Kentucky, is headquarters for Ashland Inc. and AK Steel. The downtown is scattered with ornate mansions built by wealthy industrialists.

The **Kentucky Highlands Museum** has a small display of Naomi and Wynonna Judd's stage costumes and memorabilia. 1620 Winchester Ave.; (606) 329-8888. Ashland's main square, at 16th Street and Winchester Avenue, is **Judds Plaza.** Naomi Judd returns home from time to time to help out with local fund-raising efforts.

In 1992, Billy Ray Cyrus filmed the video for "Achy Breaky Heart" at the **Paramount Arts Center,** a beautifully restored 1931 art-deco movie palace in downtown Ashland. Live performances of everything from bluegrass to Beethoven and ballet to Broadway can be seen at this outstanding venue. Free tours are offered on weekdays. 1300 Winchester Ave.; (606) 324-3175.

The ***Coalton Country Jubilee,*** 10 miles west of Ashland, offers live country music and dancing in a 400-seat theater on Saturday nights year-round. The shows begin at 8 P.M. April through October, and 7 P.M. the rest of the year. 1525 Hwy. 60; (606) 928-3110.

Ashland's five-day **Summer Motion festival,** the first weekend in July, features a country headline concert and much more. The three-day **Poage Landing Days** in late September includes a headline concert, bluegrass festival, lumberjack demonstration, art, and antiques.

GETTING THERE: Ashland is on the Ohio River, few miles north of Huntington, West Virginia. Take I-64/Exit 191 to Hwy. 23 north. Contact Ashland Area Visitors' Bureau at 728 Greenup Ave.; (800) 377-6249 or (606) 329-1007.

Carter County

FRIENDS OF TOM T. HALL

Tom T. Hall was born near Olive Hill, 40 miles west of Ashland in rural Carter County. Signs honoring Hall are posted on both ends of town, and **Sturgill's Music Center** has a Tom T. Hall display with pictures, awards, and memorabilia. "We were raised with him, so we've got a good bit of stuff," says Alma Sturgill. Her husband, Darvin Sturgill, played in Hall's band years ago. The music store sells instruments and recordings. Scott Street; (606) 286-4611.

A country music show is presented on Saturday nights (except during winter) at the **Walter Campbell Recreation Farm,** a 255-acre homestead with hay rides and sorghum-making demonstrations. North of Grayson, on Rte. 1; (606) 474-4003.

Local festivals include the four-day Shriner's Bluegrass Festival in mid-July; (606) 286-4426. At Carter Caves State Park north of Olive Hill, the two-day International Strange Music Weekend takes place in late August, followed by the five-day Fraley Family Mountain Music Festival over Labor Day weekend; (606) 286-4411.

GETTING THERE: Carter County is west of Ashland; Olive Hill is south of I-64/Exit 156 on Hwy. 60. Contact the Chamber of Commerce; (606) 286-5532.

Sandy Hook

KEITH WHITLEY FAN CLUB: "HIS MUSIC LIVES ON"

Jackie Keith Whitley was born in Sandy Hook on July 1, 1954, and died just thirty-five years later on May 9, 1989, of acute alcohol poisoning. On the verge of stardom when he died, Whitley's reputation as a singer and songwriter continues to grow. A 1995 tribute album organized by Whitley's widow, Lorrie Morgan, which includes Alison Krauss's beautiful rendition of "When You Say Nothing At All," brought his music to a still-larger audience.

A steady stream of people travel to Sandy Hook, south of Olive Hill in Elliott County, each year to pay their respects. A small museum is located in mother Faye Whitley's detached two-car garage, behind one of the houses Keith lived in as a boy. (An earlier house on the same spot was struck by lightning and burned.)

Faye Whitley (right) and her daughter-in-law Flo keep Keith Whitley's memory alive.

Don't expect a formal attraction. The garage is used for laundry and storage, and Faye pulls her car in each night. Instead, think of this as a visit with the singer's family, whose motto is "His Music Lives On." The Whitleys care deeply about keeping Keith's memory alive, and providing a support network for his fans and friends.

"[Keith] was just beginning to hit it big. He had three consecutive number-one hits when he died," says Flo Whitley, Keith's sister-in-law, who runs his fan club. "We were always supportive of him and his music, and we knew that he was talented, but it was something that we took for granted because he'd done it all his life. We did not stop to really pay attention and see how good he was until he was no longer here. I think that's also true in the country music world."

The whole Whitley family was musical. Faye Whitley played piano and guitar. Keith's grandfather played clawhammer banjo, and his older brother Dwight, married to Flo, plays guitar and sings. As a boy, Keith absorbed like a sponge the bluegrass records Dwight gave him. "Dwight would buy him a new Stanley Brothers album every week," Flo says. "When he came back the next week, Keith knew every song."

During his teens, Keith met Ricky Skaggs, from the nearby town of Cordell, at a fiddling festival in Ezel, Kentucky. The two became fast friends and bluegrass partners. "When Ralph Stanley heard them together singing the Stanley Brothers' music, he took them on the road instantly," Flo says. The young pair even released two albums covering Stanley Brothers songs.

Whitley later became the lead singer for J.D. Crowe and the New South. In the early 1980s, he landed a solo RCA recording contract and began releasing his own brand of pure country music. Among his six number-one songs were "I'm No Stranger to the Rain," "Don't Close Your Eyes," and "I Wonder Do You Think of Me."

Flo has arranged memorabilia around the garage, including Whitley's stage costumes, clothing, guitars, backstage passes, letters and cards, album covers, and personal items like speeding tickets and motel receipts. Fans have sent poems, photographs, and original artwork. In scrapbooks there are photographs of at least a half-dozen children named after Keith Whitley.

"The fan club is steadily growing," Flo says. "They are so dedicated. Keith's fans feel like they knew him personally."

Flo handles the fan club now because it became too difficult for Keith's mother. Faye Whitley lost her son Randy in a motorcycle accident in 1983, then her husband, Elmer, before Keith's apparent suicide in 1989. "I didn't love [Keith] more than anyone else," she explains. "But he had the most love for people. He had to call me every day. He'd say, 'Mom, I never intended to do anything but sing.' "

Keith struggled with alcoholism over the years, but the news of his death was a big shock to his friends, family, fans, and hometown. Sandy Hook renamed its main street Keith Whitley Boulevard, and the local tourism council plans to build a Keith Whitley Memorial Music Hall with museum and performance space. The Keith Whitley Memorial Fund is also collecting money for a bronze statue. "Keith Whitley is a hero to this town and these people now," Flo says.

The annual **Keith and Randy Whitley Memorial Motorcycle Ride,** usually Father's Day weekend, travels from Sandy Hook to Spring Hill Cemetery in Nashville. Whitley's headstone incorrectly lists his birth year as 1955. At the beginning of his contract with RCA, publicity materials mistakenly had him born in 1955 rather than 1954. With typical humor, Keith didn't correct the error because it gave him another year to reach his goal of a hit record before age thirty. (*See also:* Tennessee—Around Nashville, Nashville Cemeteries.)

On the Saturday before Labor Day, the Whitleys host a gathering at the fan club/museum with live music and an extensive exhibit of memorabilia. The **Keith Whitley Memorial Exhibit** is held in conjunction with Sandy Hook's **Tobacco Festival,** a homecoming and harvest celebration on Labor Day weekend. Main Street is closed off on Friday and Saturday for country music, bluegrass, and a traditional mutton-and-potatoes meal.

In recent years, Dwight Whitley has toured with a tribute show of his brother's music. His album of previously unrecorded Keith Whitley songs, *Brotherly Love,* is available from retailers or through Neon Records, 2412 Argillite Rd., Flatwoods, KY 41139; (606) 833-5820.

GETTING THERE: Take I-64/Exit 172 (Grayson) to Rte. 7 south, to Rte. 32 north. Or, from Exit 137/Morehead, take Rte. 32 south. The Whitley house/fan club is on Rte. 32, ⅘ mile from the intersection with Rte. 7. The white-and-black house is on the right, across the street from Betty's Pizza Place. Look for a small *Elliott County News* sign on the mailbox and "Home of Keith Whitley" painted above the garage.

Be sure to call Flo Whitley to make an appointment for a visit. Contact her for information about the memorial ride, Labor Day weekend exhibit, and fan club. Write P.O. Box 222, Sandy Hook, KY 41171-0222; or call (606) 738-5292.

For Sandy Hook/Elliott County information, call (606) 738-5821.

Van Lear
"A CABIN ON A HILL"

Through the once-thriving coal town of Van Lear, past the old company store, down a dirt road, into a narrow mountain valley, alongside a ravine, past the one-room Butcher Hollow School House and up a steep rise, is the "cabin on a hill." Made famous by Loretta Lynn's song "Coal Miner's Daughter," this is where Melvin Webb and Clara Ramey raised Lynn, Crystal Gayle (born Brenda Webb), and their six brothers and sisters.

Lynn built a replica of the Webb homeplace in Hurricane Mills, Tennessee, where she and her husband, Doolittle (Mooney) Lynn, live now. But the original is in Butcher Hollow, 10 miles south of

Paintsville in rural Johnson County. The hollow is named after the Webb children's great-grandparents, the Butchers.

"Everyone who lived in this hollow was our kin," says Herman Webb, Loretta Lynn's brother. A wiry, eager man in his sixties, he owns Webb's Grocery nearby, keeps up the cabin, and shows it to visitors. Herman is the third-born Webb child, and the only one remaining in Butcher Hollow. "I lived in Indiana for many years, but I moved back here in 1975," Webb says. "Something draws you home."

The terrain in this part of Kentucky Appalachia is rugged and densely wooded. When automobiles first arrived in Butcher Hollow they drove along the creek bed; there's a dirt road now. In her autobiography, *Coal Miner's Daughter,* Lynn said she was criticized for not paying to pave it, but won't because her daddy wouldn't have approved. "I waded out of the mud when I left Butcher Hollow and when I go back to visit I wade through the mud again. They don't need no pavement," she wrote.

The Webb homeplace was in pretty bad shape when Herman began working on it in the late 1980s. He has done a fairly complete renovation, true to the original. Webb plays a cassette of Loretta Lynn's music as he leads visitors around. There are four rooms: a living room, dining room, kitchen, and the parents' bedroom. All the kids slept in the attic, which had paper-thin walls. "You could freeze ice under your bed in the winter," he explains with a laugh.

Webb says the family didn't feel poor or deprived. "I've seen bigger families than ours living in a two-room log house with a little kitchen, right in this holler. This would've been considered a pretty good size house." In fact, the Webb place is about twice the size of the cabin where Dolly Parton grew up, and she had *ten* brothers and sisters.

The windows are boarded up since thieves broke in and stole Herman Webb's complete collection of Loretta Lynn posters, musical instruments, and other valuable memorabilia. Webb discusses the remaining items: family photos, a few of Loretta Lynn's stage costumes, and newspaper clippings. The house is furnished with original Webb family items, including furniture, a stove, and kitchen tools.

Did the family have any inkling back then that Loretta was destined for the Country Music Hall of Fame? "All the kids around here were about the same," Webb says. "She was just like any other kid. She was always good with poems and writing, little smart remarks and stuff."

The whole family was musical, he explains. Webb himself sang in a band called the Country Nighthawks for more than a decade. His brother, Jay Lee, cut a record under the name Jack Webb. "Me and Jay Lee, we used to play. He was a good musician, the one out of the family who was kind of gifted," Webb says. Brenda, the youngest, also used to sing with them. Lynn's hit, "Don't Come Home a-Drinkin' (With Lovin' on Your Mind)," was written with her sister Peggy Sue.

When the Webbs were growing up, Van Lear was a lively town with five coal mines and 10,000 people. Their father Melvin worked in the Number 5 mine at the mouth of Butcher Hollow until it closed in the late forties. "When the [mining company] pulled out of here and went to another area, the town just died," Webb says. Lynn was already in Washington State with Doolittle when the family moved to Wabash, Indiana, in 1955. Melvin died in 1959, and is buried in the family cemetery in Butcher Hollow.

About 1,600 people live in Van Lear now. The town has some handsome clapboard houses, leftovers from more prosperous times, alongside trailers and bungalows. The **Van Lear Historical Society Coal Camp Museum** depicts the area's coal-camp life. Call (606) 789-4759 for an appointment.

Van Lear is out of the way, but Webb has attracted a steady stream of visitors since he fixed the place up. "Loretta came here four years ago," he says. "She filmed a TV special. She said the house looked even better than when she lived in it."

GETTING THERE: Van Lear is 10 miles southeast of Paintsville. Take Hwy. 23 (Loretta Lynn Highway) south. Turn left on Hwy. 1107 for about $9/10$ mile, then right on Hwy. 302 for about $1\frac{1}{2}$ miles. Turn left on Miller's Creek, and bear right after the Van Lear post office. Drive about $2\frac{1}{2}$ miles to Webb's Grocery. Allow an hour. Contact Herman Webb for an appointment and prices; (606) 789-3397.

Paintsville

KENTUCKY MOUNTAIN HOME

Paintsville, the closest big town to Butcher Hollow, has a new attraction called **Mountain Home Place,** an Appalachian living history museum with a mid-eighteenth-century farm, sugarcane mill, and homestead. Special events with mountain music take place from time to time. Tickets $5. Open April through October, Wednesday through Sunday, 10 A.M. to 6 P.M. Take Hwy. 460 west, then right on Rte. 40, and right on Rte. 2275; (800) 542-5790.

Live country and bluegrass shows are presented monthly (in addition to a full movie schedule) at the 1930s **Sipp Theatre** in downtown Paintsville. Call for schedules. 336 Main St.; (606) 789-1295 or (606) 789-9014.

The **Kentucky Apple Festival** is one of the largest festivals in the state. Held the first weekend in October, it features top-name country entertainers, a parade, and much more. Fresh apple butter is made on the street, and apple pies, cakes, and other delicacies are available.

GETTING THERE: Paintsville is at Hwys. 23 and 460, 50 miles south of I-64/Ashland. Call the Chamber of Commerce; (800) 542-5790 or (606) 789-1469.

Prestonsburg

KENTUCKY OPRY

South of Paintsville down the Country Music Highway, Prestonsburg presents the Kentucky Opry at Jenny Wiley State Park. In 1997, the show is expected to move to the 1,000-seat **Mountain Arts Center,** a $7 million, state-of-the-art performance facility and recording studio in Prestonsburg.

The Kentucky Opry is a country music variety show with special guests, sparkling costumes, mountain humor, fifties and sixties music, and gospel. A highlight of the show is the "Highway 23 Medley," featuring first-rate impersonations of East Kentucky artists who grew up along the Country Music Highway, from Billy Ray Cyrus and Loretta Lynn to Dwight Yoakam and Patty Loveless. "This area is knee-deep in country music heritage," says Greg Crum, manager of the Kentucky Opry. "It's something we're very proud of." The Opry is on Monday nights late June through late August. Tickets cost $10.

Jenny Wiley State Resort Park near Prestonsburg is a wooded park with a lodge, campgrounds, lake, and golf course. A 4,700-foot sky lift to the top of Sugar Camp Mountain offers terrific views of the scenery. The Kentucky Opry and repertory theater productions are presented at the outdoor 580-seat **Jenny Wiley Theatre** throughout the summer; (606) 886-2623. Free square, folk, and country line dances are held on Friday and Saturday nights at the "dance pad," an open-air wood floor surrounded by trees, with live bands and dance lessons.

The park is named for Jenny Wiley, a pioneer woman captured by Indians in this area. After witnessing the brutal scalping of her brother and three children, she was forced to march hundreds of miles before escaping. The 163-mile Jenny Wiley trail, which traces part of her route, begins at the park and ends in Portsmouth, Ohio. *The Ballad of Jenny Wiley,* a free 35-minute play with music, tells her fascinating story. Call for times.

David Appalachian Crafts, in the town of David six miles from Prestonsburg, is a non-profit cooperative that teaches residents traditional mountain crafts and sells their beautiful quilts, split oak baskets, pottery, weaving, and wooden items. Open weekdays, 10 A.M. to 4 P.M. and by appointment. Take Mountain Parkway west from Prestonsburg to Rt. 404 south; (606) 886-2377.

Numerous festivals take place in Prestonsburg throughout the year, including the **Jenny Wiley Festival,** the second weekend in October, and the **Slone Mountain Squirrel Festival,** the Sunday after Labor Day in nearby McDowell.

GETTING THERE: Prestonsburg is 15 miles south of Paintsville at Hwy. 23 and Rte. 3. From I-75, take Daniel Boone Parkway east. From I-64, take Mountain Parkway south. The Prestonsburg Tourist Commission is at 245 North Lake Dr.; (800) 844-4704 or (606) 886-1341. Jenny Wiley State Park is off Hwys. 23/460 on Rte. 3; (606) 886-2711.

Central Kentucky

Menifee County
SWAMP VALLEY GENERAL STORE AND MUSEUM

Clayton Wells plays the pedal organ at his Swamp Valley General Store and Museum.

Swamp Valley General Store and Museum, is the domain of Clayton Wells, certified eccentric. A lifelong pack rat, Wells's eighteenth-century Civil War log cabin is stuffed from floor to rafters with his collection of—well, stuff. Junk, the interesting old kind, is piled next to valuable treasures: a Thomas Edison radio powered by sulfuric acid, a bowl of marbles, antique crystal, Appalachian furniture and artifacts, a *Dukes of Hazzard* lunch box, an invitation to President Clinton's inauguration, mementos from the Hatfield-McCoy feud, and handmade musical instruments.

A photograph on the guest-house wall shows Wells's great-aunt and -uncle, who hold the world record for the longest marriage: eighty-two years!

There is a purpose to this seeming chaos. Wells embodies the history of his kin and his beloved Menifee County, Kentucky. He is the purest of folklorists, a font of knowledge compelled to share what he knows. A large man with a gray crew cut and wide eyes, he eagerly invites visitors in, urging them to spend as long as they like and ask questions. "I got more stuff to show you," he says, and, "Now look at this!" Point to any item and he'll launch into a story. Point to the pedal organ and he'll sit down and belt out a few songs.

Wells records raw mountain-music inside a corn crib, which is decorated with photographs of Menifee County schoolchildren going back fifty years. "We close this door and we don't get any sound from the outside," Wells says. He sells his homemade tapes, with original compositions and traditional songs, for $10.

In 1988, members of the *Hee Haw* cast visited Swamp Valley for three days to make a short film called "Cardboard Corner." Wells explains, "They liked my songs 'Possum Holler Home' and 'Hang Me' and that's why they came here."

After spending several hours with Wells, the $1 admission fee seems almost beside the point. Wells needs to talk and share his collection more than most visitors need to see it. The best approach is to take it slow and simply go along for the ride.

Around the property there's also an authentic coffin-making workshop, peacocks in a cage, and a shed with a horse-drawn coach and moonshiner's bag. His general store sells 50¢ sodas from an ancient cooler, along with Moon Pies, chips, flashlights, and a few other useful items. Just down the road is the old Botts School, Menifee County's one-room schoolhouse.

GETTING THERE: Swamp Valley Museum is about 60 miles east of Lexington on Hwy. 460, between Ezel and Frenchburg. Allow an hour. Take I-64/Exit 110 (Mt. Sterling) to Hwy. 460 south; (606) 768-3250.

Natural Bridge
CLOGGING CAPITAL OF KENTUCKY

Natural Bridge State Resort Park, west of Swamp Valley in the Daniel Boone National Forest, has been a haven for clogging enthusiasts from Kentucky and beyond for more than three decades. On weekend evenings from April through October, hundreds of people flock to the park for clogging, Appalachian square-dancing, and live mountain-music on Hoedown Island, an open-air dance floor surrounded by a pretty little lake and framed by lush mountains.

Richard Jett has been calling weekly **Square Dance Frolics** here since 1962. A member of the American Cloggers Hall of Fame, Jett has called more than 1,200 traditional Appalachian square dances. "I'm just an old east Kentucky fellow. I learned my dancing when I was in the military in Washington, D.C.," Jett says. His mentor was Ralph Case, a famous dancer who taught President Truman's daughter.

Jett's weekly dances include lessons for beginners, two-steps, waltzes, line-dancing, special dances for children, and demonstrations by professional clogging teams.

Numerous **clogging and music events** are held on Hoedown Island throughout the year, including the Shindig in the Mountains Memorial Day weekend; the National Mountain Square Dance and Clogging Festival in mid-June; the Annual Music and Dance Frolic the weekend closest to July 4; the Natural Bridge Clogging Championships and Camp Clog the first weekend in August; and the Kentucky Square Dance and Music Fiesta Labor Day weekend.

GETTING THERE: Natural Bridge State Resort Park is about 50 miles east of Lexington. Take the Mountain Parkway/Exit 33 to Rte. 11 south. Square Dance Frolics begin 7:30 P.M. Saturday nights, from the end of April through October. An additional program is offered on Fridays from the end of May through August. Admission $1. Hoedown Island (606) 668-6650.

For park information, call (800) 325-1710 or (606) 663-2214.

Renfro Valley
KENTUCKY'S COUNTRY MUSIC CAPITAL

The down-home *Renfro Valley Barn Dance* has been presented in the "Old Barn" theater in rural south-central Kentucky since 1939. Historically, barn dances were radio shows performed before live audiences, without dancing. While no longer on the air, Renfro Valley's show is going strong after more than a half century. Meanwhile, the modern **Renfro Valley Entertainment Center** has been built around the Old Barn, with a variety of shows, headline concerts, festivals, and shops.

The *Renfro Valley Barn Dance* was created by John Lair, a Renfro Valley native who began his broadcasting career as a promoter for the *WLS Barn Dance.* Lair noticed people traveling hundreds of miles for the Chicago show, and thought they might support one closer to home.

He was right. Lair started his own barn dance in Cincinnati in 1937, and moved it to Renfro Valley two years later. Red Foley, Molly O'Day, the Coon Creek Girls, and Homer and Jethro entertained here in Lair's day. Known for his color-ful on-air dispatches

The Renfro Valley Barn Dance *has been going strong since 1939.*

from "this low green valley that we love," he died in 1985 at age ninety-one.

The original 1939 horn speakers still hang above the Old Barn stage, which is decorated with wagon wheels, hay, and cowboy hats. The *Renfro Valley Barn Dance* is like a second-tier *Grand Ole Opry,* with a cast of regular performers doing covers of current country hits, old-time favorites, bluegrass, and comedy. The roster includes Susan Tomes, Pam Perry Clark, Jeff Watson, and Betty Lou York.

Old Joe Clark, a Renfro Valley regular for more than fifty years, performs bluegrass with his son, Terry, who acts as straight man for his dad's ornery jokes about his wife, chiggers, and such. Several younger Renfro Valley performers have landed major recording con-tracts recently, including the New Coon Creek Girls, Tasha Harris, and Troy Gentry.

The emcee is tall and lanky Jim Gaskin, a fiddler who took Lair's place in the early eighties. "We do twelve shows a week during the full season now," Gaskin says. "People won't see the same show twice. It's different material each time."

In addition to the *Barn Dance,* visitors can enjoy the *Renfro Valley Jamboree, Mountain Gospel Jubilee,* and *Saturday Showcase.* The *Sunday Morning Gatherin',* started by Lair in 1943, is the second-oldest continuously aired radio program in America, currently heard on 200 stations in the U.S. and Canada. Clogging performances are coordinated by Richard Jett. (*See also:* Kentucky—Natural Bridge State Resort Park.)

People who remember Renfro Valley from the old days may not recognize the entertainment complex at first. In recent years, a modern 1,500-seat venue called the **New Barn** was added to accommodate headliners and an expanded show schedule. Surrounding the two show barns, **Renfro Village** has a miniature-golf course, a grist mill and pond, two restaurants, an old country church and schoolhouse, and a shopping area with souvenirs and crafts. A renovated motel and new RV park are nearby.

Don't miss the tiny **John Lair Theatre,** in which a full-size robot of Lair sits at a table, stands up, and moves his head, mouth, and arms, accompanied by the real man's voice telling the story of Renfro Valley. The fifteen-minute presentation costs $1.

After shows, performers sign autographs in the back of the **Country Music Store.** The shop sells tapes by Renfro Valley regulars and a good selection of country music. You can play tic-tac-toe with a live chicken here for 25¢. (The bird often wins.)

Renfro Valley hosts a number of **festivals** and **headline concerts.** Several take place in an adjoining field, including Old Joe Clark Bluegrass Festival the first weekend in July; Appalachian Harvest Festival the first weekend in October. The first weekend in August, an All-Night Gospel Sing is held in the Old and New Barns.

On your way to or from Renfro Valley, be sure to stop in **Berea,** a charming, progressive town with crafts galore, folk dancing, and an excellent liberal arts college. Contact Berea Welcome Center; (800) 598-5263 or (606) 986-2540.

GETTING THERE: Renfro Valley is at I-75, Exit 62, 45 miles south of Lexington. Open March through December. During the busy season, May through October, shows are presented Wednesday through Sunday with several matinees. Tickets range from $3 to $11; (800) 765-7464 or (606) 256-2664.

For area information, stop by the Renfro Valley tourist center at I-75 and Hwy. 25 next to the ticket office; (800) 252-6685 or (606) 256-9814.

ℋarrodsburg
MARTI'S GATHERING PLACE

Tucked away beside a noisy four-lane highway in downtown Harrodsburg, Marti Williamson's Gathering Place is an oasis of old-time mountain music and storytelling. Williamson is an anachronism from a simpler time, a gentle soul who has staved off pressures of the modern world by reveling in her rural upbringing.

Marti Williamson entertains visitors with traditional mountain music at her Gathering Place.

"When I look at the time I grew up, and I look at today, it's just a different world," she says wistfully. "You could run in the grass then. Sometimes I feel like I want to just step back for a while."

Williamson built her old-fashioned cabin in 1985 and tends a lovely flower garden out front. The inside is furnished with rocking chairs, quilts, an old stove, a hand-made dollhouse, antique domestic items, and vintage clothing such as her mother's wedding hat. One prized possession is a painting of the white house in Hawesville, Kentucky, where she was born.

Dressed in an old-fashioned ankle-length dress with high collar, Williamson talks to visitors, tells stories about her childhood, and sings traditional songs while playing dulcimer harp, or autoharp. "I've been doing music since I was a little girl," she says. "Mom and Dad taught me a lot of what I know."

In a sweet, thin voice, she sings favorites by Jimmie Rodgers, the Carter Family, Hank Williams, and Loretta Lynn. Williamson also performs original songs like "Lonely Sawmill Man," about a gentleman in her neighborhood whose wife left him when he was nineteen years old. Her best audiences are senior citizens and children. "The older folks say, 'Oh gosh, remember that?!' They go on and on," she explains. "And the kids are really inquisitive. They get so excited."

Williamson also operates **Fort Harrod Motel**, a small inn next door furnished with antiques.

Harrodsburg was first explored by Daniel Boone in 1767. Today, the Indian territory of "Kanta-ke" is known as Kentucky's oldest settlement. Area attractions include **Old Fort Harrod State Park**, across the street from the Gathering Place, with a frontier village, festivals, and outdoor dramas. Call (800) 255-PARK or (800) 85-BOONE (theater).

Shaker Village of Pleasant Hill, seven miles east of Harrodsburg on Hwy. 68, is America's largest restored Shaker community; (606) 734-5411.

GETTING THERE: Harrodsburg is 30 miles southwest of Lexington. The Gathering Place is at Hwys. 127 and 68. Admission $2 adults, $1 children. Open daily 3 to 5 P.M. June through August, or by appointment. Closed Sunday and Monday. Allow an hour. 115 S. College St.; (606) 734-4189.

For area information, contact Harrodsburg/Mercer County Tourist Commission; (606) 734-2364.

Gravel Switch
PENN'S STORE

The oldest general store in America continuously operated by the same family, Penn's Store, is smack in the middle of Kentucky. The store was built in 1845, and Dick Penn took it over in 1850. Now his twin great-great-granddaughters, Dava Osborn Jones and Dawn Osborn Graas, and their mother, Jeanne Lane, preside over its sagging floors, glass showcases, and hand-rubbed countertops by Little South Creek at Gravel Switch.

The place is pretty much the same as it has always been, although the sisters provide their own personal touch. Instead of the bologna of the old days, fresh herbs hang from the large spike nails in the ceiling. Penn's Store hosts impromptu country music jam sessions with regional artists, and an assortment of fiddlers, singers, musicians, and storytellers drop in from time to time. "Anyone who plays an instrument is welcome to come in and play, anytime," Lane says. "The better ones are those that kind of happen."

A few years ago, the sisters noticed that lots of tourists were stopping by, but there was no place for them to go to the bathroom. "People had to go out in the bushes," Jones says. "We just couldn't build a modern restroom onto our old country store. So we built an outhouse."

Thus, the **Great Outhouse Blowout** was born. The first festival, commemorating Penn's privy, took place in 1992. Chet Atkins, songwriter Billy Edd Wheeler, and about 4,000 people attended. (Atkins is a friend of Lane, who used to be a songwriter in Nashville.) Now an annual event held the first weekend in October, the Blowout features music, food, and outhouse races. (The competition consists of teams building "functional" outhouses on wheels and racing them down the street.) In 1996, Penn's Store plans to host "Kentucky's First Outhouse Olympics." Stay tuned.

Since 1971, the **Forkland Heritage Festival and Revue** has offered country music, food, a sorghum mill, pioneer exhibits, and supper theater the second full weekend in October. Forkland Community Center is on Rte. 37 near Gravel Switch; (606) 332-7897 or (606) 332-7146.

GETTING THERE: Gravel Switch is about 25 miles southwest of Harrodsburg. From Harrodsburg take Hwy. 127 south, then west on Rte. 300, and south on Rte. 37 to the store. Open 8 A.M. to 6 P.M. May through November; 9 A.M. to 5 P.M. the rest of the year. 257 Rollings Rd.; (606) 332-7715 or (606) 332-7706.

For area information, contact Danville/Boyle County Tourist Commission; (800) 755-0076 or (606) 236-7794.

Bardstown

"MY OLD KENTUCKY HOME"

Stephen Collins Foster may have grown up in Pittsburgh, but he dreamed of Kentucky. A visit to his uncle Judge John Rowan's stately plantation mansion in Bardstown, about 45 miles south of Louisville, inspired Foster to write "My Old Kentucky Home," the state's official song. *The Stephen Foster Story,* an outdoor drama about the nineteenth-century composer's life, is presented in **My Old Kentucky Home State Park** near the original mansion on Federal Hill.

Foster was prolific, finding inspiration everywhere. He wrote more than two hundred songs, including American classics such as "Oh! Susannah," "Camptown Races," "Old Folks at Home," "Jeannie with the Light Brown Hair," and "Beautiful Dreamer." Although he died in 1864, more than a half-century before country music came into its own, Foster's songs deeply influenced America's emerging popular music.

The Stephen Foster Story was written by Pulitzer prize–winning playwright Paul Green, the founder of American symphonic outdoor dramas. The play is presented in a 1,400-seat amphitheater surrounded by woods. The drama picks up Foster's life in July 1849, and follows him for a year. More than 50 songs are performed in light operatic style, by a large cast of energetic young performers in colorful period costumes.

Foster is portrayed as a boisterous and generous young man with a head full of songs, on the verge of success and acclaim. The play ends happily, although there are hints of Foster's increasing moodiness, a drinking problem, and a tendency toward depression. In real life Foster died destitute and unhappy in New York City at age thirty-seven.

The popular two-and-a-half-hour play, first performed in 1959, is an entertaining homage to America's greatest folk songwriter. In 1996 the theater was renovated, and a new director revised and updated the script. *The Stephen Foster Story* is performed nightly at 8:30 P.M. except Mondays, mid-June through Labor Day; 2 P.M. matinee on Saturdays. Tickets $12 adults, $6 children; (800) 626-1563 or (502) 348-5971. (*See also:* Florida—White Springs, Live Oak.)

My Old Kentucky Home, built in the late eighteenth century, has been open to the public since 1923. Judge Rowan, a patriotic man, designed the red-brick house with 13 front windows for the 13 original colonies. The ceilings are 13 feet high, each stairway has 13 steps, and the walls are 13 inches thick. Tours are offered daily, except Thanksgiving, Christmas week, and New Year's Day. The park has a golf course, RV hookups, and camping facilities. Springfield Road/Hwy. 150; (800) 323-7803 or (502) 348-3502.

Settled by Pennsylvanians in 1780, Bardstown is full of charming historic buildings, mansions, and elegant "great houses," many of which are now bed-and-breakfasts. The **Old Talbott Inn** on Court Square has been serving hungry travelers since the late 1800s. More than 300 buildings in Bardstown are on the National Register of Historic Places.

Bardstown is also known as the "Bourbon Capital of the World." Some 70 percent of the spirits produced in the United States are made in Kentucky, much of it here. "Kentucky bourbon whiskey" is aged for at least two years in new-charred white-oak barrels.

Whiskeys distilled in and around Bardstown include Heaven Hill, Jim Beam, Maker's Mark, Kentucky Gentleman, and Old Bardstown. Several distilleries offer free tours. The **Oscar Getz Whiskey Museum and Bardstown Historical Museum** is free and displays antique bottles, nineteenth-century advertising art, and a mock 1930 liquor store. 114 N. 5th St.; (502) 348-2999.

Festivals are held throughout the year, including the **Old Kentucky Homecoming,** a weeklong event in early June, and the **Kentucky Bourbon Festival,** a weeklong celebration beginning the second weekend in September.

White Acres Campground hosts **C.R. Wilson's Bluegrass Music Festival** the third weekend in June, three miles west of Bardstown on Hwy. 62; (502) 348-9677.

(University of Pittsburgh's Stephen Foster Museum, next to the Cathedral of Learning, includes a library and concert hall; (412) 624-4100.)

GETTING THERE: Bardstown is at Hwys. 31E, 62, and 245. Take Bluegrass Parkway/Exit 25 north and follow signs.

For area information, contact Bardstown/Nelson County Tourist Commission; (800) 638-4877 or (502) 348-4877.

Hodgenville
LINCOLN JAMBOREE

Joel Ray Sprowls's Lincoln Jamboree, billed as "Kentucky's #1 Country Music Showplace," has been in business since 1954, in Hodgenville, about 25 miles southwest of Bardstown. On Saturday nights year-round, Sprowls produces and emcees a hot variety show with his house band, featured singers, special guests, country-star impersonators, and cloggers. Every jamboree is different. Shows begin at 8 P.M. on Saturday nights, and cost $7. 2579 Lincoln Farm Rd.; (502) 358-3545.

Visitors can dine at **Joel Ray's Restaurant** and camp free if staying for the show. The **Lincoln Jamboree Museum** is Joel Ray's eclectic collection of singing-cowboy and Elvis memorabilia; old photos; stage clothing worn by Hank Williams, Roy Acuff, and Marty Robbins; the "All Star" guitar, signed by 192 artists over 35 years; and Joel Ray's Solid Gold Cadillac.

South of Hodgenville, **Abraham Lincoln Birthplace National Historic Site** is a huge granite shrine encasing the famous log cabin where the Civil War president was born. Hwy. 31E; (502) 358-3137.

GETTING THERE: From I-65, or the Bluegrass or Western Kentucky Parkways, take Rte. 61 south to Hwy. 31E.

For area information, contact Hodgenville/LaRue County Chamber of Commerce; (502) 358-3137.

Louisville Area
COUNTRY MUSIC SHOWS

West Point, established in 1789, is a tourist town on the Ohio River about 15 miles southwest of Louisville, with a unique crafts mall, antiques, bed-and-breakfasts, and restaurants.

The **West Point Country Opry,** featuring Ivan and Raymond Jennings, is a Saturday-night variety show with old-time and contemporary country music, and comedy. There's room for dancing in the 500-seat Opry hall. Tickets $6 adults, $2 children. The Opry begins at 8 P.M. on South Street; (502) 922-9393. From Louisville, take Hwy. 31W (Dixie Highway) to West Point.

Fifteen miles south of Louisville, the **Shepherdsville Country Music Show** takes place Saturday nights in a large hall with church-pew seating. The show features a house band and special guests. During the winter, C. R. Wilson presents a bluegrass show on Friday nights. Admission $5. Take I-65/Exit 117 to Rte. 44W; (502) 968-6358.

(*See also:* Indiana—Corydon Jamboree.)

West Kentucky

Owensboro
BILL MONROE AND BARBECUED MUTTON

If it's fiddles or hickory-smoked mutton you're looking for, search no more. Owensboro, the "Bluegrass and Barbecue Capital of America," has a surfeit of both, and folks here are happy to share.

Overlooking the Ohio River, Owensboro is 20 miles north of Rosine, hometown of the bluegrass pioneer, Bill Monroe. The International Bluegrass Music Association (IBMA) has been based here since 1985, and the first-rate International Bluegrass Music Museum and Hall of Honor opened in mid-1996 (*see page 92*).

Dozens of restaurants and take-out joints serve delectable pork, beef, and chicken; regional specialities include barbecued mutton and "burgoo," an unusual mutton soup.

Moonlite Bar-B-Q Inn, a celebrated local favorite, serves a diet-busting all-you-can-eat buffet with barbecued mutton, ribs and chicken, burgoo, fried shrimp, baked ham, macaroni and cheese, buttery vegetables, a salad bar, cornbread and sorghum, and at least a dozen desserts. 2840 W. Parrish Ave.; (502) 684-8143. Another popular haunt is **Shady Rest Barbecue Inn,** the oldest barbecue restaurant in Owensboro. 3955 E. 4th St.; (502) 926-8243.

The **International Bar-B-Q Fest** serves 10 tons of mutton, 3,000 chickens, and 1,500 gallons of burgoo in mid-May. More than 40,000 people attend the two-day extravaganza, which includes a barbecue competition, bluegrass music, and arts and crafts; (502) 926-6938.

Owensboro offers entertainment (*see below*), a fine-arts museum, a science and history museum, theater and symphony companies, numerous parks, and an unusual structure called the **Cigar Factory Complex,** the largest wooden building in the world. 1100 Walnut St.; (502) 684-2692.

GETTING THERE: Owensboro is on the Ohio River in northwestern Kentucky, 125 miles north of Nashville and 115 miles west of Louisville. Take one of the following: Green River or Audobon Parkway; Hwy. 431 or 231; or Rte. 54 or 60. Contact Owensboro/Daviess County Tourist Commission; (800) 489-1131 or (502) 926-1100.

INTERNATIONAL BLUEGRASS MUSIC MUSEUM AND HALL OF HONOR—"IT'S BLUEGRASS IF YOU THINK IT IS"

Just what is bluegrass music? Described variously as "folk music in overdrive," "high lonesome," and "the jazz of country music," traditional bluegrass is a form of commercial country music with complex instrumentation and high-pitched vocals. The bluegrass sound was defined by Bill Monroe and his Blue Grass Boys around 1945; the classic bluegrass instruments are acoustic guitar, fiddle, mandolin, bass, Dobro, and banjo. For many Americans, bluegrass is "Dueling Banjos" or the theme song for *The Beverly Hillbillies.*

Today, there are so many exciting styles of bluegrass that it's virtually impossible to pigeonhole the genre. Bluegrass prodigy Alison Krauss's sweep of four Country Music Association awards in 1995 demonstrates how outdated the classic definition of bluegrass has become.

"Bluegrass is an evolving, ethereal form," says Thomas Adler, executive director of the International Bluegrass Music Museum and Hall of Honor in Owensboro. "There's a level where you have to say, it's bluegrass if you think it is."

International Bluegrass Music Association (IBMA) headquarters and the museum are located in Owensboro's brand-new **RiverPark Center,** centerpiece of the city's revitalized downtown. If the completed museum is anything like the excellent "preview exhibit" I saw, it will rival the Country Music Hall of Fame in Nashville.

While honoring its pioneers and practitioners, the museum seeks to test preconceived notions about bluegrass. An interactive computer exhibit called "The Sound of Bluegrass . . . You Be the Judge!" plays a piece of music and lets you rate "how bluegrass" the song is on a scale of 0 to 100 percent. For example, how bluegrass is Flatt and Scruggs's version of Bob Dylan's "Like a Rolling Stone"? The Osborne Brothers' album covering Ernest Tubb songs? Elvis Presley's recording of Bill Monroe's "Blue Moon of Kentucky"? Or the Beatles' "I've Just Seen a Face" performed by the Charles River Boys? The computer tallies each visitor's vote to come up with a current average. "We wanted folks who came to the museum not only to take but to give something back," says Dan Hays, IBMA's executive director.

Thomas Adler, executive director of the International Bluegrass Music Museum and Hall of Honor, is building an archive of bluegrass documents and artifacts.

One of the most interesting items in the collection is a banjo donated by the Red River Valley Boys, a Russian bluegrass band that relied solely on photographs to construct their first instrument. During the 1991 siege of the Russian Parliament building, they played the banjo atop barricades in defiance of a ban on displays of Western culture.

Another coup was the acquisition of an original poster from "the first bluegrass festival," when Carlton Haney of Roanoke, Virginia, decided to put several performers on one bill over Labor Day weekend, 1965. Festivals have since become a staple of bluegrass culture.

The pièce de résistance is a fiddle that belonged to Pendleton Vandiver, an old-time square-dance fiddler. Vandiver was Bill Monroe's mentor and the subject of one of his most popular songs, "Uncle Pen."

Long-range plans for the museum—contingent on an aggressive $4 million fund-raising campaign—include a recording studio, broadcast station, instrument-making and repair workshops, a library, and a reading and listening area. The main exhibit will be a multimedia Bluegrass History Timeline, showing its progress from 1830 to the present.

Adler is also building the definitive archive for historical documents and bluegrass artifacts. He relies heavily on fans for donations of 78s and LPs, old tickets, snapshots, posters, tapes of shows, equipment, noncommercial recordings, and instruments. "A lot of important items are out there in the hands of fans, and get discarded, lost, and destroyed every year," Adler says. Before throwing anything bluegrass-related away, contact the museum. "There's never been a place that was really concerned with the preservation [of bluegrass]," Adler says. "We are."

On the second and fourth Thursday evenings of every month, IBMA stays open late for free jam sessions in the adjoining **Woodward's Bluegrass Cafe.** All are welcome to listen or bring an instrument, and the exhibits are open for viewing.

The **IBMA FanFest,** in conjunction with the **IBMA Awards Show** and a weeklong trade show and convention, is held in late September. More than 30 top-name acts donate their talent for the three-day event.

GETTING THERE: From the Hwy. 231 bridge over the Ohio River, go one block to RiverPark Center. Admission $4 adults; free, ages 16 and under. Allow two hours. Call for current schedule. 207 E. Second St.; (502) 684-9025.

GOLDIE'S BEST LITTLE OPRY HOUSE IN KENTUCKY

Beverly "Goldie" Payne, mistress of Goldie's Best Little Opry House in Kentucky, is a bona fide celebrity in western Kentucky and southern Indiana. She's been serenading the Owensboro area for more than 20 years, from jam sessions in her living room to the old Windy Hollow Country Music Jamboree to her own theater. Payne's a real character with brassy blonde hair, a wide smile, and a rowdy, hyperfriendly personality.

Shows at Goldie's are a spirited mix of country, bluegrass, and comedy, with Payne introducing the acts, razzing band members, cracking jokes, and taking $5 requests for charity. On Saturday nights, she books regional country artists. On Friday nights, anyone with the nerve can perform with Goldie's Backstage Band. Although an inveterate cutup, Payne treats all her aspiring talent with respect. "When we call you up, you're the star of the show," she says.

One graduate of amateur night at Goldie's is Jon Brennan, formerly of MTV's *The Real World.* Brennan was the token country guy in the cast. Now he has a national recording contract, and Goldie's is headquarters for the Jon Brennan Fan Club. He always plays here when he's not on the road with his "Real Tour" band.

Goldie's Opry House is a family affair. Payne's husband does the sound, sister manages the ticket booth, daughter sings and helps with the emceeing, and a boisterous assortment of children and grandchildren handle the snack bar, bookkeeping, lights, and cleanup. Payne's father, in his late eighties, tears tickets and watches the show from the front row. "It's entertainment for us," Payne explains, "as well as other people."

GETTING THERE: Friday and Saturday nights, shows at 8 P.M. Tickets $7. Downtown at 418 Federica St.; (502) 926-0254.

WINDY HOLLOW RESTAURANT AND COWBOY MUSEUM

It all started in 1972, when Sunset Carson decided to film a movie in the Owensboro hills called *The Marshal of Windy Hollow,* starring Ken Maynard and Tex Ritter. For complicated legal reasons the movie was never released, but Hal Miller, the local restaurateur who hosted the film crew, was bitten by the Western bug.

Hal Miller has filled his rustic Windy Hollow Restaurant and Cowboy Museum with memorabilia.

Come by Miller's Windy Hollow Restaurant and Cowboy Museum any weekend for dinner, and you can warm your toes by the wood-burning fireplace, watch an old Gene Autry flick, and look over Miller's extensive collection of cowboy memorabilia.

"This place has kind of grown into a museum that serves food," says Evelyn "Rooster" McCarthy, Miller's daughter and sidekick.

The rambling, rustic restaurant was once an antique shop and coal-mining museum. Gas lights, kerosene lanterns, mining tools, and wagon-wheel chandeliers hang from the rough-hewn wood rafters. The walls are lined with colorful original movie posters, many signed by the stars.

Musty display cases are filled with Tom Mix's chaps, Gene Autry guitars, a shirt worn by Tex Ritter in the 1940 movie *Take Me Back to Oklahoma,* a Roy Rogers and Dale Evans lunch box, Sunset Carson's gun and holster, and Ken Maynard's white hat. Miller says Maynard is his favorite Western star. "He wore the white hat. He was a good one, like me."

In his mid-seventies, Miller is a bundle of energy. He rushes here and there, pointing out photos of the movie shoot, snapshots taken when Ernest Tubb ate here in 1975, a cue card used by Minnie Pearl, and a class picture of Florence Henderson, who graduated from a local high school in 1951. A World War II veteran, Miller also displays memorabilia from his time overseas with the 297th Engineers Combat Battalion.

Open Friday and Saturday nights from 5 to 9 P.M. Dinners (ranging

M Y   H O M E T O W N

Marty Brown on Maceo

"I wrote a song about Maceo—it goes, 'We're about as old-fashioned as a buttermilk biscuit / If you blink twice, you just might miss it.' But it's Home Sweet Home to me. We've got about three hundred people there. We've got a post office, a railroad track and store, and that's about it. It's small-town America.

"When I go home, I like to fish and write songs, and basically just hang out with people I haven't seen in a while. I think that's probably why I stay back home, because there's no fake people. I don't have to put on no airs, 'cause they've seen me at my worst and they've seen me at my best."

GETTING THERE: Maceo is about 15 miles northeast of Owensboro on Hwy. 60.

from $5.95 for chicken to $10.95 for steak) come with vegetables, salad bar, and banana pudding. On Sunday mornings, a country ham breakfast buffet is served from 7 A.M. to 1:30 P.M. for $5.45.

The restaurant is next to **Windy Hollow Recreation Area,** a complex with a NASCAR speedway, campground, swimming hole, and pay fishing lakes. 5141 Windy Hollow Rd.; (502) 785-4150. Although no longer owned by the Millers, the area was developed by Hal and his twin brother, Tom, who died in 1974. Miller explains, "We used to ride ponies and play cowboys and Indians back in these hills as kids."

GETTING THERE: Windy Hollow Restaurant is about 10 miles southwest of Owensboro. Take Hwy. 81 west to Old Hwy. 81, to Windy Hollow Road. Follow the signs. 5251 Windy Hollow Rd.; (502) 785-4088.

Rosine
BIRTHPLACE OF BLUEGRASS

The Father of Bluegrass, Bill Monroe, and his mentor, Pendleton Vandiver ("Uncle Pen"), were born in Rosine, a tiny town south of Owensboro in Ohio County. Vandiver and other Monroe family members are buried in **Rosine Cemetery;** his monument depicts a map of the town and the lyrics to Monroe's song "Uncle Pen," a bluegrass standard.

Bratcher's Grocery hosts the *Old Barn Jamboree* on Friday nights at 7:30 P.M. Local bluegrass bands appear for free. You can also stop by Bratcher's for a snack or directions to Uncle Pen's grave. Rosine hosts **bluegrass festivals** in May, June, July, and the third weekend in September.

The Rosine Association is in the process of building a monument to Monroe and restoring the house where he grew up. For information or to join, contact Hoyt Bratcher, General Delivery, Rosine, KY 42370; (502) 274-3551.

Line dancing and **barn dances** take place weekly at **Ohio County Park** in Hartford, just west of Green River Parkway/Exit 48 on Rte. 69. The park has 50 campsites, RV facilities, nature trails, trap shoots, and sprint-car races; (502) 298-4466.

GETTING THERE: Rosine is about 25 miles south of Owensboro. Take Green River Parkway/Exit 48 (Hartford). Go left on Rte. 1543 to the end, then left on Hwy. 62 eight miles. Contact the Ohio County Chamber of Commerce; (502) 298-3551.

Central City
THE EVERLY BROTHERS GO HOME

Don was born in Brownie, Kentucky, and Phil in Chicago, but the Everly Brothers grew up in Central City, an old coal town with quiet tree-lined streets, and trim brick and clapboard houses. Despite their pop crossover success, the brothers were raised on country; their father, Ike,

The Everly Brothers monument credits the brothers with taking the music of Kentucky around the world and "bringing it back home to Central City."

was one of the local guitar pickers who taught Merle Travis to play. The Everly Brothers' hits include "Bye, Bye Love," "Wake Up, Little Susie," and "All I Have to Do Is Dream," penned by Felice and Boudleaux Bryant, members of the Country Music Hall of Fame.

A **marble monument** in front of Central City's red-brick city hall, dedicated in 1988, has engraved likenesses of the brothers. Inside, the foundation sells Everly Brothers souvenirs and displays gifts from fans, photographs, and memorabilia. 203 N. 2nd St.; (502) 754-9603.

In the late 1980s, the Central City Police Department needed new radios until Don Everly, living in Nashville, found out. "[The brothers] came up here and bought us some new radios," says Valerie Edmonds of the Everly Brothers Foundation. "Things just kind of took off from there. We've had a concert every year since."

Up to 15,000 people attend the **Central City Music Festival and Everly Brothers Homecoming,** held every Labor Day weekend in the west-central Kentucky city. With paid admissions from the Saturday-night headline concert, the foundation funds college scholarships for students from Muhlenberg County's two high schools. The Everly Brothers perform most years.

The foundation has purchased land in Central City to build an Everly Brothers Complex, which will eventually include a museum and amphitheater.

GETTING THERE: Central City is 35 miles south of Owensboro and 90 miles north of Nashville. Take West Kentucky Parkway/Exit 58 to Hwy. 431 north. Contact Central City Chamber of Commerce; (502) 754-2360.

Drakesboro
LAND OF GUITAR LEGENDS

A few miles south of Central City, Drakesboro (pop. 565) spawned more than its share of country music stars and legendary thumb-pickers. Highway 431 through town is called "John Prine Avenue," while stretches of Route 176 are named "Mose Rager Boulevard" and "Merle Travis Highway."

Mose Rager Memorial Park is dedicated to Drakesboro's rich musical heritage. Next to a gazebo and fountain, a black marble monument pays tribute to Rager, who died in 1986. He is remembered as a "unique personality and legendary country-music thumb-picker who was known as Kentucky's Shy Guitar Master. . . . " Merle Travis once said of Mose, "We're all imitations of the best." Several pictures of Rager playing guitar are engraved on the back of the monument. The park, which also honors Travis, Ike Everly, and Kennedy Jones, is on Route 176, a half-mile west of Highway 431. On the second Saturday of every month, local thumb-pickers gather in Drakesboro's city building, across the street from the park, for a **country music jamboree.** All are welcome to the free show, which begins about 5 P.M.; (502) 476-8986.

About two miles past Mose Rager Park on Route 176 (Merle Travis Highway), the **Merle Travis Memorial** at Ebenezer Church honors the amazing honky-tonk guitarist, singer, and composer of dozens of hit songs, including "Sixteen Tons" and "Smoke! Smoke! Smoke! (That Cigarette)." Travis's ashes were strewn about the stone statue after his death in 1983. Every year on the Saturday after Thanksgiving, the **Merle Travis' Birthday Celebration,** a memorial service, supper, and festival, takes place in Central City.

GETTING THERE: Drakesboro is 10 miles south of Central City. Take Western Kentucky Parkway/Exit 58 to Hwy. 431 south. Contact the Greenville / Muhlenberg County Chamber of Commerce; (502) 338-5422.

Benton
KENTUCKY OPRY

The *Kentucky Opry,* in Benton near Kentucky Lake, is the premier country-music show in the state's southwestern region. The show features Clay Campbell and his young sons Clayton, Cody, and Casey, who sing and play a number of instruments, as well as a cast of talented regional performers. The fast-paced variety show includes country, gospel, a harmonizing men's quartet, bluegrass, and comedy. The *Opry* is presented on Saturday nights year-round and Friday nights from June through August, and in December.

Campbell, the *Opry's* owner and emcee, got his start more than 30 years ago in Lee Mace's *Ozark Opry* in Missouri, one of the nation's first country shows. Throughout the year, he books headliners from the *Grand Ole Opry* and entire shows from Branson, Missouri. Special events include talent searches, free bluegrass jam sessions, and Christmas shows.

GETTING THERE: Take I-24/Exit 24, Purchase Parkway south. Turn left on Hwy. 68, then left on Hwy. 641. Admission $8.50 for the *Opry,* and up to $17 for special events. Shows begin at 8 P.M. 88 Chilton Rd.; (502) 527-3869.

Louisiana

Ruston
DIXIE JAMBOREE

Every Saturday night Jimmy Howard kicks off his down-home *Dixie Jamboree* in historic downtown Ruston, the peach capital of Louisiana. The show is a laid-back country concert, presented in a renovated 1928 theater with plush, comfortable seats and a dance floor in front of the stage. The audience is a dancing crowd, up and two-stepping as soon as each song begins. The eight-piece house band plays contemporary country and standards with a cast of regular singers and guests. Showtime is 7 P.M, and 7:30 during daylight savings time.

Tons of peach ice cream are served during Ruston's **Louisiana Peach Festival** in June, along with a parade, auction, cooking contests, and country entertainment. Call (318) 255-2031 for details.

GETTING THERE: Ruston is 70 miles east of Shreveport. Admission to Dixie Jamboree $5. Take I-20 to Hwy. 167 south. Turn left on Alabama St. 206 N. Vienna St.; (318) 255-6081.

Beech Spring
JIMMIE DAVIS TABERNACLE

The Jimmie Davis Tabernacle, on a quiet shady country road in northern Louisiana, is a church and community meeting place dedicated to the beloved two-time Louisiana governor and member of the Country Music Hall of Fame. Davis's signature song was the sentimental favorite "You Are My Sunshine," but he also had hits with honky-tonk and gospel songs. (On the campaign trail, he often preferred to sing, rather than pontificate.)

Davis, ninety-six years old in 1995, was born in Beech Spring near Quitman, and now lives in Baton Rouge. He built the red-brick tabernacle with friends in 1965, and donated it to Jackson Parish in 1995. "We're real proud," says Sylvia Tucker of the Chamber of Commerce. The tabernacle can be rented for religious events such as weddings and revivals. It's not open all the time, but feel free to stop by and look around. In front of the tabernacle, a pedestal with a sundial reads, "I count none but sunny hours." Davis's original home place is next door, and is open during special events and by appointment. The Peckerwood General Store, a relic from Davis's boyhood, is across the street. Davis will be buried in a small cemetery in back. The words "I'll See You on the Other Side" and "You Are My Sunshine" already are etched on his stone. His wife, Alvern Adams, died in 1967 and is buried in the plot.

The **Jimmie Davis Homecoming** takes place on the tabernacle grounds the first Sunday in October, with country gospel bands from around the country and an old-fashioned potluck dinner. Thousands of people attend. "This year, everyone was just waiting and waiting for Jimmie to go onstage," Tucker says. "When he finally sang, 'You Are My Sunshine' and 'Suppertime,' you could hear those people all the way to Jonesboro."

GETTING THERE: Beech Spring is in north-central Louisiana, about 15 miles south of Ruston. Take I-20 to Hwy. 167 south to Quitman and follow the signs to the Tabernacle on Rte. 542. Contact the Jackson Parish Chamber of Commerce; (318) 259-4693.

Marthaville
LOUISIANA COUNTRY MUSIC MUSEUM

Louisiana is a unique melting pot of musical styles, with New Orleans jazz, Cajun, and zydeco on the bayous, and Mississippi Delta blues. The northern part of the state is a hotbed of country music. Shreveport's Louisiana Hayride, "Cradle of the Stars" in the late 1940s and the 1950s, helped launch the careers of Hank Williams, Jim Reeves, and Elvis Presley.

Nestled—you could even say hidden—in the state's northeast piney woods, the Louisiana Country Music Museum salutes the state's country music heritage and home-grown stars like former governor Jimmie Davis, *Grand Ole Opry* star Jimmy C. Newman, Shreveport-born Hank Williams, Jr., and cousins Jerry Lee Lewis and

Mickey Gilley. This fine museum has been sadly underadvertised and undervisited.

The building is shaped like a musical note, with a small but professionally designed museum in the round part. The exhibits employ audio, memorabilia, text, maps, and photographs to illustrate the impact of Louisiana's land, people, culture, and religious heritage on its country music. The tour begins with a 14-minute film.

Roy Acuff donated a fiddle and a yo-yo, which are on display. In a letter, he wrote, "As you know, I do not give a lot of my fiddles away, so I hope the people who visit the museum at Rebel Park will enjoy it."

There is a small recording studio, as well as a listening room, library, and outdoor amphitheater. Future plans call for a walk of stars, "dog trot" stage, and regular musical performances. The **Louisiana State Fiddling Championship** takes place the first Saturday in April. Bluegrass, country, and gospel **jams** are held on the second Saturday afternoon of each month, April through November.

The museum is in the **Rebel State Commemorative Area,** which honors an unknown Confederate soldier who was separated from his unit and killed by Union cavalrymen. A local family buried the young man and tended his grave for 100 years, until the establishment of a state park during the 1960s.

Louisiana's oldest city, **Natchitoches,** is 25 miles east of Marthaville on the Cane River. Established as a French outpost in 1714, the picturesque city has block after block of centuries-old plantation homes and townhouses with ornate French cast-iron grillework. It has appeared in several movies, including *Steel Magnolias* and *Man in the Moon.* Tours can be arranged at the Visitors' Center, next to the statue of St. Denis at 781 Front St.; (318) 352-8072.

The nationally recognized **Lasyone's Meat Pie Kitchen** specializes in hearty golden-crust meat pies, "dirty" rice, red beans, and sinful "Cane River cream pie." 622 2nd St.; (318) 352-3353. Take I-49 to Hwy. 6 east to Natchitoches.

GETTING THERE: Marthaville is 75 miles south of Shreveport. The museum is open 9 A.M. to 5 P.M. year-round except Thanksgiving, Christmas, and New Year's Day. Admission $2. Allow an hour. Take I-49 to Hwy. 6 west at Natchitoches, to Rte. 120 north, through Marthaville to the museum on Rte. 1221; (318) 472-6255.

Eunice

"LE GRAND NEW OPRY"

Eunice, Louisiana's "Prairie Cajun Capital," takes great pride in preserving French Acadian culture. The small city northwest of Lafayette represents Louisiana in the Southern Arts Federation and was recognized as one of the top ten rural cities for cultural tourism. Year-round Eunice offers authentic music, festivals and food, and that famous "joie de vivre" Cajun hospitality.

Rendez-Vous des Cajuns, a Cajun/country music show almost entirely in French, is presented weekly in the renovated 1924 **Liberty Theatre Center for the Performing Arts.** Dubbed *"Le Grand New Opry," Rendez-Vous des Cajuns* takes place from 6 to 8 P.M. on Saturday nights, with Cajun and zydeco musicians, dancing, humorists, and a "living recipe corner." The Opry is also broadcast live on local radio and television. Admission $2. S. 2nd St. and Park Ave.; (318) 457-7389.

Next door to the Liberty Theatre, the **Prairie Acadian Cultural Center** is a hands-on museum with historical artifacts, video, slide shows, and crafts workshops. Legendary regional musicians perform Saturdays at 3 P.M., and Cajun **jam sessions** are Sundays at 3 P.M. Open daily 8 A.M. to 5 P.M., with free admission. 250 W. Park Ave.; (318) 457-8499.

Additional attractions include the Eunice Museum in a restored railroad depot, Cajun and zydeco dance halls, restaurants, and sausage kitchens. Two crawfish processors offer tours by appointment.

Eunice's **annual festivals** include the World's Championship Crawfish Étouffée Cook-off the last Sunday in March, Louisiana Folklife Festival in the fall, and the Cajun Music Festival the second Sunday after Easter.

GETTING THERE: Eunice is about 40 miles northwest of Lafayette. Take I-49/Exit 19 to Hwy. 190 west, or I-10 to Rte. 13 north. Call (800) ACADIANA or (318) 457-2565.

Lafayette
CAJUN COUNTRY

In the mid-1700s, French-speaking Acadians from Nova Scotia refused to pledge allegiance to the British monarchy. Driven from their homes, they wandered for decades before settling in southern Louisiana.

These French Acadians, who came to be known as Cajuns, brought a unique culture to the region's international ethnic mix, which included Creoles, transplants from Africa and the West Indies. Although their children were later forced to speak English in school, the Cajun and Creole people kept their cultures alive through music, dance, food, and traditions.

Vermilionville in Lafayette is a living history museum and village that faithfully and authentically preserves the nineteenth-century culture of the Cajuns and Creoles. Visitors walk through a working village on the banks of two bayous. Louisiana natives in costume run a real farm, cook, weave, and demonstrate period crafts and trades.

Lively Cajun and Creole zydeco music is performed every afternoon, and a restaurant serves traditional cooking (not too hot or spicy). Open daily, 10 A.M. to 5 P.M., except Christmas and New Year's Day. Admission $8 adults, $5 children. Allow two hours. Take I-10/Exit 103A (Evangeline Thruway). 1600 Surrey St.; (800) 99-BAYOU or (318) 233-4077.

Acadian Village is another fine living-history and folklife museum in the Lafayette area, with nineteenth-century homes furnished in period antiques. The village is on ten secluded acres of gardens and woodlands.

Hank Williams fans will be interested in **LeBlanc House,** birthplace of the huckster who invented a cure-all (mostly alcohol) elixir called Hadacol. During the 1950s, state senator Dudley LeBlanc hired entertainers to hawk the tonic in "Hadacol Caravans." The traveling shows featured the likes of George Burns, Jack Benny, Mickey Rooney, and Jimmy Durante.

A sponsor of Hank Williams's "Health and Happiness" shows, LeBlanc booked him to headline a Caravan tour. On one memorable occasion, Williams upstaged Bob Hope, who made the best of the situation by donning a cowboy hat and introducing himself as "Hank Hope."

Open 10 A.M. to 5 P.M., except major holidays. Take I-10/Exit 97 to Rte. 93 south, then right on Ridge Rd., and left on W. Broussard. Admission $5.50 adults, $2.50 children. Allow two hours. 200 Greenleaf Rd.; (800) 962-9133 or (318) 981-2364.

Original Mulate's Cajun Restaurant is 10 miles east of Lafayette in Beaux Bridge, known as the "Crawfish Capital of the World." The restaurant serves fresh crawfish and catfish, accompanied by live Cajun music and two-stepping seven days a week. The place is more than seventy-five years old, constructed out of native cypress wood and decorated with Acadian art. Meals cost between $8 and $14. Open Monday through Saturday 7 A.M. to 10:30 P.M., and Sundays 11 A.M. to 11 P.M. Take I-10/Exit 109 to Hwy. 94. 325 Mills Ave.; (800) 42-CAJUN, (800) 634-9880 (in Louisiana), or (318) 332-4648.

GETTING THERE: Lafayette is 135 miles west of New Orleans at I-10 and I-49. Call the Tourist Commission; (318) 232-3808.

Abita Springs
PINEY WOODS OPRY

Across Lake Ponchartrain from New Orleans, Abita Springs' Piney Woods Opry presents old-time country music on the third Saturday of the month during spring and fall. The show is broadcast live from Abita Springs Town Hall on KSLU 90.9 FM. Mayor Bryan Gowland acts as emcee for most performances, which feature regional bands and special guests. Admission $3. Shows begin at 7 P.M. Take I-12 to Rte. 59 north. Call to confirm schedules; (504) 892-0711.

Maine

Brunswick

THOMAS POINT BLUEGRASS FESTIVAL

Thomas Point Bluegrass Festival, begun in 1979, attracts the biggest names in bluegrass as well as fine regional and local bands. The three-day festival takes place over Labor Day weekend in a scenic, wooded park on the Maine Atlantic coast. There's full-service camping, a rustic lodge, restaurants, playground, and a small permanent stage. Park owner Pat Crooker says Thomas Point has a "reputation as a family traditional festival. We get people year after year, from around the corner, and all over the country and the world."

GETTING THERE: Brunswick is on I-95, about 30 miles north of Portland. Thomas Point is at Rte. 24 and Cooks Corner; (207) 725-6009.

Maryland

Festivals Across Maryland

Maryland's two biggest and best country-music festivals are held on opposite ends of the state. The **Tangier Sound Country Music Festival** takes place on the southeastern shore of Chesapeake Bay in Crisfield. For one or two days the third weekend in June, the biggest contemporary country stars perform in an outdoor amphitheater at Hammock Point. The festival also includes children's activities, a juried crafts showcase, dance tent, and fresh local seafood. From Washington, D.C., take Hwy. 50 or Hwy. 13 to Rte. 413; (800) 521-9189 or (410) 651-2968.

The **Rocky Gap Music Festival**, up in the mountains of northwestern Maryland near Cumberland, attracts 15,000 people each year for three days of performances by country music's top stars. The festival takes place the first weekend in August at Rocky Gap State Park. The stage, with a 75-foot "star ramp" into the audience, is beside a pretty lake. There's also an autograph booth, arts and crafts, workshops, local bands, dancing, and a children's music stage. Take I-68/Exit 50; (800) 50-VISIT or (301) 777-5905.

Massachusetts

Lowell
LOWELL FOLK FESTIVAL

The largest free folk festival in the country takes place the last full weekend of July in Lowell, an industrial city in northeast Massachusetts near the New Hampshire border. The **Lowell Folk Festival** draws more than 150,000 people to downtown Lowell. All day Saturday and Sunday, country, bluegrass, gospel, New Orleans jazz, and traditional ethnic music is presented on five stages; at night there are large headline concerts from 7:30 to 10 P.M.

GETTING THERE: Lowell is 30 miles north of Boston. Take I-495/Exit 36 to Lowell Connector, to Exit 5N (Thorndike St.); (508) 970-5000.

Webster
NEW ENGLAND'S HOME OF COUNTRY MUSIC

Every summer on the shores of Lake Chargoggagoggmanchauga-goggchaubunagungamaugg, also known as Webster Lake, **Indian**

Ranch books the finest entertainers in country music. Headline shows are presented outdoors on Sunday afternoons Memorial Day through September allowing guests to enjoy the park. Located in the pine woods of New England, Indian Ranch has picnic areas, grills, a cocktail lounge, and lake swimming. (The lake's name, which holds a world record for its length, means, "You fish on your side, I fish on my side, no one fishes in the middle.")

Annual festivals include the Memorial Day Country Music Festival featuring regional bands; Father's Day Special Concert in June; and Country Fest the last weekend in September.

GETTING THERE: Webster is in south-central Massachusetts, over the Connecticut border. Tickets $6 to $25. Take I-395/Exit 2 to Rte. 16; (508) 943-3871.

Watertown

COMING ATTRACTIONS: THE NEW ENGLAND COUNTRY MUSIC HALL OF FAME, MUSEUM, AND LIBRARY

Gordon Brown, president of the New England Country Music Historical Society, works tirelessly to preserve this area's place in country music history. Yodelin' Slim Clark, Dick Curless, Joe Val, and Georgia Mae are among New England's better-known singers. (In 1995, Clark was honored with a star at the Country Music Hall of Fame in Nashville.) NECMHS is raising funds for a New England Country Music Hall of Fame, Museum, and Library, which will be based in Watertown, west of Boston. To join or make a donation, contact Brown at P.O. Box 575, Watertown, MA 02272-0575; (617) 876-6638.

Contact Brown for information on active country music associations in Connecticut, Massachusetts, Maine, New Hampshire, and Rhode Island.

Minnesota

Hibbing
HOMETOWN OF BOB DYLAN

Bob Dylan made a lasting impression on Nashville during his short stay. He cut three albums there in the late sixties and appeared on the first Johnny Cash television show. His songs have been covered by country singers from Cash and June Carter to John Anderson and Nanci Griffith. Cash told the *Journal of Country Music* that when he first heard Dylan, "I loved it so much that I wrote him a letter. I thought he was the best hillbilly singer I'd ever heard. I really did. I thought, he's got to be from Mississippi, the best writer that ever came out of Mississippi."

Dylan was actually born in Hibbing, a mining town in northeast Minnesota's "Iron Range." Attractions around Hibbing have names like the Hill Annex mine, Soudan Underground mine, Hull Rust Mahoning mine, Minntac mine, and the Minnesota Museum of Mining.

For the record, the Chamber of Commerce provides the following history of Bob Dylan and Hibbing:

- Born on May 24, 1941 in Duluth and named Robert Allen Zimmerman.
- Moved to Hibbing in 1946.
- Hibbing address: 2425 7th Ave. E.
- Graduated from Hibbing High School in 1959 (yearbook is in locked cabinet at Hibbing Public Library).
- Dropped out of university in 1960 and moved to New York.
- June 5, 1968, father Abraham [Zimmerman] died and Bob returned to Hibbing for the funeral.

Hibbing Public Library will attempt to answer any questions concerning Bob Dylan, and allows public use of their **Bob Dylan Collection Materials.** Open Monday through Thursday, 10 A.M. to 8 P.M.; Friday and Saturday 10 A.M. to 5 P.M. 2020 E. 5th Ave.; (218) 262-1038.

Ironworld U.S.A. in Chisolm is a theme park of iron-ore mining and European immigrant cultures. Headline country concerts take place regularly in the park's 1,600-seat amphitheater. **Annual festivals** include International Polkafest the last weekend in June, Iron Country Hoedown Labor Day weekend, and Minnesota Ethnic Days in mid-July. Open mid-April through October. Admission $6.75 adults, $4.75 children. Five miles east of Hibbing on Hwy. 169; (800) 372-6437 or (218) 254-3321.

GETTING THERE: Hibbing is 85 miles northwest of Duluth on Hwy. 169. Contact the Chamber of Commerce; (218) 262-3895.

Mississippi

Nesbit
JERRY LEE LEWIS RANCH

The gate to Jerry Lee Lewis Ranch features an iron piano.

The first thing visitors to the Jerry Lee Lewis Ranch see is a tall white fence with security cameras and an big iron piano on the gate. A half-hour tour of the Killer's two-story red-brick house includes photographs, memorabilia, gold records, cars, and pianos. The highlight is Lewis's swimming pool, shaped like a baby grand, with black and white piano-key steps.

GETTING THERE: Nesbit is in northwest Mississippi, about 15 miles south of Memphis. Tours $10 by reservation; $20 if you show up without calling first. Call for hours. Take I-55/Nesbit Rd. exit. Go east on Nesbit Road to second stop sign, then right on Malone. 1595 Malone Rd.; (601) 429-1290.

Clarksdale
DELTA BLUES MUSEUM

Sometimes called "white man's blues," country music is currently performed almost exclusively by white people, yet the influence of African-Americans and the blues on country's early development is unmistakable. Jimmie Rodgers, famous for his "blue yodels," listened to and jammed with black workers while he worked the Mississippi railroad lines during the 1920s. One of the first *Grand Ole Opry* stars was DeFord Bailey, an extremely popular black harmonica wizard in the 1930s. Hank Williams often credited a black street singer known as "Uncle Tee-Tot" with teaching him how to sing.

The fine Delta Blues Museum celebrates Mississippi's rich blues heritage and examines its influence on country, jazz, and rock and roll. Clarksdale is in the heart of the Mississippi Delta, where the blues began. Legendary bluesmen W.C. Handy, Robert Johnson, and Muddy Waters grew up around here, as well as country stars Conway Twitty (Friars Point) and Charley Pride (Sledge).

The museum relies primarily on text, photos, and a choice selection of memorabilia to tell its story. (A major renovation was underway in 1996.) One display states that country music is "more than an extension of folk ballads and fiddle tunes brought by settlers from England, Ireland, and Scotland. Its flavor was enhanced by gospel music, black string bands, blues, and the popular music of tent shows." For example, the banjo, an instrument developed in Africa, was associated exclusively with black performers before the mid–nineteenth century.

Open Monday through Saturday 10 A.M. to 5 P.M. Free. Take Hwy. 61 to DeSoto Ave., to 1st Ave., 114 Delta Ave.; (601) 627-6820.

Although the audience for country music is increasingly diverse, few black singers and musicians have succeeded except for Charley Pride, the most popular black country artist ever. The radio waves carrying country music to the Pride family's old Philco radio did not discriminate. "The music I chose, personally, to listen to was country music," Pride is quoted as saying in a museum exhibit. "I don't know why it was exactly. . . . Like whether you were pink or purple or whatever really should determine, in some kind of absolute way, the kind of music you like. That's kind of silly, isn't it? I mean it's all American music, anyway."

Pride grew up in **Sledge,** a rural community between Clarksdale and Memphis. A highlight of Pride's stage show is a medley of his songs about Mississippi, accompanied by a film of the folks in his hometown. Sledge is at Rtes. 3 and 315. Rte. 3 is called "Charley Pride Highway" in Sledge.

Clarksdale's motto is "We've got the blues . . . and a whole lot more!" The city's attractions include tours of mechanized cotton harvesting and fish farming, as well as dozens of stately late-nineteenth- and early-twentieth-century homes in a historic district.

The Stackhouse, a record store and recording studio, sells an excellent selection of blues, country blues, jazz, gospel, and country music. A sign over the register warns tourists not to ask for directions to "The Crossroads": No one knows where the legendary birthplace of the blues is, exactly. 232 Sunflower Ave.; (601) 627-2209.

Funky **juke joints** in and around Clarksdale, such as the Rivermount Lounge, often present live music on weekends. The Stackhouse staff can fill you in on where to hear the blues.

The Delta Blues Museum hosts blues jams, workshops, and several annual festivals, including the three-day **Sunflower River Blues and Gospel Festival** in mid-August.

Clarksdale's annual three-day **Delta Jubilee** offers a pork barbecue contest, antique cars, historic homes tour, and live music, the first full weekend in June. Playwright Tennessee Williams went to school here and is honored with a citywide festival in mid-October.

South of Clarksdale in Greenville, the **World Championship Hot Tamale, BBQ, and Catfish Cook-off and Bluegrass Picnic** takes place in mid-May; (800) 467-3582.

GETTING THERE: Clarksdale is 75 miles south of Memphis, at Hwys. 61 and 49.

For area information, call Clarksdale/Coahoma County Tourism Commission; (800) 626-3764 or (601) 627-7337.

Tupelo
ELVIS SLEPT HERE

While visiting Graceland, I was struck by Elvis's limited view of what success can buy. The King's Dream House is a modest brick mansion, decorated in a lovable campy style that would embarrass most self-respecting millionaires. But after seeing the shotgun shack in Tupelo, Mississippi, where Elvis was born, I understand. Anyone who doubts that Elvis was a country boy at heart need only make the pilgrimage to Tupelo and walk through the tiny white house.

Elvis Presley was born in this two-room house built by his father.

It's a two-hour drive from Memphis, where the King died in Graceland on August 16, 1977, to Tupelo, where he and twin brother Jesse Garon were born on January 8, 1935. (Jesse died at birth.) An easy day trip from Memphis, there's plenty in the shady Southern town (pop. 30,000) to keep Elvis-o-philes happy. **The Elvis Presley Center** includes the house, the Elvis Presley Museum, and a meditation chapel in a 15-acre park with gardens and sheltered picnic tables. Attractions include an Elvis driving tour, **Elvis Presley Lake and Campground,** and an Elvis-themed McDonald's (*see page 117*).

To do Tupelo right, start with the birthplace. Elvis's father, Vernon, built the two-room East Tupelo home with $180 he borrowed for materials. Repossessed by the time Elvis was three, the house had to be almost entirely rebuilt because fans ripped the place apart. In the early 1970s, Tupelo's East Heights Garden Club restored the home to the way it looked in the 1930s. The wood floors, fireplace, doors, and windows are original, while furniture and household items were donated by locals. Baby Elvis slept with his parents in a cast-iron bed that fills the front room, and a small kitchen is in the back.

The **Elvis Presley Museum** next door features memorabilia and personal items collected by Presley family friend Janelle McComb. Visitors are not allowed to carry a camera or video recorder into the "Times and Things Remembered" exhibit, or even take notes on a pad. "Everything is copyrighted," a stern guard explained. In light of the fanaticism of some Elvis fans, visitors aren't allowed to touch the glass, and museum staff keep watch with eagle eyes.

After Elvis lost his beloved mother, Gladys, McComb became a mother figure to him. Her private collection includes handwritten notes, stage costumes, personal items, souvenirs, and snapshots. A large volume of material is intelligently displayed in a small space, with explanatory placards.

Among the bizarre, remarkable items on display are a hammer used by Vernon to build the shack in 1934, proudly displayed on a marble pedestal. There are several maudlin poems composed by McComb at Elvis's request, including one dedicated to four-year-old Lisa Marie, the signature smeared by tears. McComb also displays a towel and coffee cup obtained by a female fan who bribed a guard with $40 after Elvis left his hotel room. Apparently the towel was still wet, and the fan kept it in her freezer for 17 years until McComb convinced her to thaw it out for the museum.

Next door is the **Elvis Presley Memorial Chapel,** built with donations from fans and friends. The small, tasteful meditation chapel has three rows of oak pews, stained glass, and an organ. It is available for prayer, special events, and weddings. Special events are held at the center on **Elvis Presley Commemoration Day,** the first weekend in July.

The center can supply the route for a four-mile **driving tour** of places Elvis often visited as a boy. Starting from the birthplace, the tour includes:

- Assembly of God church, on Adams Street, where the Presley family attended services.

- Lawhon School, on Lake Street, where Elvis attended grades one to five. Mrs. Grimes, his fifth-grade teacher, entered him in the local talent contest; he won second place singing "Old Shep."
- Tupelo Fairgrounds, behind East Main Street, where Elvis played concerts in 1956 and 1957.
- Tupelo Hardware on East Main Street, where Elvis bought his first guitar. Downtown Tupelo hasn't changed much since Elvis was a boy. The brochure asks, "Who knows what might have happened if the hardware store had stocked drums instead of guitars?"
- Milam Junior High School, on Gloster Street, where Elvis attended grades six and seven and "45 days of the eighth" before moving to Memphis. He made A grades in music.

One place that isn't on the official city tour, but should not be missed, is the **Elvis-themed McDonald's** on South Gloster Street. Janelle McComb supplied the B-grade Elvis memorabilia. The walls are covered with photos, news clippings, and copies of "The Priceless Gift," McComb's poem to Lisa Marie. Display cases show fanclub buttons, programs, album covers, and souvenir plates. Table dividers display renderings of the King in frosted glass. From downtown Tupelo, make a left from E. Main St. onto S. Gloster and watch for the restaurant on the left side of the street.

Elvis Presley Lake and Campground is located 2½ miles northeast of Hwy. 78 and Veterans Blvd. The 350-acre lake is in an 850-acre park with primitive camping and RV hookups. Hiking, swimming, boating, fishing, and picnic facilities are available; (601) 841-1304.

The campground hosts the **Lee County Shriners Bluegrass Festival,** a two-day event with headline bands and local talent, the first weekend in August; (601) 841-2324 or 844-4790.

(*See also:* Tennessee—Memphis.)

GETTING THERE: Tupelo is in northeast Mississippi, 100 miles south of Memphis. Take Hwy. 78 (Elvis Aron Presley Memorial Highway). The Elvis Presley Center is on Elvis Presley Drive, off Hwy. 6/Main St. (Signs are posted.) Open 9 A.M. to 5 P.M., Monday through Saturday (until 5:30 P.M. May through September); 1 to 5 P.M. Sundays. Separate admissions are charged for the birthplace ($1 adults,

50¢ children) and the museum ($4 adults, $2 children); (601) 841-1245.

For area information, contact the Tupelo Convention and Visitors' Center; (800) 533-0611.

Smithville
Rod Brasfield Days

Rod Brasfield, a native of Smithville (pop. 870) and member of the Country Music Hall of Fame, has been honored with the annual Rod Brasfield Days in his hometown since 1981. Brasfield was a favorite comedian on the *Grand Ole Opry* for fourteen years and Minnie Pearl's comedy partner for a decade. He died in 1958.

Several years ago, Pearl invited Smithville's festival committee to Nashville and gave them Brasfield's Hall of Fame award, which is on display in Smithville's City Hall. A memorial marker in Smithville Park depicts Pearl and Brasfield; he is buried in a cemetery about five miles away.

The free festival, the fourth weekend in August, kicks off with a parade, and includes music, a talent contest, crafts, and food.

GETTING THERE: Smithville is about 35 miles southeast of Tupelo. Take Hwy. 78 to Rte. 28 south; (601) 651-4456.

Meridian
Jimmie Rodgers—The Father of Country Music

Waiting for the Jimmie Rodgers Museum in Meridian, Mississippi, to open one morning in July, I met a middle-aged man from Southern California on his way to a car convention in Atlanta. We admired the marble Jimmie Rodgers monument, a locomotive donated by the Railroad Men of Meridian, and a flagpole dedicated by Ralph Peer. I asked why he had stopped. "I stumbled across Jimmie Rodgers about 35 years ago in a record store," Jack told me. "In those days they would play the record for you. Everyone in the store thought I was crazy. Since then, I've listened to him continuously. There was no way I could miss this."

My story was similar. I fell in love with Jimmie Rodgers's music about five years ago, after hearing him on a friend's record player. His jaunty style, catchy, humorous lyrics, and expressive yodels appealed to me. His recordings were a revelation, a lush variety of emerging American styles, yet entirely original. Rodgers incorporated folk, country blues, Hawaiian ukuleles, and even Louis Armstrong's trumpet. A small-town charmer with big-city aspirations, he had charisma and style.

Rodgers was born near Meridian on September 8, 1897, and succumbed to tuberculosis on May 26, 1933, in New York City. In between, he worked the rails, recorded 110 songs, and became the first hillbilly superstar. When his body was brought back to Meridian on a railroad car, fans lined the sides of the tracks.

On May 26, 1953, the people of Meridian joined Ernest Tubb and Hank Snow in dedicating "The **Monument in Memory of James Charles Rodgers**" in Meridian's Highland Park. It reads:

> His is the music of America. He sang the songs of the people he loved, of a young nation growing strong. His was an America of glistening rails, thundering boxcars and rain-sweet nights, of lonesome prairies, great mountains and bright blue skies. He sang of the bayous and cotton fields, the wheated plains of the little towns, the cities and the winding rivers of America.
> We listened; we understood.

Rodgers was virtually penniless when he was discovered by Peer in 1927 in Bristol, an Appalachian train town straddling the Tennessee-Virginia border. By the early 1950s, he had sold more than 10 million 78 rpm singles. The impact of Rodgers's distinctive voice and bluesy yodel on modern country music cannot be overstated. In 1961, he was the first artist inducted into the Country Music Hall of Fame. "Jimmie Rodgers has probably affected country music more profoundly than any other singer in the history of the genre," the Country Music Association wrote on his plaque. Billed in his day as "The Singing Brakeman" and "America's Blue Yodeler," Rodgers is remembered as the "Father of Country Music."

Bill Monroe's first hit was a souped-up version of Rodgers's "Muleskinner Blues," recorded in 1939. Ernest Tubb and Hank Snow began their careers imitating him. The first songs young Hank Williams learned were Jimmie's. Merle Haggard's homage, "Same Train, Different Time," introduced Rodgers's music to a whole new generation. Covers of "T for Texas," "In the Jailhouse Now," and "My Carolina Sunshine Girl" are familiar to millions of country fans, while Marty Brown, Junior Brown, and Jimmie Dale Gilmore carry the Rodgers flame today.

Rodgers was inducted into the Rock and Roll Hall of Fame in 1984, received the W.C. Handy (blues) Award in 1985, and was honored with a U.S. postage stamp in 1978.

The Singing Brakeman's 1928 Martin guitar is kept in a safe at the Jimmie Rogers Museum.

The **Jimmie Rodgers Museum** was opened in 1975 with funds raised from annual festivals. Housed in a mock train depot, the one-room exhibit features dozens of fascinating Rodgers items. Many were donated by his daughter, Anita Rodgers Court, who died in 1993. On display are his Levi's jeans jacket, handmade straight-back chairs, letters written on hotel stationery, Shriners and Mason hats, a traveling trunk with "America's Blue Yodeler" scrawled on the side, rare sheet music, and railroad memorabilia.

The Singing Brakeman, a short Hollywood film produced in 1930, is shown on a TV at the back of the museum, along with a 30-minute documentary featuring Rodgers's co-songwriter and sister-in-law, Elsie McWilliams. A section of the museum is devoted to McWilliams, the Meridian native who wrote eighteen songs including "You and My Old Guitar" and "My Old Pal" for Rodgers on a piano displayed here.

The centerpiece of the museum is a 1928 Martin guitar, the one Rodgers holds in the famous "thumbs-up" photo, with a mother-of-pearl "Jimmie Rodgers" inlaid on the neck and a big "THANKS" on the back.

"It was supposed to go to the Smithsonian," says Jean Dollar Bishop, director of the museum. "They had two representatives on their way to pick it up. But [Anita] changed her mind at the last minute. Of course, more people would see it there, but it means more to have it here in his hometown." Bishop says the guitar is valued at $100,000, but it "really is priceless." It is displayed behind glass in a safe with eight-inch-thick walls.

The **Jimmie Rodgers Memorial Festival,** during the week of May 26, includes headline performances at the historic Temple Theater, jam sessions, talent contest, and beauty pageant. "We have people coming from Australia, England, India, and Japan," Bishop explains. "The festival is like a big reunion. People come back year after year." Call (601) 483-5763 for information.

The Jimmie Rodgers Museum is in Highland Park on 39th Ave. Admission $2. Open Monday through Saturday, 10 A.M. to 4 P.M.; Sundays 1 to 5 P.M. Closed Thanksgiving, Christmas, and New Year's Day; (601) 485-1808.

Rodgers's grave is in Bonita, in a quiet cemetery next to the Oak Grove Baptist Church. Rodgers's and his wife Carrie's simple headstones read "America's Blue Yodeler" and "First Lady of Country Music." Their daughters June, who died as a baby, and Anita are buried nearby, as are Elsie and Dick McWilliams. (Ask for directions at the museum.)

Additional attractions in Meridian include a stately downtown, with Victorian mansions, and museums.

Weidmann's, a family-run restaurant founded in 1870, serves fish, steak, Wiener schnitzel, salads, and lunch specials, all moderately priced. The decor is German, with dark wood, cuckoo clocks, and beer steins. 210 22nd Ave.; (601) 693-1751.

The **Causeyville General Store,** opened in 1895, sells stone-ground corn and hoop cheese, and has a free musical museum. Eight miles south of Meridian on Hwy. 19; (601) 644-3102.

GETTING THERE: Meridian is at I-20 and I-59 in east-central Mississippi. Contact the Meridian/Lauderdale Partnership; (800) 748-9970 or (601) 483-0083.

Jackson

MISSISSIPPI MUSIC HALL OF FAME

The Mississippi Music Hall of Fame was scheduled to open in late 1996 at the **Jim Buck Ross Mississippi Agriculture and Forestry/ National Agricultural Aviation Museum** in Jackson. The music museum, honoring artists born in Mississippi, will include a 700-seat performance space. The first inductees for country are Jimmie Rodgers (Meridian), Tammy Wynette (Itawamba County), Charley Pride (Sledge), and Jerry Clower (Liberty). Other artists honored in 1996 included Elvis Presley, Jimmy Buffett, Bo Diddley, B.B. King, Robert Johnson, the Blackwood Brothers, Mississippi Mass Choir, and the Staple Singers. Major displays on the current year's inductees are supplemented by permanent exhibits, videos, and music.

The 40-acre complex is the brainchild of Jim Buck Ross, Mississippi's Commissioner of Agriculture and Commerce for three decades. The living history museum celebrates Mississippi's rural agricultural heritage with a working sugarcane mill, 1892 cotton gin, and a 1920s-era small town. Other attractions include Indian artifacts, guns, farm tools, and "perhaps the world's largest pencil collection."

The **Mississippi Country Western Dance Association** holds dances at the museum monthly.

GETTING THERE: Jackson is in central Mississippi, 95 miles west of Meridian. Take I-55/Exit 98B. Open year-round, Monday through Saturday, 9 A.M. to 5 P.M.; Sunday 1 to 5 P.M. Admission $3 adults, $1 children. 1150 Lakeland Dr.; (800) 844-TOUR or (601) 354-6113.

Liberty

JERRY CLOWER MUSEUM

"The Mouth of Mississippi," Jerry Clower, and his wife, Homerline, live on a large spread in Liberty less than a mile from the much humbler domicile where he was born. A popular comedian on the *Grand Ole Opry* since 1973, Clower has recorded more than twenty-five albums of stories about rural characters and country living.

The Jerry Clower Museum, in his backyard, displays hundreds of personal items, photographs, awards, and gifts from fans. The road between Liberty and McComb in southwest Mississippi is called Jerry Clower Highway. (The *Grand Ole Opry* is responsible for litter control on a two-mile stretch.)

In Yazoo City north of Jackson, the **Triangle Cultural Center** has a permanent display of Clower memorabilia with gold records and other items. 332 N. Main St.; (800) 381-0662 or (601) 746-1815.

GETTING THERE: Liberty is in the southwest corner of Mississippi. Take I-55/Exit 15 to Rte. 48 west. The museum is open Monday through Friday. You must make an appointment. One Amazing Grace Lane; (601) 684-8130.

Missouri

Branson

Taken at face value, Branson is nothing short of a phenomenon. Less than ten years ago, this quiet Ozark Mountains resort town had fewer than 5,000 residents, a few theme parks, and a handful of family-run music shows. Today, it's a mini–Las Vegas with 25,000 residents, 40 theaters with 57,000 seats, and nearly 6 million visitors a year.

How did this happen? With country music soaring to new levels of popularity in the 1980s, several aging celebrities put down roots in Branson, including Roy Clark, Sons of the Pioneers, and Boxcar Willie. By opening their own theaters, the stars avoided the grind of the road while providing inexpensive, high-quality stage productions for fans. In a town already friendly to tourism, the simple but brilliant idea took off. Today, Glen Campbell, Charley Pride, Anita Bryant, Mickey Gilley, Mel Tillis, Wayne Newton, the Osmonds, and Andy Williams all own theaters. The hottest—and most expensive—ticket in town is a Japanese bluegrass fiddler named Shoji Tabuchi.

However, Branson is and always has been much more than a place to see live country music. Vickie Dixon Cushman, whose family runs Mutton Hollow theme park, sums up Branson's history as "a river, a book, and a train." The White River was dammed in the 1950s, creating Table Rock Lake and Lake Taneycomo; Harold Bell Wright's million-selling 1907 novel, *Shepherd of the Hills,* drew curious literary fans; and the train arrived early in the twentieth century, carrying visitors to the downtown depot.

Decades before the eighties explosion, Branson attractions included Silver Dollar City, Shepherd of the Hills Theatre and Park, and the College of the Ozarks. Music shows by the Mabe and Presley families have been going strong since the 1950s. "This area was really thriving before the whole music thing happened," Cushman explains.

Another misconception is that Branson appeals only to country fans. Most shows here cater to all musical tastes, and there are numerous "noncountry" attractions like the Lawrence Welk and Tony Orlando theaters, Broadway shows such as *Pump Boys & Dinettes* and *The Will Rogers Follies,* stand-up comedians and magic shows, outdoor recreation and fall foliage, conference facilities, factory outlets, and crafts malls.

The main drag is Hwy. 76, known as "76 Parkway" or "76 Country Music Boulevard." This five-mile glittering strip of flashing neon is lined with motels, restaurants, theaters, helicopter rides, high-rise hotels, outlet stores, bungee-jumping, water parks, miniature golf, ice-cream stands, T-shirt shops, steak houses, fast food, and video arcades.

Despite all the hype, Branson is still pretty scenic. It's built on rolling ridgetops overlooking green valleys. The development, while intense, is fairly well contained. Views of the Ozark Mountains from Hwy. 76 are lovely, and it's possible to drive off in any direction and be back in the country in a few minutes.

Then, there have always been the friendly folks of the Ozarks.

"It's amazing what's happened since I started coming here," says Dolly Parton, who opened her Dixie Stampede dinner attraction here in 1995. Parton says she's visited Branson since way before it became a boomtown. "The folks here are very similar to the folks back home. I can't see any difference in the way that people are in their hearts, the way that they talk and feel and act. This part of the country reminds me a lot of east Tennessee. So, I like it here."

"Branson has a charm about it that other places have tried to reproduce," Cushman adds. "They can't do it."

GETTING THERE: Branson is in the heart of the Missouri Ozark Mountains, 40 miles south of Springfield, 250 miles south of St. Louis, and 175 miles north of Little Rock, Arkansas. Take I-44 to Hwy. 65 south. Contact Branson/Lakes Area Chamber of Commerce; (417) 334-4136.

Getting Help

Where to begin? If you're not traveling with a tour group, go straight to the **Branson Chamber of Commerce,** where the friendly staff will help you get started. This one-stop wonder has free maps, rows and rows of brochures, lists of free attractions, coupon books, telephones, vending machines, cold water, souvenirs, and free coffee.

For accommodations, the center has a sophisticated but easy-to-use system that has never failed to locate lodging within fifteen miles of Branson. A computer lists dozens of hotels, motels, lodges, inns, bed-and-breakfasts, campgrounds, and RV parks. Free phones are available for checking prices and making reservations. The computer prints out driving directions, and a large wall map helps you get your bearings.

Don't rule out accommodations several miles away, such as campgrounds at Table Rock Lake or motels in Hollister, which are quieter and provide a respite from the Branson bustle.

There is no dearth of information to help you navigate Branson. Virtually every business establishment, from convenience stores and gas stations to theaters and restaurants, has stacks of free maps and kiosks with dozens of glossy brochures. At least a half-dozen books have been published about Branson that provide detailed information about accommodations, food, shows, and theaters, down to the fabric on the seats and the number of stalls in the bathroom.

Perhaps the best advice can be obtained from fellow travelers and residents.

- "Take time. There are so many shows," fiddler Shoji Tabuchi says. "Try to come for a week to see all the places."
- "The biggest shows are not necessarily the best," offers Jim Owen, star of a Branson morning show. "Talk to the locals, they'll tell you the truth."
- "See everything that you can," says Jennifer Wilson, star of another popular morning show. "Don't stay in the room. Make an effort to go all day long. You'll have a blast!"

GETTING THERE: The Branson Chamber of Commerce is at Hwy. 65 and Rte. 248, about a mile north of Hwy. 76. Open year-round 8 A.M. to 6 P.M.; (417) 334-4136.

Getting Around Branson

Stories about Branson's traffic are legendary. Anyone who spends a significant amount of time here will get caught in backups and snarls, but it's not as bad as it sounds. Branson's infrastructure is slowly catching up with the city's growth. A $10 million road project was approved by voters in 1991, and new multilane highways are being built.

Unfortunately, in 1995 there was still no viable form of public transportation in Branson. The sidewalks were shamefully inadequate, even lacking curb cuts for wheelchairs in some places. (Virtually all attractions are accessible to the disabled, though.)

Keep in mind these pointers when driving in Branson:

- Allow plenty of time to arrive at shows, particularly in the evenings.
- Avoid busier thoroughfares, such as 76 Parkway. Before you leave, check maps for color-coded alternative routes.
- Be a courteous driver.
- Do not drive in the center lane of Parkway, which is designated for turns.
- Plenty of parking is available at all attractions, with attendants directing traffic.

Choosing a Show

Dozens of different shows are offered in Branson every morning, afternoon, and night. If you have the energy, it's possible to see four shows in one day! The live entertainment season generally runs from March through December, although a growing number of theaters and attractions are open year-round.

Most theaters present several shows at one time. For example, in 1995 Don Williams, the Oak Ridge Boys, and Jimmy Travis all performed at the Charley Pride Theatre. Remember that although a star's name is on the marquee, he or she might not be performing during your visit. If there's someone in particular you want to see, call ahead to find out if they'll be in town.

The mix is constantly changing, with artists and productions coming to town or leaving every season. Guides listing current schedules and performances can be picked up at the Chamber of Commerce and around town.

Many theaters offer free gospel shows and musical worship services on Sunday mornings.

Special events include the Branson Jam, which kicks off the annual show season at the end of March. The festival features three days of celebrity showcases at area theaters; (417) 334-4136. State of the Ozarks Fiddlers Convention, at Compton Ridge Campground, takes place in mid-May and mid-September; (417) 338-2911. In downtown Branson, the free Old-Time Fiddle Festival, with $2,000 in prize money, is the third Saturday in August; (417) 334-1548.

BUYING SHOW TICKETS

Prices for live entertainment range from $26 for Shoji Tabuchi and $25 for Wayne Newton, to $13 for the Braschlers or Sons of the Pioneers. Most other shows cost between $15 and $20. Children are often admitted free, and some discounts are offered to seniors.

It's usually easy to obtain tickets. Most shows don't sell out and competition for audiences is intense, with many offering specials or discount coupons. Simply call ahead to reserve seats, or stop by the theater beforehand. Box offices are open daily.

Tickets can be purchased through dozens of tour and ticket services, some of which deliver. Be sure to inquire in advance about service fees.

BRANSON THEATERS

Branson theaters come in all shapes and sizes, from the 4,000-seat Grand Palace to the tiny 275-seat Owens Theater downtown. Virtually all have comfortable seating, decent sound, concessions, souvenirs, and ample parking. The newer venues have state-of-the-art lighting and sound, large lobbies, "crying rooms" for babies, restaurants, and other amenities. Most "celebrity" theaters display awards and memorabilia in the lobby. Feel free to visit theaters beforehand to check out the facilities, gift shops, or lobby displays.

The following list of theaters, addresses, and phone numbers is current as of early 1996. Area code is 417 for all phone numbers.

- 50s Variety Theater (720 seats). 3105-H Hwy. 76; 337-9829.
- 76 Music Hall (550 seats). 1935 W. Hwy. 76; 335-2484.
- Andy Williams's Moon River Theatre (2,000 seats). 2500 W. Hwy. 76; 334-4500.
- Anita Bryant Theatre (800 seats). 3446 W. Hwy. 76; 339-3939.
- Baldknobbers Jamboree Show (1,700 seats—restaurant and motor inn). 2835 W. Hwy. 76; 334-4528.
- Barbara Fairchild Theatre (650 seats). 3115 W. Hwy. 76; 336-4718.
- Bobby Vinton's Blue Velvet Theatre (2,000 seats). 2701 W. Hwy. 76; 334-2500.
- Boxcar Willie Theater (900 seats—motel, museum). 3454 W. Hwy. 76; (800) 942-HOBO or (417) 334-8696.
- Branson Mall Theater (500 seats). 2206 W. Hwy. 76; 335-3500.
- Branson's Magical Mansion (3,000 seats—Van Burch & Welford). 517 Shepherd of the Hills Expressway; 336-3986.
- Braschler Music Show (700 seats—Sons of the Pioneers). 3044 Shepherd of the Hills Expressway; 334-4363.
- Charley Pride Theatre (2,000 seats). 755 Gretna Rd.; 33-PRIDE.
- Country Tonite Theatre (2,000 seats). 4080 W. Hwy. 76; (800) GO-TONITE or (417) 334-2422.
- Cristy Lane Theatre (1,100 seats). 3600 W. Hwy. 76; 335-5111.

- Dixie Stampede (1,000 seats—dinner theater). 1527 W. Hwy. 76; (800) 520-5544 or (417) 336-3000.
- Gettysburg Theatre (920 seats—musical historic drama). 2211 Hwy. 248; 334-8400.
- Glen Campbell Goodtime Theatre (2,200 seats). Hwy. 65 at Hwy. 248; 336-1220.
- Grand Palace (4,000 seats—headliners). 2700 W. Hwy. 76; (800) 952-6626 or (417) 33-GRAND.
- Jennifer's Americana Theatre (950 seats). 2905 W. Hwy. 76; 335-8176.
- Jim Stafford Theatre (1,100 seats). 3440 W. Hwy. 76; 335-8080.
- Lawrence Welk Champagne Theatre (2,300 seats) and Welk Stagedoor Canteen (400 seats). 1984 Hwy. 165; (800) 505-WELK or (417) 337-7469.
- Lowe's Fall Creek Dinner Theatre (600 seats). Hwy. 165 and Fall Creek Rd.; (800) 21-LOWES or (417) 334-0428.
- Mel Tillis Theater (2,700 seats). 2527 Hwy. 248; 335-MMEL.
- Mickey Gilley Theatre (950 seats—Jim Owen). 3455 W. Hwy. 76; (800) 334-1936 or (417) 334-3210.
- Mutton Hollow Revue Theatre (550 seats—breakfast and lunch shows). W. Hwy. 76 and Shepherd of the Hills Expressway; 334-4947.
- Osmond Family Theatre (1,200 seats). 3216 W. Hwy. 76; 336-6100.
- Owens Theater (275 seats—downtown Branson). 205 S. Commercial; 336-2112.
- Presleys's Jubilee (1,600 seats). 2920 W. Hwy. 76; 334-4874.
- Pump Boys and Dinettes Dinner Theatre (500 seats). Hwy. 165 and Green Mountain Dr.; 336-4319.
- Roy Clark Celebrity Theatre (1,100 seats). 3425 W. Hwy. 76; 334-0076.
- Shepherd of the Hills Outdoor Theatre (1,800 seats). W. Hwy. 76 near Hwy. 265; 334-4191.
- Shoji Tabuchi Theatre (2,000 seats). 3260 Shepherd of the Hills Expressway; 334-7469.
- Showboat Branson Belle (650 seats—cruise, meal, and show). Table Rock Lake at Hwy. 165; (800) 227-8587 or (417) 336-7171.
- Thunderbird Theatre (700 seats). 2215 W. Hwy. 76; 336-2542.

- Tony Orlando Yellow Ribbon Music Theatre (2,000 seats). Hwy. 165 at The Falls; (800) 560-TONY or (417) 335-TONY.
- Wayne Newton Theatre (2,700 seats). 3701 W. Hwy. 76; 33-WAYNE.
- Who Dunnit Murder Mystery Dinner Theater (250 seats). 3050 Green Mountain Dr. at the Settle Inn; 335-4700.
- Will Rogers Theatre (2,200 seats). Hwy. 65 at Hwy. 248; (800) 687-4752 or (417) 336-1333.

Jennifer

WHO'S THAT GIRL?

First-time visitors to Branson can't help wondering: Who's that beautiful gal beaming down from huge billboards all over town? It's Jennifer.

Jennifer, a.k.a. Jennifer Wilson, is an all-American woman with million-dollar legs and a winning personality. She's got a show at Jennifer's Americana Theatre called *The Jennifer Show*. Every day, Jennifer sings her heart out, dances, clogs, and changes costumes between numbers. A terrific entertainer, Jennifer won the All-American Music Award for Female Entertainer of the Year in 1993, 1994, and 1995. (By the way, "Jennifer" is a registered trademark.)

Visitors to Branson can't miss Jennifer, an all-American entertainer. (JanBill Ltd.)

Hardworking and ambitious, Jennifer spent five years with Missouri's *Salt River Opry*, earned a master's degree in psychology, and owned a dance studio before her career took off. Jennifer is also a professional model and aspiring actress whose manager is Bill Dailey, husband of best-selling romance novelist Janet Dailey. In 1995, the USO chose Jennifer from hundreds of applicants to re-create Betty Grable's famous World War II pinup poster. Jennifer closes her Branson show with all the U.S. military service songs (including the Coast Guard's!), tap-dancing in a spangled, sequin-encrusted, red, white, and blue miniskirt.

Jennifer's number-one fan is John Ward, who always sits front-row center. On July 14, 1995, John, seventy-one, saw Jennifer's show for the 139th time. "I'll be back Wednesday," Ward says. "It's the only show I come to. She's got the best and prettiest and sweetest show in town."

Jennifer isn't a great singer, but she is an exceptionally nice and enthusiastic person who would like to personally welcome visitors to Branson. "We love having you," she says. "Branson is still old-fashioned. We're based on God, family, and country."

PERSONAL PICKS AND PANS

It would be impossible for one traveler to see every show in Branson. On my visit, I saw four celebrity shows, one family-run variety show, three morning shows, and Shoji Tabuchi, who is in a class by himself. The level of entertainment was uniformly high, with excellent production values and professional performances.

Nonetheless, there's a definite formula for Branson shows, with an overreliance on tried-and-true crowd pleasers. Almost every show includes a rendition of the fiddle tune "Orange Blossom Special," a Sons of the Pioneers and/or Lennon Sisters medley, and a "rube" comedian wearing a silly hat. I heard certain jokes repeated more than once (one about cowboys squatting on their spurs comes to mind). I found myself wondering why there weren't more female musicians or nonwhite people on stage.

With these complaints aired, I can offer some recommendations. Of the celebrity shows, **Charley Pride**'s has genuine warmth and impressive supporting musicians and backup singers (Charley's Angels). Pride, dressed in casual slacks and a sweater, does a powerful medley of his "Mississippi" songs including "Mississippi Cotton-Pickin' Delta Town," accompanied by a video of the folks in his hometown of Sledge, Mississippi. During one number, Pride gamely attempts to shake hands with everyone in his large audience.

The original **Sons of the Pioneers,** regulars in Branson since the mid-eighties, are simply delightful. Fresh and original yet heart-warmingly familiar, the Sons will surprise you. While other shows imitate them, the real Sons sing beautiful, haunting harmonies on "Ghost Riders in the Sky" and "Tumbling Tumbleweeds," knocking your socks off with their virtuoso musicianship and side-splitting physical comedy. Sons of the Pioneers have performed continuously with various members for seven decades; Dale Warren has been with the group for more than forty years. The performance includes a historical slide show and a moving tribute to Roy Rogers, one of the group's founders.

Of the "noncelebrity" shows, try the *Jim Owen Morning Show.* Owen is the premier Hank Williams, Sr., imitator in the country. He's also a songwriter whose credits include several Mel Tillis hits. He does impersonations, and gives a moving talk about Williams's drug abuse. The big surprise, though, is Owen's knack for stand-up comedy, especially his routines about "M-Mel Tillis," family, and marriage.

Comedy is the best thing about the **Baldknobbers** show, presented by three generations of the Mabe family. The fast-paced variety show may be a little slick for some tastes, but the comedy team of "Stub" and "Droopy Drawers" are showstoppers, worth the price of admission.

You won't see anything like **Shoji Tabuchi**'s show on earth. The Japanese fiddler routinely sells out in Branson with his big, Broadway-style production. While still in Japan, Tabuchi fell in love with Roy Acuff's fiddling. He came to the United States and paid his dues working in restaurants and clubs from San Francisco to Louisiana before finding his audience in Missouri.

Tabuchi's show has grown to baroque proportions. It includes a twenty-piece band, dozens of dancers and backup singers, smoke, laser lights and fireworks, elaborate sets, and dance numbers. Tabuchi gives people what they want with a mix of show tunes, big band, country, polka, jazz, pop, and classical music. "We try to play every kind of music," Tabuchi says.

Tabuchi's lavish art-deco pink-and-purple theater is famous for its crystal chandeliers, and the red billiard table in the men's room. Like Liberace on the piano, Shoji *isn't* the world's best fiddle player, but he is the consummate showman.

Where to Eat

Branson is full of chain restaurants, fast-food outlets, and "feeding troughs," inexpensive all-you-can-eat buffets with decent to mediocre food. Several casual family restaurants and pubs are located in downtown Branson.

Some good food can be found if you look for it, however. At the **Hard Luck Diner,** the waiters and waitresses are all aspiring country singers. In between taking and delivering orders, they pick up microphones and sing, working the room like professionals. Several even have their own fan clubs. The decor is a brand-new fifties-style diner with shiny chrome, booths, and Formica counters. The food is inexpensive (nothing priced higher than $9) and excellent: piled-high sandwiches, blue plate specials (meat loaf, roast beef, catfish), burgers, salads, ice-cream sodas, and killer desserts. It's in Grand Village, an upscale shopping area across from the Grand Palace Theater. 2800 W. Hwy. 76; (417) 336-7217.

The **Friendship House Restaurant/Rose O'Neill Tea Room** is run by enthusiastic students of the College of the Ozarks. Overseen by professionals, they cook and serve decent, reasonably priced breakfast, lunch, and dinner buffets, with homemade breads, salads, meats, vegetables, and a slew of delicious desserts. There's also a full menu of sandwiches, burgers, salads, and dinner entrées. The students are friendly and attentive, eager to answer questions and offer travel advice. It's a relaxing place to eat, and you can feel good about supporting a fine liberal-arts college. Two miles south of Branson on Hwy. 65; (417) 334-6411, ext. 3341.

Mickey Gilley's **Texas Cafe,** next door to the singer's theater, serves barbecued ribs, chicken, and pork, "wild bull chili," fajitas, burgers, salads, and steaks. The red-hot chile poppers are a spicy "wow" treat: jalapeño halves filled with cream cheese, breaded, fried, and dipped in pepper jam. The restaurant has attractive Southwestern decor and a full bar/cantina. 3457 W. Hwy. 76; (417) 335-2755.

Dolly Parton's $14.5 million **Dixie Stampede** dinner attraction is identical to her successful theaters in Pigeon Forge, Tennessee, and Myrtle Beach, South Carolina. Guests eat a four-course barbecue meal in a 1,000-seat arena, while a rodeo-style North-South rivalry is enacted below. 1527 W. Hwy. 76; (800) 520-5544 or (417) 337-9400.

Branson Attractions
COLLEGE OF THE OZARKS
RALPH FOSTER MUSEUM—SMITHSONIAN OF THE OZARKS

Ralph Foster was a radio pioneer dedicated to promoting the region's musical talent. Foster's flagship station was KWTO (Keep Watching The Ozarks), begun in the mid-1930s. The *Ozark Jubilee,* a popular weekly radio/television show starring Red Foley, was produced by Foster's Crossroads TV company and helped launch the careers of Slim Wilson, Porter Wagoner, Homer and Jethro, and many others.

The fascinating Ralph Foster Museum, self-proclaimed "Smithsonian of the Ozarks," is on the College of the Ozarks campus. The museum houses Foster's vast collection of Indian artifacts, a model of his office, and much, much more. The rambling, eclectic exhibits, on three floors in a large plain building, include displays of Rose O'Neill's Kewpie dolls, clocks, and pocket watches; paintings by Thomas Hart Benton and Harold Bell Wright; farm implements and tools; hundreds of rifles and pistols; and an extensive wildlife and natural-history room with stuffed moose, bears, and dozens of birds. For $7.95, visitors can even have their pictures taken on the original *Beverly Hillbillies* truck.

Fans of the *Ozark Jubilee* will enjoy the **Si Siman Music Room** on the first floor. Siman started his career with Foster at KWTO, and became a successful music publisher and impresario. He "put the

Ozarks on the map" with the *Jubilee,* bringing the area and its music to a national audience. As Wagoner's manager, Siman bought the singer his first suit and tie; he published "The Clown," "Always on My Mind," and dozens of hit country songs. The room is filled with Siman's personal collection of memorabilia and photographs.

Upstairs on the third floor, there is a "before and after" display on the history of music tourism in Branson. One side is the old Branson, which pays tribute to Mary Herschend, who built Silver Dollar City in the late 1950s, and Mary Trimble, responsible for the Shepherd of the Hills Outdoor Drama and Homestead. "These two women were so strong in their resolve. They were responsible for bringing tourism to this area," says Bob Esworthy, director of the museum.

Photos of early music shows featuring the Collins, Plummer, Presley, and Mabe families are on display. "They played from May to October, and charged four dollars to get in," Esworthy says. "Families would come here and relax and fish and have a nice time.

"Well, *Hee Haw* came to town," he continues, referring to Roy Clark's stage-show venture in 1983 that ignited the city's phenomenal growth. For the new Branson exhibit, Esworthy has collected items such as Andy Williams's Christmas sweater, Jim Stafford's guitar, Moe Bandy's boots, and Barbara Fairchild's stage costume.

GETTING THERE: The Ralph Foster Museum is open Monday through Saturday, 9 A.M. to 4:30 P.M. Call for winter hours. Closed Christmas Day through the last week in January. Admission $4.50; students and children free. Allow two to three hours for the museum, or a half day for the museum and campus tour. Two miles south of Branson off Hwy. 65; (417) 334-6411.

SHEPHERD OF THE HILLS—BRINGING A VERY OLD STORY TO LIFE

"This, my story, is a very old story," begins Harold Bell Wright's 1907 book *Shepherd of the Hills,* the first American novel to sell a million copies. "This, my story, is the story of a man who took the trail that leads to the lower ground, and of a woman, and how she found her way to the higher sunlit fields. In the story, it all happened in the Ozark Mountains, many miles from what we call civilization."

Wright, a minister born in upstate New York, suffered from tuberculosis and traveled to the Ozarks for his health. The people he met and the countryside around what is now Branson, including Inspiration Point, Mutton Hollow, and Old Matt's Cabin, inspired him and were featured in the novel.

The simple love story is an uplifting parable about prejudice, spirituality, and personal honor. People began visiting "Shepherd of the Hills Country" as soon as the book was published. *Shepherd of the Hills* was the subject of four Hollywood movies, including one starring John Wayne.

At **Shepherd of the Hills Homestead and Outdoor Theatre,** opened in 1960, the tale is reenacted nightly by a large cast in an 1,800-seat amphitheater. The realistic production features the shepherd herding live sheep, evil Baldknobber vigilantes thundering in on horseback, and a burning cabin. During intermission, the audience is invited to a square dance with live music in a barn.

The **homestead park** is open during the day. The tour includes the original "Old Matt's Cabin" and a 1901 church. On site, there's also a 255-foot observation tower, playground, trail rides, excursions in Clydesdale-drawn carriages, several restaurants and crafts shops, and the popular **Precious Moments Chapel** and gift gallery.

GETTING THERE: Shepherd of the Hills is open daily from the end of April through the end of October. The drama is performed nightly at 8:30 P.M. (7:30 P.M. after Labor Day). The homestead park is open 9 A.M. to 5:30 P.M. (until 4:30 P.M. after Labor Day). The park is also open from mid-November through mid-December for a Christmas show. Admission $17 for the drama, $13 for the homestead and observation tower, and $4 for the tower only. Combination tickets are available. South of Hwy. 265 on W. Hwy. 76; (417) 334-4191.

MUTTON HOLLOW ENTERTAINMENT PARK AND CRAFTS VILLAGE
HAROLD BELL WRIGHT MUSEUM

A lovely change of pace in Branson, **Mutton Hollow** is a gentle, laid-back entertainment park and crafts village with live entertainment, trail rides, and a vintage Ferris wheel and carousel. "We're what Branson used to be," Director Vickie Dixon Cushman says. "We've changed less than other places. Families come here and they're not afraid to let go of the kids' hands."

Bruce Grimes, the "yodeling blacksmith," entertains visitors at the Mutton Hollow crafts village.

The park gets its name from Harold Bell Wright's *Shepherd of the Hills.* Mutton Hollow is where the old shepherd lives down "the trail that is nobody knows how old."

The Cushman family has run Mutton Hollow since the late sixties, and completed a million-dollar renovation in 1991. The park is beautifully landscaped, with well-tended flower beds of everything from hibiscus to pansies. The Cushmans' secret recipes for lye soap and apple butter are cooked in kettles, and friendly craftspeople demonstrate their skills. Bruce Grimes, the "Yodeling Blacksmith," spins yarns and sings while constructing iron farm tools with an anvil and coal fire.

More than a half-dozen different live music performances, including breakfast and lunch shows, are presented throughout the day in small covered theaters and an air-conditioned indoor pavilion. The $5 lunch show is a terrific bargain, with barbecue chicken, fish, beans, cornbread, slaw, fruit, and spirited music from the Platters quartet.

On the Mutton Hollow grounds, the **Harold Bell Wright Museum and Theater** displays personal items, original manuscripts, and paintings. A sound-guided tour is narrated by Norman Wright, the author's only surviving son. Wright, a writer and director for Walt Disney, has produced an entertaining 30-minute film, shown at the museum, which tells Harold Bell Wright's life story and stars his grandson Michael. Allow an hour. The museum entrance is in the Mutton Hollow parking lot. A separate admission of $3.75 is charged; (417) 334-0065.

GETTING THERE: Mutton Hollow is open daily, April through December, 9 A.M. to 6:30 P.M. (gates open at 7:30 A.M. for breakfast show). Allow a half to a full day. Admission to the park is free, with separate tickets for some shows and rides. W. Hwy. 76 and Shepherd of the Hills Expressway; (417) 334-4947.

SILVER DOLLAR CITY

Silver Dollar City is a popular amusement park on the same scale as the Opryland theme park in Nashville, with live music, food, costumed craftspeople, and a lot of things to buy. Opened in 1960 by the Herschend family, Silver Dollar City combines an 1890s frontier mining village with modern attractions and rides, including roller coasters and flumes. **Marvel Cave** is underneath the park; a tour is included with admission.

The park's charming older attractions include a weird haunted mansion and the flooded shooting mine, where visitors ride around in little boats and shoot at moving targets with air guns. **McHaffie's Homestead** is a realistic rustic farm with chickens, roosters, and pigs, where frontiersmen build log cabins with axes and hand tools.

Ten different **shows** are presented daily, including *Country America's Top 100 Hits* in the Echo Hollow amphitheater, and *Listen to the River* in the 1,000-seat indoor Opera House.

With 1.7 million visitors a year, Silver Dollar City can get crowded during the peak season. But it's a pretty, wooded park with lots of trees and shaded benches.

Special events include Silver Dollar City Music Festival in June, with performances by musicians from around the country. The National Festival of Craftsmen takes place from mid-September through the end of October, with hundreds of artists displaying and demonstrating their handiwork.

GETTING THERE: Silver Dollar City is open early April through late October, and mid-November through December. Call for early-

and late-season hours. In season, open 9:30 A.M. to 6 P.M. Allow a half to a full day. Admission $23.50 adults, $14 children ages 4 to 11, and free for under 4, with discounts during the Christmas season. Four miles northwest of Branson, on Hwy. 265; (800) 952-6626 or (417) 336-7100.

ADDITIONAL BRANSON ATTRACTIONS

There's plenty to do in Branson, and new attractions are opening all the time. The following is only a selection of activities.

A stroll through **downtown Branson** along Main Street and Commercial Avenue reveals several flea markets, clothing stores, shops, cafes, family restaurants, ice-cream parlors, and candy stores. **Dick's Old-Time 5 & 10** sells a large selection of colorful tin signs, household items, fabric, hardware, toys, model cars, cheap souvenirs, and candy (103 W. Main St.; (417) 334-2410). **Branson Scenic Railway** is a forty-mile, two-hour train excursion into the heart of the Missouri and Arkansas Ozark Mountains (206 E. Main St.; (800) 2-TRAIN-2 or (417) 334-6110).

Historic **Bonniebrook** mansion displays the work of Rose O'Neill, a turn-of-the-century artist, novelist, poet, and creator of the adorable Kewpie doll. Guests can stroll the estate's flower gardens, sample Bonniebrook wines, and dine at the elegant Rose Garden Restaurant. The International Rose O'Neill Club meets every April at Bonniebrook for the **Kewpiesta,** a five-day festival. Bonniebrook is 9 miles north of Branson. Take Hwy. 65 north to Rose O'Neill Rd.; (800) 539-7437 or (417) 336-3230.

The largest ship ever constructed for a land-locked lake is Kenny Rogers's *Showboat Branson Belle,* a huge new paddle-wheeler with a 650-seat multilevel dinner theater. All tickets include a meal, show, and cruise on Table Rock Lake. (Rogers does not perform regularly.) The *Showboat* is docked 8 miles west of Branson. Take Hwy. 165 to Table Rock Dam; (800) 227-8587 or (417) 336-7171.

Ride the Ducks is a 70-minute sightseeing tour on an amphibious vehicle that drives around Branson, then rolls into Table Rock Lake for a cruise. Open May through December. Tours depart from W. Hwy. 76, near Green Mountain Dr.; (417) 334-DUCK.

On the lake's northeast shore, **Table Rock State Park Lake** is a 356-

acre public facility with camping, RV hookups, a fully equipped marina, fishing, boating, scuba-diving, picnicking, and swimming. Seven miles west of Branson on Hwy. 165/265; (417) 334-4704.

For information about additional accommodations, outfitters, and attractions on Table Rock Lake, visit the Chamber of Commerce Visitors' Center on Hwy. 13 in Kimberling City; (417) 739-2564.

Shoppers can choose from dozens of factory outlet stores, specialty gift shops, arts and crafts galleries, and T-shirt and souvenir emporiums. The **Engler's Block** crafts mall contains more than thirty shops selling woodcarvings, handcrafted leather, jewelry, blown glass, and more. 1335 W. Hwy. 76; (417) 335-2200.

The **Ernest Tubb Record Shop No. 5** sells country-music recordings, books, posters, and videos, including many rare and hard-to-find items. Branson Mall (next to Wal-Mart), 2200 block of W. Hwy. 76; (417) 336-5605.

BRANSON SURVIVAL TIPS

- Allow plenty of time to drive to theaters.
- Use discount coupons for shows and attractions, available at the Chamber of Commerce and around town.
- Dress comfortably. Branson is casual.
- Theaters and restaurants are over–air-conditioned. Carry a sweater.

Springfield
REMEMBERING THE *OZARK JUBILEE*

Long before Branson became the Ozark Mountains' country music headquarters, Springfield's *Ozark Jubilee* brought national attention to the region and boosted the careers of Porter Wagoner, Brenda Lee, and many others.

Si Siman started the *Ozark Jubilee* on KWTO Radio (*see* Branson— Ralph Foster Museum). From 1954 to 1960, the show was broadcast on ABC-TV with *Grand Ole Opry* star Red Foley as host, from the 1910 Jewell Theater in downtown Springfield.

The theater has since been torn down. A few years ago, a commemorative stone was placed on the spot by an anonymous "friend of the Ozarks." It reads, "The *Jubilee* favorably introduced millions of viewers to talented Ozarkers and inspired those visitors to travel to the Ozarks, where they experienced the beauty of Springfield and the entire area."

GETTING THERE: Springfield is an hour north of Branson at Hwy. 65 and I-44. The marker is in Park Central East, between Jefferson and Campbell Aves. Take Hwy. 65 to Chestnut Expressway west. Turn left on Grant Avenue, then left on Olive Street to the park. Contact the Springfield Visitors' Bureau; (800) 678-8766.

Sedalia
HOMETOWN OF LEROY VAN DYKE

In Sedalia, a small city between Kansas City and Columbia, an avenue is named for native son Leroy Van Dyke near the Ramada Inn, at 3501 W. Broadway/Hwy. 50. Van Dyke, whose hits include "Walk On By" and "The Auctioneer," joined the *Ozark Jubilee* in Springfield in 1956. The singer lives in the area, and occasionally serves as the real auctioneer for local civic functions.

Sedalia is home of the **Mississippi State Fair,** which draws 300,000 people every August. Popular **bluegrass festivals** are held at the fairgrounds in June and August, with headline and local bands. The four-day **Scott Joplin Ragtime Festival** in June is the world's only classical ragtime event, with music and symposia. The groundbreaking composer lived in Sedalia in the 1890s. A commemorative mural is downtown at 207 S. Ohio, and the **Scott Joplin Archives** are in State Fair Community College Library, 3201 W. 16th St.

GETTING THERE: Take I-70/Exit 70 to Hwy. 65 south. For Sedalia information, call (800) 827-5295.

Missouri Music Shows

Beyond the panoply of shows in Branson, Missouri hosts several dozen Oprys, jamborees, and family music shows around the state. Most are performed on weekends during the summer season and cost $3 to $10 per person. Schedules often change, so be sure to call ahead before planning a trip. The following are listed by location, generally from north to south and east to west.

In Mark Twain's hometown of Hannibal, on the Mississippi River in northeast Missouri, **Ebers River City Opry** features country, comedy, and clogging. On weekends, April through October, Allen and Shelia Ebers, and their seven children, ages 12 to 24, star in the show. Take Hwy. 36 or 61. 101 N. Main St.; (573) 267-3678 or 221-2477.

North of Mark Twain Lake, Bob Vanderback's **Salt River Opry** features country and gospel music, clogging, and comedy on Saturday nights April through October. (Branson's Jennifer Wilson got her start here.) Different shows are presented weekly, with a regular cast and special guests. The complex, near Monroe City just north of Cannon Dam, includes a motel, restaurant, and the **Missouri Pure Country and Bluegrass Music Hall of Fame,** recognizing achievements among the state's thriving music-show community. Take Hwy. 36 to Rte. J south; (573) 735-4461.

In Macon near Long Branch Lake, **Wilcox Country Opry Barn** presents headline acts, local bands, and talent shows the second and fourth Saturday night of every month. Hwy. 63 south; (816) 385-2304 or -6428.

In Kirksville, **Chariton Valley Opry** is open Saturday nights April through mid-December with country music and comedy. Take Hwy. 63 to Hwy. 6 west to the McMain Building; (816) 665-3085.

In north-central Missouri, **Cuzn Pud's Jamboree** is a variety show with special guests, presented April through November. The theater is on Main Street in Laredo. Take Hwy. 65 to Rte. 6 east to Rte. E south; (816) 286-2305.

Near Pony Express Lake, Cow Pasture Amphitheater in Osborn offers country music on Saturday nights as well as camping, fishing, and golf. May through October. Three-day festivals take place in July and September. Take Hwy. 36 to Hwy. 33 north; (816) 449-2039.

In St. Joseph on the Missouri River, **Pony Express Opry** is a fast-paced professional music show presented twice-daily (except Sunday), with Nick Zane, a fifteen-member band, and restaurant. Open year-round, near the city's historic downtown. 210 N. 4th St.; (816) 232-0955.

The Lake of the Ozarks region in central Missouri has been a popular vacation resort and country music magnet for decades. The following shows are in towns surrounding the lake. All are open April through October, with shows nightly at 8 P.M. (For area information, contact Lake Area Chamber of Commerce; (573) 348-2730.)

Lee Mace's Ozark Opry, begun in 1953, was the first family music theater of its type in the United States, located in Osage Beach. Lee Mace died in 1985; his wife Joyce owns and manages the popular Opry. Closed Sunday. Take I-44/Exit 129 to Rte. 5 north, to Hwy. 54 north/east at Mace Road; (573) 348-2270 or -2702.

Also in Osage Beach, **Main Street Opry** showcases modern and traditional country, bluegrass, gospel, and rock and roll. Closed Mondays, additional shows in November and December. Hwy. 54, ½ a mile west of Grand Glaize Bridge; (800) 843-9713 or (573) 348-4848.

South of Lake Ozark in Camdenton, **Kin-Fokes Country Music Show** is a high-spirited mix of "hand clappin', toe-tappin' " music and comedy. Closed Sunday. On Camdenton Square. Take I-44/Exit 129 to Rte. 5 north; (573) 346-6797.

In the Kansas City area, Davis Theater in Higginsville features **Sundowners Country Music Show** Saturday nights year-round. Take I-70/Exit 52 to Rte. 213 north. 2008 Main St.; (816) 584-2999.

Northtown Opry is in North Kansas City, a small town on the Missouri River. The Saturday-night shows feature a ten-piece band and special guests year-round. Take I-35 north to Armour Road west. 408 Armour Rd.; (816) 471-6779.

Edgerton, between Kansas City and St. Joseph, is home of the **Union Mill Opry.** In its fourth decade, the Saturday-night variety show has a cast of fifteen performers and special guests. Take Hwy. 169 to Rte. Z west; (816) 227-3733 or (in Kansas City) (816) 790-3733.

At the north edge of the Mark Twain National Forest, the **Meramec Country Music Show** in Steelville serves up music, comedy, and even magic. Open Friday and Saturday nights, May through October. Downtown, at Rtes. 8 and 19. Take I-44/Exit 208 to Rte. 19 south; (573) 775-5999.

Montana

Montana Festivals

Lewistown, a town of 6,000 smack in the middle of Montana, hosts the "Wild and Woolly" **Montana State Cowboy Poetry Gathering** the third weekend in August. For three days, the Treasure State's most eloquent gather for poetry workshops, Western arts and crafts, and evening music performances. Daytime events are held at the Yogo Inn, 211 E. Main St., and evening concerts at the Fergus Center for the Performing Arts, 201 Casino Drive. Lewistown is 125 miles northwest of Billings. Take Hwy. 87. Contact the Chamber of Commerce; (406) 538-5436.

The fourth weekend in July, fiddlers from around the nation pour into Polson for the **Montana State Old-Time Fiddlers' Contest.** The gathering and competition take place in northwest Montana on the shores of Flathead Lake, the largest natural freshwater lake west of the Mississippi River. The town itself is in a beautiful natural amphitheater created by the steep 500-foot walls of the Flathead River gorge. Polson is 70 miles north of Missoula. Take I-90/Exit 96 to Hwy. 93 north; (406) 883-5969.

Nebraska

Omaha

ANDERSEN'S RED BARN OPRY SHOWHOUSE

Florence Andersen has presented live shows every weekend from a big red barn in Omaha since 1979. Her appropriately named Red Barn Opry Showhouse features an unrehearsed traditional country and bluegrass jamboree on Friday nights, and a professional stage show with the house band, regular cast, and special guests on Saturday nights. Andersen's annual talent contests draw competitors from around the nation; the winner gets to perform on *Ernest Tubb's Midnight Jamboree* in Nashville.

The Red Barn is actually a comfortable, air-conditioned, 500-seat hall. "I play bass, my son plays steel, and my two grandsons play everything," says Andersen. "And the rest of my band is terrific."

GETTING THERE: Omaha is on the eastern border of Nebraska. Tickets $3 on Fridays, $5-7 on Saturdays. Shows begin at 8 P.M. Take I-80/Exit 440 to Hwy. 50 north. Turn right on service road. 10318 Sapp Brothers Dr.; (402) 895-5939.

Nevada

West Wendover
THE GREAT AMERICAN COWBOY COOK-OUT AND WILD WEST SHOW

Lorraine and Brad Merl's Great American Cowboy Cook-out and Wild West Show in West Wendover offers covered-wagon excursions through the Nevada desert to an old-fashioned cowboy campsite. Along with a show, there's steak, baked potatoes, beans cooked in a Dutch oven, and marshmallows to roast over an open fire. Year-round, weather permitting. Reservations required. I-80 at Utah border; (801) 665-2674.

Elko
HOME OF THE ORIGINAL COWBOY POETRY GATHERING

When folklorist Hal Cannon, director of the Western Folklife Center in Elko, put together the first cowboy poetry gathering in 1985, he could not have anticipated the wave of appreciation and respect for Western ranch culture that resulted; now hundreds of cowboy poetry and music festivals take place every year, in big cities and small towns around the country. Cannon says his goal was simply "to dispel the myth of the lone cowboy, a rugged individualist with no way to express himself. It's simply not true."

Several thousand cowboy poets, cowboy singers, real cowboys, and cowboy wanna-bes make the pilgrimage to Elko, in the mountains of northeast Nevada, for the **Cowboy Poetry Gathering** the last week of January—often in subzero temperatures. The festival offers readings, workshops, concerts, dances, autograph sessions, films, and special art exhibits, at sites all over town. Michael Martin Murphey, Waddie Mitchell, Riders in the Sky, Tish Hinojosa, Ian Tyson, and the Texas Playboys are among the regular performers.

In 1996, the June **Cowboy Music Gathering,** which attracts more than 10,000 people a year, will expand into a month-long season of folk and country shows, and cowboy poetry readings. Eventually, Cannon hopes to offer live entertainment all summer long. If you plan to attend either event, book well in advance. Tickets and hotel rooms are snatched up quickly.

The Western Folklife Center was founded in the late 1980s to provide a forum for studying ranching and agricultural cultures, and to produce festivals, books, recordings, and exhibits of Western culture for a wide audience.

In 1992, the Center moved to the 1912 Frontier Hotel in downtown Elko. The **Western Folklife Center** has changing exhibits in a small gallery "based on reality, rather than the myth, of the cowboy," Cannon says; the Pioneer Saloon; a small music hall; and the popular Folk Arts Shop. Plans are under way to expand the gallery into a museum, and add an audio-visual theater and performance space.

Elko loudly trumpets its crowning as "Best Small Town in America" in a 1992 book. Attractions include a handful of low-key casinos and the **Northeast Nevada Museum,** which displays the state's largest gun collection, dioramas of Western living, and exhibits on regional wildlife.

The city is located in a desert basin surrounded by foothills and the snowcapped Ruby Mountains. Hunting, fishing, boating, camping, hiking, horseback riding, and wildlife viewing are excellent in nearby parks and refuges. Two historic mining towns are within driving distance.

Elko is fairly isolated, in the kind of country where you can see the entire length of a freight train moving across the desert floor. In the old days, traveling across these expanses on horseback would take weeks, allowing plenty of time for cowboys to absorb the dramatic scenery and transform the feelings into art and poetry. It's beautiful country, well worth the effort of a visit.

GETTING THERE: Elko is 235 miles west of Salt Lake City and 120 miles east of Winnemucca. Take I-80/Exit 301. For area information, contact Elko Visitors' Bureau; (800) 248-3556 or (702) 738-4091.

The Western Folklife Visitors' Center is generally open Tuesday through Sunday, 10 A.M. to 6 P.M., with extra days and hours during busy seasons. Call for cowboy festival information. 501 Railroad St.; (702) 738-7508.

Las Vegas

AMERICA'S SHOWTOWN

Everything in Las Vegas just keeps getting bigger and bigger. Around 5,000 people move into the area every month, pushing the desert city's population to over a million, while nearly 34 million people visit annually. To keep up with the growth (and compete with the explosion in legal gambling around the country), Las Vegas has turned to "mega-resorts."

These monolithic theme resorts, which now line the world-famous glittering Las Vegas Strip (Las Vegas Boulevard), are self-contained entertainment parks with noisy casinos, thousands of hotel rooms, amusements, cheap buffets, shows, restaurants, and stores. Each one is larger and more ostentatious than the next.

Las Vegas boasts more live entertainment than any other city in the world. In addition to superstars, comedians, magicians, and a variety of stage shows, country music entertainment abounds. The **Fremont Street Experience** is Las Vegas' newest mega-attraction, a four-block-long canopy of two million light bulbs, the largest electric sign in the world. An awesome six-minute sound-and-light show called the **Downtown Hoedown,** with country music, is presented several times a night, drawing tourists to the city's revitalized downtown area.

Names like WILLIE, DOLLY, and REBA appear regularly on the flashing hotel marquees, and there are several glittery "hot country" shows and lounges with live bands and dancing.

Ticket prices vary widely, from minimal cover charges at dance clubs and $20 to $25 for stage shows, to as much as $1,000 for superstars like Barbra Streisand. (Prices usually include one or two drinks.) Call (702) 225-5554 for current show schedules.

Among the country music offerings in Las Vegas is the Aladdin Hotel's **Country Tonite,** also seen onstage in Branson, Missouri. This fast-paced variety show is presented twice nightly, except Tuesday. The four talented and precocious Moffat Brothers first appeared here in 1993. Tickets $19.25, or $23.55 with a buffet; (702) 736-0111.

Country Fever plays at the Golden Nugget, featuring the Posse Band, the Definitely Denim Dance Troupe, comedy, and star look-alikes. There are two shows nightly, except Friday. Admission

$22.50, with an appetizer and drink; (800) 777-4658 or (702) 386-8100.

At the Excalibur, **Wild Bill's** lounge offers country bands and dancing nightly; (800) 937-7777 or (702) 597-7600.

A **Country Star Restaurant** was expected to open in 1996, on the Strip and Harmon Avenue. (*See also:* California—Hollywood.)

In addition to gambling and entertainment, **area attractions** include the awesome Hoover Dam, art and natural-history museums, the Liberace Museum, and the Debbie Reynolds Hollywood Movie Museum.

GETTING THERE: Las Vegas is in southern Nevada, 290 miles east of Los Angeles on I-15. Contact the Las Vegas Visitors' Authority; (702) 892-0711.

New Jersey

Waretown
SOUTH JERSEY'S ALBERT MUSIC HALL

Back in the 1950s, Joe and George Albert used to go fox hunting from their rustic cabin in the pine woods near Waretown, an isolated seaside town on the New Jersey shore. On Saturday nights, they would get out their instruments and pick and sing country music with a few friends.

"The people in South Jersey are very much like people in the Appalachians," says Elaine Everett, a volunteer for the music show at Albert Music Hall. Before the Garden State Parkway was built, she says, residents eked out their meager livelihoods by fishing and collecting pinecones. "Families tended to play music and sing, and that was their entertainment."

More and more people started showing up at the Albert brothers' cabin, and the weekly event evolved into a treasured ritual for the community. With the brothers getting older, a nonprofit group formed to make sure the event continued and preserved New Jersey's musical heritage.

To accommodate crowds the group rented a space, which was called Albert Music Hall. Every Saturday night from 8 to 11:30 P.M., amateur bands and singers perform twenty-minute sets of mostly acoustic country, bluegrass, and folk music. A old-timey band called the Pineconers, from the Albert brothers days, always performs before the break. Band members include several older women and "Mr. Spoons," a gentleman who taps out rhythms on hand-carved cherrywood utensils.

The devoted patrons of Albert Music Hall never miss a Saturday night. When the original building burned down in 1992, they put on a show in the parking lot. A few weeks later, Frederic Priff School donated its gym, and the community set to work raising money for a new hall, which is scheduled to open next door in 1996.

"We're an all-volunteer organization. No one gets a cent," Everett says. "We have an awful lot of very loyal people."

Albert Music Hall holds four festivals annually, including the **Ocean County Bluegrass Festival,** the Sunday after Labor Day.

GETTING THERE: Waretown is on the South Jersey shore, about 35 miles north of Atlantic City. Admission $4. Take Garden State Parkway/Exit 69 to Rte. 532 east (¼ mile west of Rte. 9). Wells Mill Rd.; (609) 971-1593.

New Mexico

Red River
MOUNTAIN COWBOY MUSIC

Red River is a Western resort town in the mountains of north-central New Mexico. In the off-season, when he's not busy with his West-Fests, Cowboy singer Michael Martin Murphey performs acoustic cowboy music at the Red River Inn's **Mineshaft Theater.** Murphey lives in a cabin with his family about ten minutes from town. "During the summer, I ride my horse to work," he says. "People get a big kick out of it." 300 W. Main St.; (800) 365-2930.

Murphey says there's terrific downhill and cross-country skiing, and ample access to wilderness, while "country music is played up and down the streets." The **Aspengate Arts and Crafts Festival,** with live entertainment, takes place the last full weekend in September.

GETTING THERE: Red River is about 40 miles north of Taos. Take I-25/Exit 419 to Rte. 58 west, to Rte. 38 north. Contact Red River Chamber of Commerce; (800) 348-6444 or (505) 754-2366.

Las Vegas
THE REAL OLD WEST

Las Vegas, New Mexico, is a real Old West town with more than 900 buildings on the National Register of Historic Places. Billy the Kid, Doc Holliday, and Jesse James used to frequent Las Vegas, once among the roughest towns in the West. The entire town is an outdoor museum, a relic from one of the last frontiers on the Santa Fe Trail. It's also in a beautiful mountain setting with access to parks and wildlife refuges, lakes, golf, and ski resorts.

Honoring the town's history as a major rail and roundup center, the three-day **Rails and Trails** festival the second weekend in June features a fiddle contest, Western street dance, melodramas, rodeo, art show, and live entertainment.

GETTING THERE: Las Vegas is 65 miles east of Santa Fe on I-25. Contact the Chamber of Commerce; (800) 832-5947 or (505) 425-8631.

Clovis
NORMAN PETTY STUDIOS

In 1957, two upstart west Texas musicians made their respective ways over to Norman Petty Studios in Clovis, New Mexico: Roy Orbison and Buddy Holly. Petty produced "That'll Be The Day," "Peggy Sue," "It's So Easy," and "Every Day" with Holly, as well as Orbison's first hit "Ooby Dooby."

The original studio, closed in the early sixties, is nearly a shrine for some Holly fans. Original recording equipment, Holly's Fender amplifier, and other memorabilia are on display. The studio, at 1313 W. 7th St., can be toured by appointment. Contact Kenneth Broad, (505) 356-6422.

The **Clovis Music Festival,** in mid-July, acknowledges Petty's and Clovis's place in pop and country music history.

(*See also:* Iowa—Clear Lake; Texas—Lubbock, Wink.)

GETTING THERE: Clovis is 90 miles west of Lubbock, Texas, and 220 miles east of Albuquerque. Hwy. 60 and 70/84; (505) 763-3435.

Ruidoso
MUSIC SHOWS AND COWBOY SYMPOSIUM

Memorial Day through Labor Day weekend, several country music and Western shows are presented daily around Ruidoso, a town in the heart of Billy the Kid territory in south-central New Mexico. Tickets $10–13; call for reservations.

The Castle Music Show is a family variety show with country, blues, clogging, comedy, and yodeling, performed in a 300-seat theater. Special shows are offered occasionally in the off-season. Hwy. 70 west; (505) 257-6180.

Bent Tree Jamboree offers a mix of contemporary country and Western music, along with steak meals in a dinner theater north of Ruidoso. Take Rte. 48 to Airport Rd.; (505) 336-4076.

The **Flying J Ranch,** in its second decade, also serves authentic chuckwagon dinners, followed by a Western show. On Rte. 48; one mile north of Alto Country Club turn-off; (505) 336-4330.

Ruidoso Downs hosts the rollicking three-day **Lincoln County Cowboy Symposium** the second weekend in October. The festival features cowboy poetry and music, square-dancing, a chuckwagon cook-off, team roping, crafts, and trail rides; (505) 378-4142.

Nearby attractions include the Ruidoso Downs Racetrack, the Anne C. Stradling Museum of the Horse, and the Mescalero Apache Indian Reservation.

GETTING THERE: Ruidoso is 150 miles southeast of Albuquerque. Take I-25/Exit 139 to Hwy. 380, to Hwy. 37, to Hwy. 48; (800) 253-2255 or (505) 257-7395.

New York

New York City
COWGIRL HALL OF FAME BAR-B-Q

The Cowgirl Hall of Fame Bar-B-Q is a funky Texas outpost in downtown Manhattan. The restaurant is affiliated with the Cowgirl Hall of Fame and Western Heritage Center in Fort Worth, Texas, a wonderful institution dedicated to securing the nation's cowgirls and Western women their rightful place in history.

The restaurant is cluttered with antler chandeliers, colorful Western murals, lassos, bandannas, and guitars. Photos of "guest cowgirls" line the walls by the bar, from June Carter and Debbie Garrison (1979 Miss

Rodeo America) to Patty Loveless, Patsy Montana, Bonnie Raitt, and RuPaul. During the 1992 Democratic Convention, Chelsea Clinton and thirty friends went slumming here; former Texas governor Ann Richards booked the whole restaurant for the Texas delegation's party.

The rich Southern food is tasty, and there's plenty of it: huge portions of dry ribs, black beans, fried chicken, Frito pies, meat and vegetarian chili, and burgers, as well as some variations on traditional fare. (The gourmet items are good, although it's doubtful that America's cowgirls ate many eggplant fritters on the range.) For dessert there are pies, cobblers, and the Cowgirl's "original ice cream baked potato."

The Center supplies the restaurant with new mini-museum displays four times a year on Hall of Fame inductees such as rodeo champions, Western artists, writers, and frontier women. Country music plays constantly, and live performances are booked occasionally. A popular event is the annual Patsy Cline lookalike contest on "St. Patsy's Day," March 17. (A second restaurant is located in Santa Fe, New Mexico; (505) 982-2565.)

GETTING THERE: Cowgirl Hall of Fame Bar-B-Q is open Monday through Thursday; for lunch, noon to 4 P.M., and dinner, 5 to 11:30 P.M; until 12:30 A.M. Fridays and Saturdays. Weekend brunch 11:30 A.M. to 4 P.M. Entrees $6 to $12. Reservations accepted. 519 Hudson; (212) 633-1133.

Festivals in New York State

North of New York City, where the Berkshire Mountains meet the Hudson River Valley, **Winterhawk Bluegrass Festival** on the Rothvoss Farm offers four days of the nation's top bands in mid-July. The festival is advertised as a "100% Family Festival" with a children's tent, square-dancing, and teen programs, in addition to bluegrass band contests and workshops. In Ancramdale, near the Massachusetts/Connecticut/New York border on Rte. 22; (513) 390-6211.

The **Buckwheat Harvest Festival** takes place in Penn Yan, about 125 miles east of Buffalo in New York's Finger Lakes region. Held

MY HOMETOWN

Terry Radigan on Brooklyn, New York

"I'm from the Flatlands in Brooklyn, 36th Street and Avenue P. My grandparents emigrated there from Ireland. The neighborhood was lower-to middle-class, blue collar, Irish and Italian Catholic. There was so much happening. It made me real nosy. You get to watch stuff, which helped my songwriting.

"In New York there are a lot of singer/songwriters, which to me is country music. I played the **Bitter End, The Bottom Line,** and a lot of little bars. Greenwich Village has places where you see people with their guitars. The **Red Lion** next to the Bitter End has a wonderful mix of music."

GETTING THERE: The Bitter End is a 200-seat club in Greenwich Village. 147 Bleecker St.; (212) 673-7030. The Red Lion tavern is at 151 Bleecker St.; (212) 473-9560. The Bottom Line is downtown near New York University. 15 W. Fourth St.; (212) 777-2370.

the third weekend in September, the three-day festival features headline concerts by top country artists, buckwheat pancakes, continuous live entertainment, and parade. Penn Yan is on the north shore of Keuka Lake, south of Geneva. Take New York State Thruway (I-90)/Exit 42 to Rte. 14 south, to Rte. 24 south, to Rte. 54. Yates County Fairgrounds; (315) 536-7434.

North Carolina

Mount Airy
HOMETOWN OPRY IN "MAYBERRY"

For more than a decade, Frank Bode has hosted the popular *Hometown Opry* on the third Saturday night of every month in Mount Airy's 400-seat **Andy Griffith Playhouse.** The old-time country-music and bluegrass show begins at 7:30 P.M. and costs $5. Local and regional talent as well as occasional headline acts perform. Once a month, the Surry County Arts Council books professional bluegrass bands at the Playhouse or **Downtown Cinema Theatre.**

Andy Griffith grew up near Mount Airy, which inspired the television town of Mayberry. The local arts council offers $2 tours of the "Mayberry" City Jail, Wally's gas station, and Floyd's barbershop. In late September, the popular **Mayberry Days** take place, with a headline concert, parade, and Andy Griffith trivia and "look-alike" contests.

The two-day **Bluegrass and Old-Time Fiddlers' Convention,** an annual event since the early 1970s, is held in Mount Airy's Veterans Memorial Park the first weekend in June; (910) 786-6830.

GETTING THERE: Mount Airy is 40 miles north of Winston-Salem near the Virginia border on Hwy. 52. The Surry County Arts Council/Andy Griffith Playhouse is at 218 Rockford St.; (800) 286-6193 or (910) 786-7998.

Wilkesboro

MERLE WATSON MEMORIAL FESTIVAL

One of the largest country festivals anywhere, **MerleFest** celebrates legendary guitar picker Doc Watson's son Eddy Merle, who was named for Eddy Arnold and Merle Travis. Through the sixties, seventies, and eighties, Doc and Merle Watson were a popular duo, recording and performing folk, bluegrass, country, and traditional music. An excellent guitar player, Merle died in a tractor accident in 1985.

The four-day festival, held the last weekend in April at Wilkes Community College, features headline country and bluegrass acts, regional and local artists, music contests, crafts, storytelling, dance, and food. The Merle Watson Memorial Garden is open year-round.

GETTING THERE: Wilkesboro is about 50 miles west of Winston-Salem. Take I-77/Exit 73 to Hwy. 421 west; (800) 343-7857 or (910) 651-8600.

Asheville

MOUNTAIN MAGIC

Extraordinary mountain scenery, well-preserved art deco and early twentieth-century architecture, and a hip, lively arts community make Asheville an excellent base for exploring western North Carolina. The city is nestled in a high valley where the Blue Ridge and Great Smoky Mountains meet, and is surrounded by more than a million acres of national forest.

Asheville's attractions include crafts, clogging, mountain music, and numerous festivals, author Thomas Wolfe's boyhood home, and George Vanderbilt's extravagant 250-room **Biltmore House;** (800) 543-2961.

Every Saturday night in July and August, Asheville's City-County Plaza downtown comes alive with **Shindig-on-the-Green,** with free mountain music and square-dancing; (704) 258-6107.

Aficionados of clogging, square-dancing, and bluegrass won't want to miss the **Mountain Smoke House.** After feasting on barbecue, diners are treated to live music and dancing. Entertainment is Tuesday through Saturday, April through December. From I-240 bypass, take Charlotte St. exit south. Turn right on College, left on Oak Street, and right on Marjorie. 20 South Spruce St.; (704) 253-4871.

At Lake Junaluska, west of Asheville next to Great Smoky Mountain National Park, the **Smoky Mountain Folk Festival** is presented over Labor Day weekend; (704) 452-1688. Fifteen miles east of Asheville, **Camp Rockmont** at beautiful Black Mountain hosts mountain-music festivals Memorial Day weekend and in mid-October; (704) 669-6813.

GETTING THERE: Asheville is at the juncture of I-40, I-26, and the Blue Ridge Parkway. Contact the Asheville Travel and Tourism Office; (800) 257-1300 or (704) 258-6109.

Maggie Valley
CLOGGING CAPITAL OF THE WORLD

Maggie Valley is the epicenter of clogging culture in America. An old-fashioned resort town which locals call "Maggie," it's in a pretty little valley surrounded by mountains. Apple cider and fresh-boiled peanuts are sold from stands by the roadside.

Clogging is a fast and lively dance with deep roots in Appalachia, thrilling to watch. "It's a combination of the Irish jig and buck-dancing," explains Mary Sue Edwards, owner of the **Stompin' Ground** in Maggie. Teams of cloggers, clad in colorful costumes, move in ever-changing formations, a kaleidoscope of boxes, lines, and circles. The dancers' upper bodies remain steady while their feet tap out complicated rhythms.

Buck-dancing, which is even faster, used to be called "buck-and-wing dancing," with buck-dancing for gents and wing-dancing for gals; in Canada, it's called step-dancing. At bluegrass festivals, down-home buck-dancers and cloggers can be seen hoofing it on a piece of board by the side of the stage.

If Maggie is the "Clogging Capital of the World" (like the sign says), then Stompin' Ground is its state house. Inside a large barn, Stompin' Ground has continuous live music and dancing, interspersed with performances by some of the area's best clogging teams. (John and Audrey Wiggins, along with Clinton Gregory, were the house band here for most of the 1980s.) "The audience gets out there to line-dance, two-step, waltz, square-dance, free-style clog, or whatever," Edwards says.

Stompin' Ground hosts **America's Clogging Hall of Fame Clogging Competition** the third full weekend in October with teams from all over the country. Open nightly at 8 P.M. from May to October. 9 Soco Rd. (Hwy. 19); (704) 926-1288.

Maggie Valley Opry House is the home of Raymond Fairchild, a five-time World Banjo-Pickin' Champion. Performers on his show include the Maggie Valley Boys, the Crowe Brothers, and guests from the

The Stompin' Ground hosts performances from some of Appalachia's best cloggers.

Grand Ole Opry, doing bluegrass, mountain music, and clogging. Tickets $7. Nightly at 8 P.M., May through October, on Hwy. 19; (704) 648-7941 or 926-9336.

In addition to clogging, Maggie offers low-key attractions such as Ghost Town in the Sky (*see below*), a small zoo, crafts and antiques shops, festivals, and easy access to golf, fishing, skiing, horseback riding, and other outdoor activities.

GETTING THERE: Maggie Valley is 35 miles west of Asheville and 90 miles east of Knoxville. Take I-40/Exit 20 to Hwy. 276 south, to Hwy. 19 west. Maggie Valley Chamber of Commerce is on Hwy. 19; (800) MAGGIE-1 or (704) 926-5426.

THE SHOW MUST GO ON

Ghost Town in the Sky

To reach Ghost Town in the Sky, an Old West theme park, visitors must take a dramatic chairlift or incline railway up the steep side of a mountain. During the ascent, views of the Smokies and Maggie Valley become increasingly panoramic.

The park, located on the mountain top, looks fun. But before exploring, let's go straight to the **Country Music Hall.**

The scene: a plain, poorly lit room with plywood walls and folding metal chairs.

The stage: A strange setup with three unusual groupings of instruments.

The star: Eddie Nash, an ordinary fellow about fifty years old, in dull street clothes. He is barefoot.

Showtime: Nash sits down at a set of instruments with "ONE-MAN BAND" on the front spelled out with stick-on letters.

Face set in stony concentration, he breaks into a rousing rendition of "Crying My Heart Out Over You," an old country standard.

Arms and legs working together in perfect synchronization, Nash is playing
- rhythm guitar, with both hands;
- harmonica, when he's not singing;
- electric bass, with his right big toe;
- steel guitar, with his left heel;
- organ, with his left toes;
- keyboard, with his left knee;
- chimes and cymbal, with the end of his guitar neck;
- pre-programmed electronic drum machine, trombone, and trumpet.

During a 25-minute show, Nash plays dozens of instruments in various combinations. In addition to country songs, he performs "Dueling Banjos" (both parts), a frantic "Orange Blossom Special," and a vaudevillian version of "Sweet Georgia Brown" triple-time on a piano. Throughout, Nash does not crack a smile. The audience is warmly appreciative of his rare, off-beat musical gift.

Nash has been plying his unusual trade in relative obscurity atop this 4,600-foot mountain since the day Ghost Town in the Sky opened in 1961. Except for a few years off in the mideighties, he has been performing up to seven times a day, seven days a week, six months of every year. That's nearly 40,000 shows.

Why has he stuck with the Maggie Valley gig for so long?

"I enjoy it," explains Nash, a man of few words. "I can't travel with all the equipment," he continues. The other six months of the year, he is understandably "too tired to do anything else."

Back outside the Country Music Hall, Ghost Town is as doggedly resistant to change as Nash. Walking down its Main Street, there are models of a Western bank, jail, and hotel, with dressed-up dummies propped behind bars and counters. The rides include a roller coaster and "county fair"–type attractions: Tilt-a-whirl, Ferris wheel, shooting gallery, bumper cars, kiddy rides, a ghost mine, and carnival games.

There are live gunfights (Clinton Gregory once worked here as a stunt man), Indian dances, and cancan girls. Burgers, grilled cheese sandwiches, soft pretzels, ice cream, fudge, and beer are available.

Ghost Town is refreshingly ordinary, relying on its beautiful setting, old-fashioned amusements, and tried-and-true entertainers like Eddie Nash. It's charming, and yes, a lot of fun.

GETTING THERE: Ghost Town is open daily from early May to late October. Hours vary, but are generally 9:30 A.M. to 6 P.M. Admission $16.95 for ages 10 and over, $11.95 for ages 3 to 9. Allow at least a half day. Take I-40/Exit 20 to Hwy. 276 south to Hwy. 19 west; (800) 446-7886 or (704) 926-1140.

Cherokee Country

The **Cherokee Indian Reservation,** next to the Smokies at the southern end of the Blue Ridge Parkway, is a scenic base for a vacation in **Great Smoky Mountain National Park.** Compared to the bustling Tennessee gateway towns of Pigeon Forge and Gatlinburg, it's refreshingly rustic. It has easy access to the outdoors for hiking, horseback riding, white-water rafting, tubing, and fishing, while fine accommodations are available in dozens of motels, cabins, and campgrounds.

In addition, the 56,000-acre reservation known as "Qualla Boundary" provides the opportunity to explore the fascinating history of the Cherokees, with powwows, Native American arts and crafts, and educational attractions such as museums and an historical drama.

Country music is extremely popular among Native Americans, and the Cherokees are no exception. Live country music is performed nightly during the summer in the town of Cherokee on a tiny outdoor stage between a leather-crafts shop and Arrowhead Family Amusement Center on Hwy. 441. Look for the sign. Bands get started between 7 and 8 P.M.

Also in Cherokee, Rick Morris's **Smoky Mountain Jamboree,** billed as a "country music extravaganza," is a variety show featuring local entertainers. It's presented nightly, June through October, and on weekends in April, May, and November. Hwy. 441 at Acquoni Rd. in Great Smokies Center; (704) 497-5521.

The annual **Cherokee Bluegrass Festival** takes place in late August at Happy Holiday Campground with a full lineup of bluegrass legends and local artists. Four miles east of Cherokee on Hwy. 19; (800) 633-2977 or (704) 497-7250.

(*See also:* Tennessee—Sevierville, Pigeon Forge, and Gatlinburg.)

GETTING THERE: Cherokee is at Hwy. 441 and Hwy. 19/74. The Cherokee Visitors' Center is on Main Street in downtown Cherokee; (800) 438-1601 or (704) 497-9195.

Ohio

Cleveland

ROCK AND ROLL HALL OF FAME AND MUSEUM

Rock and roll has its roots in a high-energy fusion of rhythm and blues, country, honky-tonk, and rockabilly music. Early rock pioneers such as Elvis Presley, the Everly Brothers, Jerry Lee Lewis, Roy Orbison, Carl Perkins, and Johnny Cash grew up on country and bluegrass music, and all had hits on the country charts early and late in their careers. All of the above also happen to be members of the new Rock and Roll Hall of Fame in Cleveland, as are Jimmie Rodgers (the "Father of Country Music"), Hank Williams, Woody Guthrie, and Bob Dylan. (It should be noted that this Hall of Fame is inducting new members at a furious rate, about ten every year since 1986. By comparison, the Country Music Hall of Fame selects one, two, or occasionally three new members annually.)

The museum opened its doors in 1995, in a modern new structure designed by I. M. Pei. Exhibits focus on the origins of rock and roll, its heroes and legends, and the music's impact on society and culture. The galleries include multimedia exhibits on the early influences on rock, Sam Phillips's Sun Records, and "One-Hit Wonders." Many displays are interactive, including "The 500 Songs That Shaped Rock and Roll."

The site also features an archives, library, free films, a broadcast studio, and the two-floor Hall of Fame itself.

The Rock and Roll Hall of Fame is open daily, Memorial Day to Labor Day; closed Mondays the rest of the year. Hours are 10 A.M. to 5:30 P.M., with some seasonal changes and late hours. Closed Thanksgiving, Christmas, and New Year's Day. Admission $13 adults, $9.50 children. In downtown Cleveland, at Ohio St. and North Coast Harbor; (800) BUCKEYE or (216) 781-7625.

Attractions in Cleveland include an extensive parks system, art and history museums, and a zoo. The entertainment scene is lively, with everything from symphonies and opera to rock, jazz, country, and blues.

The annual three-day **Cleveland Country Music Festival** at Cuyahoga County Fairgrounds in Berea in mid-June includes headline acts, Western dancing, an old-time fiddlers' contest, demolition derby, and crafts. Take I-71/Bagley Rd. west to the fairgrounds; (216) 247-4FUN.

GETTING THERE: Cleveland is on Lake Erie in northeast Ohio. Take I-71, I-77, or I-90. For general information, contact the Visitors' Bureau; (800) 321-1004 or (216) 621-4110.

Bradford
WALLY'S SERVICE STATION

Bradford, Ohio, may not be Mayberry, but it's small-town America enough for Wally's Service Station, a full-scale re-creation of the filling station where Goober and Gomer worked on *The Andy Griffith Show.*

Bob Scheib, a dedicated member of the *Andy Griffith Show* Rerun Watchers Club, converted an old tobacco shed on his three-acre property in west-central Ohio into a real-life Wally's several years ago. The station has vintage gas pumps, soda cooler, and cigarette machine. An exact replica of Andy's squad car sits out front, and Floyd the Barber's chair is inside.

In mid-July, Scheib hosts the annual **Mayberry Squad Car Rendezvous.** Several thousand *Andy Griffith* fans and more than a dozen *Andy Griffith* squad cars converge for a day of hayrides, music, checkers, and displays of Mayberry memorabilia. Contests include Mayberry character look-alikes and sound-alikes, and theme-song whistling. Former stars of the show also attend.

(*See also:* North Carolina—Mount Airy.)

GETTING THERE: Wally's Service Station is about 30 miles north of Dayton. Take I-75/Exit 73 (Rte. 55) and follow the signs. (Between Bradford and Pleasant Hill off Hwy. 36.) Call in advance for an appointment. 10870 Circle Hill Rd.; (513) 473-5606.

Portsmouth
WHERE HAPPY TRAILS BEGIN

Roy Rogers, the beloved singing cowboy, grew up in Portsmouth, a small industrial city overlooking the Ohio River. Portsmouth is at the northern terminus of east Kentucky's Country Music Highway, about 25 miles northwest of Flatwoods (hometown of Billy Ray Cyrus). A small exhibit of Rogers memorabilia and other Western stars can be viewed at the Portsmouth post office, by appointment.

You can also drive by Rogers's boyhood home at **Duck Run** in Rush Township, 12 miles north of Portsmouth. Take Hwy. 23 north 10 miles to Lucasville. Turn left (west) on Rte. 348. Drive several miles until you see the Duck Run sign. Turn right on Duck Run, then make the first right onto Roy Rogers Road. The house is on the left, at the top of a hill. The Roy Rogers Society owns a triangle of land here for tourists to stop and take pictures. A marker is on the spot. (The house is privately owned and occupied.)

At least one member of the Rogers family attends Portsmouth's annual three-day **Roy Rogers Festival** the first weekend in June. For collectors of Rogers memorabilia, this is the main event. Western movie actors and actresses attend, and there's a banquet on Saturday night with musical entertainment.

(*See also:* California—Los Angeles area; East Kentucky—The Country Music Highway.)

GETTING THERE: Portsmouth is 120 miles east of Cincinnati. From I-64, take Hwy. 23 north. Contact the Portsmouth Visitors' Bureau; (614) 353-7647.

For appointments to see the Roy Rogers exhibit or festival information, call the Roy Rogers Society; (614) 353-0900.

Oklahoma

Northeast Oklahoma

Grand Lake o' the Cherokees

Plenty of country music is happening around Grand Lake o' the Cherokees in the northeast corner of Oklahoma.

The town of Langley (pop. 400), on the lake's southwest shore, is the official "Bluegrass Capital of Oklahoma" and self-proclaimed "Fiddling Capital of the World." Several festivals take place annually at Powderhorn Park, including the four-day **World Series of Fiddling Contest** Labor Day weekend. The **National Fiddlers' Memorial** is located in the park. Langley is between Hwys. 58 and 69, on Rte. 82/28. Powderhorn Park is at 4th St. and John Dahl Ave.; (918) 782-9850.

Two Oprys are offered in Grove, on the lake's eastern shore, as well as a huge free historic park called Harbor Village. *Kountry Kuzins Jamboree* features a twelve-member cast performing comedy and "some old country and some new." The show is presented weekend evenings late March through October and scattered matinees and evenings in November and December. Tickets $10. 3659 N. Hwy. 59; (800) 292-1974 or (918) 786-9458.

The *Grand Lake Opry* is a professional variety show in a new 1,000-seat theater at the lakeside. Shows feature a house band and special guests Friday and Saturday nights, April through December. The complex includes a restaurant and lake cruises. Tickets $10. Take Hwy. 59 to the foot of Sailboat Bridge; (918) 786-5754.

Dewey

TOM MIX, KING OF THE COWBOYS

Tom Mix, the first King of the Cowboys, appeared in 300 films over thirty years between the turn of the century and the 1930s. Galloping on Tony the Wonder Horse, Mix rescued damsels, snagged villains with his lasso, and performed feats of bravery. He made quite a splash in Hollywood, too, wearing flashy clothes, driving custom cars, and throwing huge parties.

The **Tom Mix Museum and Western Theater,** operated by the Oklahoma Historical Society, is in Dewey, where Mix served as deputy town marshal in 1912. Mix's third wife, Olive, was a native of Dewey and the couple had a ranch west of the town. (Mix was born in Pennsylvania.) The museum features artifacts, memorabilia, photographs, and silent movies.

(A statue marks the spot where Mix crashed his yellow Cord convertible and died on October 12, 1940, on Hwy. 79 between Phoenix and Tucson, Arizona. Contact the Pinal County Visitors' Center; (602) 868-4331.)

GETTING THERE: Dewey is 30 miles north of Tulsa on Hwy. 75. Open Tuesday through Friday, 10 A.M. to 4:30 P.M., and Saturday and Sunday 1 to 4:30 P.M. Free. Allow an hour. 721 N. Delaware; (918) 534-1555.

Claremore

WILL ROGERS MEMORIAL AND MUSEUM

More than sixty years after Will Rogers's death in a plane crash, Americans are still captivated by the humorous "poet lariat." In the 1990s, the Broadway musical *The Will Rogers Follies,* at various times starring Keith Carradine, Larry Gatlin, and Pat Boone, brought Rogers's wit and wisdom to new generations. Rogers, a native Oklahoman and part Cherokee, entertained with terrific style, passion, and charisma.

Rogers was a real cowboy, expert with a rope. He wowed the vaudeville circuit, broadcast commentary over the radio, and starred in more than seventy motion pictures. His weekly syndicated column appeared in six hundred newspapers. In his spare time, Rogers was a model husband and father, traveled all over the world, and devoted enormous energy to charitable causes. (For example, Rogers did a series of benefits with yodeler Jimmie Rodgers in the early 1930s for Dust Bowl victims.)

"People are looking for a role model," says Gregory Malak, manager of the excellent **Will Rogers Memorial and Museum** in Claremore. "Honesty, integrity, hard work—he personified those. We open our files to researchers here, and there are no skeletons in Rogers's closet. He's a true honest man."

Rogers died in a plane crash at Point Barrow, Alaska, in 1935. (There are markers in downtown Barrow and at the crash site 16 miles away. Contact the city of Barrow; (907) 852-5211.) He is buried in a tomb overlooking Claremore on property purchased for his retirement. "I never met a man I didn't like"—his most famous quote—is engraved on the stone.

The spacious, seven-gallery museum tells Rogers's multifaceted story with dioramas of his life, art, memorabilia, personal artifacts, original manuscripts, and interactive exhibits. Visitors read Rogers's witticisms, hear his radio shows, and watch movies in comfortable screening rooms. There's even a hands-on children's museum. Rogers's kindly face peers out from everywhere.

The **Oologah Historical Museum** in the restored downtown displays some additional Rogers memorabilia; (918) 443-2790.

Dog Iron Ranch, where Rogers grew up, is 12 miles away in Oologah. The ranch is a living history museum with longhorn cattle and the Rogers family's log house, overlooking Oologah Lake. Free. Rte. 88 north; (918) 275-4201.

Claremore's **Will Rogers Days** are held the second weekend in June and the first weekend in November, with music, arts and crafts, parades, rodeo, and other events; (918) 341-2818.

(*See also:* California—Los Angeles area.)

GETTING THERE: Claremore is 30 miles northeast of Tulsa. The museum and ranch are free. Allow two hours for the museum, and an hour for the ranch. Open daily 8 A.M. to 5 P.M. Take I-44 (Will Rogers Parkway)/Exit 254 to Rte. 20 west. 1720 W. Will Rogers Blvd.; (800) 828-9643 or (918) 341-0719.

Tulsa
BOB WILLS'S CAINS BALLROOM

Across the railroad tracks from downtown Tulsa, the legendary **Cains Ballroom** sits proudly on a desolate, boarded-up stretch of North Main Street. During the thirties and forties, Cains hopped with the Western Swing of Bob Wills and his Texas Playboys. The old-time dance hall still looks the same inside and out, and a variety of shows are presented year-round except during the summer. (Cains Ballroom is not air-conditioned.) Down the street on "Bob Wills Main Street" are several "hip" art galleries and restaurants. 423 N. Main St.; (918) 584-2309.

Tulsa is a growing cosmopolitan city, with world-renowned art-deco architecture, fine art museums, dozens of parks, and a zoo. More than a thousand oil-related companies are based in and around the city.

Rodgers and Hammerstein's famous Broadway show *Oklahoma!* is performed nightly (except Sundays) during the summer at Discoveryland's outdoor amphitheater, preceded by a Western barbecue. W. 41st St. and Rte. 97; (918) 742-5255.

The annual three-day **Bluegrass and Chili Festival** takes place the weekend after Labor Day at Tulsa's downtown Williams Center Green; (918) 583-2617.

GETTING THERE: Tulsa is in northeast Oklahoma at Muskogee and Turner Turnpikes and Hwys. 75 and 412. Contact Tulsa Visitors' Bureau; (918) 585-1201.

Cains Ballroom is a landmark in downtown Tulsa.

Central Oklahoma

Oklahoma City
COWBOY CITY

Oklahoma City, the state capital, is a sprawling metropolis with modern attractions such as theme parks, a zoo, and art, science, and history museums. Cowboys and country music, however, really take center stage. A sign at the airport welcomes visitors to the hometown of Vince Gill. A world-class cowboy museum revels in all things Western, while across town real ranchers move cattle through the world's largest stockyards.

The **Oklahoma Opry** has been dedicated to nurturing young country-music talent since the late 1970s. Founder Grant Leftwich regularly auditions aspiring artists, and presents the cream of the crop on Saturday nights, accompanied by the ten-piece house band. "We put on a professional show," Leftwich says. "We could sell out every week if we used big names, but what I've undertaken is a showcase for new stars." One *Oklahoma Opry* graduate is rising star Bryan White. "He's just a super nice kid. He has that charisma," Leftwich says. Open year-round in the Capitol Hill neighborhood. Admission $7. 404 W. Commerce; (405) 632-8322.

The **National Cowboy Hall of Fame and Western Heritage Center** is much more than a place that honors cowboys. The top-notch museum, opened by a consortium of seventeen Western states in 1958, is dedicated to preserving the arts and cultural heritage of the Old West. A $36 million expansion will triple its size by 1996. An extensive collection of Western art is displayed, including works by Frederic Remington and Charles M. Russell, and the original plaster sculpture for James Earl Fraser's famous *End of the Trail* statue.

The Rodeo Hall of Fame pays tribute to more than 200 of the sport's greatest athletes, while the Hall of Great Westerners immortalizes hundreds of explorers, ranchers, writers, and politicians. The Hall of Western Performers displays portraits and memorabilia from dozens of popular entertainers including Tom Mix, Reba McEntire, Rex Allen, Roy Rogers and Dale Evans, and Sons of the Pioneers. The John

Wayne Gallery houses the movie star's personal collection of Asian, Western, and Native American art, with a screening room showing an entertaining montage of film clips.

Special events at the Cowboy Hall of Fame include the **Cowboy Poetry Gathering** in mid-April, **Cowboy Chuckwagon Gathering** the last weekend in May, and the **National Children's Cowboy Festival** in mid-October. Open 9 A.M. to 5 P.M., Labor Day through Memorial Day; 8:30 A.M. to 6 P.M. the rest of the year. Closed Thanksgiving, Christmas, and New Year's Day. Allow three hours. Admission $6.50 adults, $3.25 ages 6 to 12. Take I-44 to the Martin Luther King Drive exit, and follow the signs; 1700 N.E. 63rd St.; (405) 478-2250.

For real cowboys in action, visit the **Oklahoma National Stockyards.** Founded in 1910, this is one of the largest cattle and livestock markets in the world, moving more than a million head a year. Auctions are held Mondays and Tuesdays beginning at 8 A.M. Tours are also available; call for times. 2500 Exchange Ave.; (405) 235-8675.

Just outside the market gates, **Stockyards City** is headquarters of the International Professional Rodeo Association. Numerous restaurants and businesses including saddleries, tack shops, bootmakers, and clothing stores, are patronized by modern cowboys and tourists alike. The area used to be pretty rough-and-tumble; however, only one bar remains from those days, and redevelopment efforts are transforming the historic district into a popular tourist destination. Take I-40 or I-44 to Stockyards City. S.W. 15th St. and Agnew; (405) 235-7267.

Cattlemen's Steakhouse has been serving juicy slabs of beef in Stockyards City since 1910. According to legend, George Wade rolled a "hard six" (33) in a craps game and won the entire restaurant from Hank Fry in 1945. 1309 S. Agnew; (405) 236-0416.

GETTING THERE: Oklahoma City is in the center of Oklahoma at I-35, I-40, and I-44. The Visitors' Center is downtown at 123 Park Ave.; (800) 225-5652 or (405) 297-8912.

MY HOMETOWN

Bryan White on the Oklahoma Opry

(Peter Nash)

"The *Oklahoma Opry* is a great music place for young people to get started. I started there when I was sixteen years old. My dad let me sing every weekend. It's also a better place for kids to go and hear music. Grant [Leftwich] was always helpful. I can remember a few times that he let me borrow his guitar. He was like a grandfather." (*See page 170.*)

Del City

OKLAHOMA COUNTRY-WESTERN HALL OF FAME
AND MUSEUM

The Oklahoma Country-Western Hall of Fame and Museum opened its doors in 1995 in Del City, a suburb southeast of Oklahoma City. "Look where all your country music singers are from," says Del City mayor John Stamps, rattling off a list that includes Vince Gill, Reba McEntire, and Garth Brooks. "We've got museums for everything in the world, why not country music?"

In 1994, the Hall of Fame inducted Vince Gill, Bob Wills, and Bob Wood, a performer and local music-store owner. The museum, which consists mainly of memorabilia, is a nonprofit project of Del City Lions Club and the Chamber of Commerce. Located in the converted Lions Club hall, the museum has a performance hall in back that seats up to 450 people. The **Oklahoma Country Music Association** sponsors shows on the first Sunday afternoon of every month, **jam sessions** every Thursday night, an annual awards ceremony, and special events.

Bob Wood's Del City Music Store and recording studio are a few blocks away. The sidewalk in front has cement handprints of McEntire, Gill, Conway Twitty, Shoji Tabuchi, John Anderson, and others. 2908 Epperly (off S.E. 29th); (405) 677-8777.

GETTING THERE: Del City is just outside Oklahoma City limits. Call for museum hours and schedules. Take I-40 east to Sunny Lane exit. Turn right on Sunny, and right on S.E. 29th. 3925 S.E. 29th St.; (405) 677-3174.

Yukon

HOMETOWN OF GARTH BROOKS

In addition to being a Route 66 town, the "Czech Capital of Oklahoma," and a stop on the famed Chisholm Trail, Yukon is hometown of country music mega-superstar Garth Brooks. "Home of Garth Brooks" is painted on the Yukon water tower, along with the city's state champion high-school teams. The tower is visible from I-40 at

West Vandament, but there's no easy access for viewing or photography. Garth Brooks Boulevard also runs through town.

The **Chisholm Trail Festival,** the first weekend in June, is known for its nineteenth-century living history cowboy encampments. The popular festival features cowboy singing and poetry, Western art, and collectibles.

GETTING THERE: Yukon is a western suburb of Oklahoma City. Take I-40/Exit 136 north to Hwy. 92. For city and festival information, call (405) 354-3567.

Southern Oklahoma

Hugo
BLUEGRASS IN CIRCUS CITY

The oldest bluegrass festival west of the Mississippi River is **Grant's Blue Grass Music Festival** in Hugo. Bill Grant first staged the five-day extravaganza in 1969. In fact, Grant says his festival is one of the three oldest continuously running bluegrass festivals in America.

Grant's festival brings together top national, regional, and local musicians for more than seventy hours of entertainment. "We've had all the greats in bluegrass music come across our stage," says Grant, a mandolin player and half of a bluegrass duo with Delia Bell. It always takes place the first weekend in August, with a two-day "Early Bird" event in late March. Grant has RV hookups, camping, and modern facilities. From Hugo, take Bus. Hwy. 70 east 1 mile to Bill Grant Rd. Go north for 1½ miles to Salt Creek Park; (405) 326-5598.

The Carson & Barnes and Kelly-Miller Brothers circuses are based in Hugo, giving the town its nickname, "Circus City, U.S.A." Circus performers are buried under unusual headstones at **Mt. Olivet Cemetery** in the Showman's Rest section, reserved for "all the showmen under God's big top."

GETTING THERE: Hugo is in southeastern Oklahoma near the Texas border. Take Indian Nation Parkway to Hwy. 70 east. For area information, call (405) 326-7511.

Gene Autry
BACK IN THE SADDLE AGAIN

When Gene Autry bought the Flying A Ranch near Berwyn, the 200 Berwyn residents were so excited that they officially renamed the town "Gene Autry" in 1941. The ceremony, attended by the cowboy movie star himself, attracted tens of thousands of people.

Unfortunately, World War II intervened and Gene Autry abandoned the Flying A several years later, never to return. "We invite him every year," longtime resident Elvin Sweeten explains. Nonetheless, the name stuck.

The 1990s found the population of Gene Autry down to fewer than 100 people. After the local school closed, the building was vandalized. "We didn't want it to be an eyesore," Sweeten says. "We got together to save the community. I said, 'I'll put a museum in there.' "

Sweeten began collecting memorabilia from Gene Autry and all of Hollywood's singing cowboys, including Ken Maynard, Tom Mix, Roy Rogers, Rex Allen, and Tex Ritter. Hundreds of items are now beautifully displayed in the **Gene Autry Oklahoma Museum of Local History**: movie posters, photographs, album covers, hats, guitars, books, and toy guns and holsters. The Local History room tells the town's colorful history, while the old gym in the center of the building serves as a screening room.

Legend has it that late one night in Chelsea, Oklahoma, cowboy humorist Will Rogers walked into the Frisco Railroad office where a teenaged Autry was working as a telegrapher and strumming on his guitar. Rogers asked Autry for a few songs. "You've got something, boy," he said. "Work hard, and you may go somewhere." Encouraged, young Autry soon landed a spot on Tulsa's KVOO radio as "Oklahoma's Yodeling Cowboy."

Autry went on to star in nearly one hundred B Westerns between 1935 and 1953; his popular recordings include "Back in the Saddle Again" and "Rudolph the Red-Nosed Reindeer." He was inducted into the Country Music Hall of Fame in 1969. An astute businessman, Autry made a fortune in real estate and co-owns the California Angels baseball team. He recently built a beautiful Western museum in Los Angeles' Griffith Park.

While many Gene Autry residents still idolize the singing cowboy, others have hard feelings towards him for not visiting in more than fifty years, Sweeten says. Nonetheless, the museum is a great source of pride for the community and is becoming a magnet for singing-cowboy fans from all over the world.

The annual **Gene Autry Film and Music Festival** the last weekend in September features live music, appearances by Western stars, and Gene Autry film screenings. Sweeten hopes the money raised will help pay for air-conditioning and a new roof for the museum.

The **Flying A Ranch** is still intact in private hands, and can be seen from Rte. 53, 2 miles west of Gene Autry. Look for two long stone barns.

Autry was born in Tioga, Texas, a hamlet about 65 miles south of Gene Autry on Hwy. 377. His kin are buried in the local cemetery.

(*See also:* California—Los Angeles.)

GETTING THERE: Gene Autry is in South-central Oklahoma, north of Ardmore. Museum hours vary; call ahead. Free, with donations requested. Allow an hour. Take I-35/Exit 40 to Rte. 53 east. At the airport, turn right on Gene Autry Rd. Go through town and follow the signs; (405) 389-5335 or 294-3155.

Pennsylvania

West Grove
SUNSET PARK

Founded by "Uncle Roy" Waltman in 1941, Sunset Park in West Grove is one of the best-loved and most successful country music parks in the nation. Sunset Park is nestled in the woods of Pennsylvania Dutch country not far from the Maryland-Delaware border.

Concerts take place on Sunday afternoons, and feature a headline country or bluegrass artist and a local band. (Marty Stuart, Bill Monroe, and Waylon Jennings have been regular visitors over the years.) The Waltman family also offers home-cooked meals all day, and crafts vendors. The season runs from May through September.

GETTING THERE: West Grove is about 30 miles southwest of Philadelphia. Call for schedule. Take I-476 to Hwy. 1 west. 102 S. Jennersville Rd. (Rte. 841); (610) 869-3513.

Pennsylvania Festivals

The **Wind Gap Bluegrass Festival** takes place the second full weekend in June, with four days of top bluegrass stars and regional bands, workshops, and camping at Mountain View Park. Guests also can take a free tour of the Martin guitar factory nearby. Owned by the Appalachian Fiddle and Bluegrass Association, the park is in Wind Gap, about 20 miles north of Allentown and the Delaware River–New Jersey border. From Allentown, take Hwy. 22 to Rte. 512 north; (215) 584-2324.

Granite Hill Campground west of Gettysburg hosts its four-day **Bluegrass Camporees** in early May and the end of August. The nation's top bluegrass stars perform, and there are workshops, band contests, crafts, food, and jam sessions. Gettysburg is 80 miles north of Washington, D.C., and 120 miles west of Philadelphia. Take I-83 to Hwy. 30 west, to Rte. 116 west; (800) 642-TENT or (717) 642-8749.

Rhode Island

The two-day Ben & Jerry's **Newport Folk Festival** in early August is one of the nation's oldest folk-music events. Eight major folk and country artists are presented from 11 A.M. until dusk, by the water at Fort Adams State Park. Ten thousand tickets are sold, and sellouts are common. Newport also hosts popular jazz and music festivals every summer; (401) 847-3700 (phone line opens in June).

Newport, a small seaside city settled in 1639, is best known for a row of magnificent estates built by wealthy industrialists during the nineteenth century. A three-mile "cliff walk" on the edge of Rhode Island Sound provides magnificent views, and many of the mansions are open for tours.

GETTING THERE: Newport is 30 miles south of Providence. Take I-195/Exit 8A to Hwy. 24 south. Contact Newport County Visitors' Bureau; (800) 326-6030 or (401) 849-8098.

South Carolina

Myrtle Beach
BRANSON EAST

First there were the beaches: miles and miles and miles of clean white sand and sparkling blue water on the South Carolina coastline.

Then there was "the Shag." During the forties and fifties, droves of South Carolina teenagers rushed to Myrtle Beach as soon as school let out to soak up the sun by day and dance the Shag, a combination of the lindy hop and jitterbug, by night.

Next came the golf courses. By the year 2000, there will be 100 public golf courses here, making Myrtle Beach heaven on earth for hackers and an attractive vacation and retirement destination.

Fast forward to 1984. Calvin Gilmore, a real-estate developer/musician from the Missouri Ozarks (remember Branson?), took a vacation at Myrtle Beach and noticed a dearth of evening entertainment. Within two years, Gilmore opened the *Carolina Opry,* a country music variety show in the Branson tradition.

Today, Myrtle Beach, which attracts some 12 million visitors a year, is the East Coast's burgeoning country music mecca. By 1995, there were a half-dozen theaters here, bearing the names of the Gatlin Brothers, Ronnie Milsap, and Alabama, with plans for at least a dozen more.

Myrtle Beach encompasses several towns along 60 miles of beach, from North Myrtle Beach to Pawley's Island. The main north-south thoroughfare is Hwy. 17, between the Atlantic Ocean and the Intracoastal Waterway.

A full-service, year-round resort area, "The Grand Strand" serves up amusement parks and water parks, miniature golf, video arcades, souvenir shops, more than 1,200 restaurants and all-you-can-eat buffets, high-rise hotels, and cheap motels. **Brookgreen Gardens** in Murrells Inlet has the world's largest collection of outdoor statues with 400 pieces in lovely, well-kept gardens. Open 9:30 A.M. to 5:30 P.M. daily. 1931 Brookgreen Dr.; (803) 237-4218.

The Myrtle Beach show season is year-round, with fewer performances in the winter. Tickets $20 to $25. Call ahead for schedules.

Gilmore's dynasty now includes two theaters, and he is currently expanding his enterprises south to Charleston. *Carolina Opry* in Myrtle Beach, presented in a 2,200-seat state-of-the-art venue, is a fast-paced variety show of country, pop, rock and roll, gospel, and comedy, at 8901 Hwy. 17 N. *Legends in Concert* features impersonations of the biggest stars in pop and country music, in Surfside Beach at 301 Hwy. 17 S. For tickets or information about these shows, call (800) THE-OPRY or (803) 238-8888.

Fantasy Harbour is a 400-acre $250 million entertainment and shopping complex in Myrtle Beach, which will eventually offer 11 theaters, 12 theme restaurants and dinner theaters, four hotels, a 1,500-seat amphitheater, and an aquarium. It is already home to Myrtle Beach's number-one tourist attraction: Waccamaw, a huge outlet shopping center with 125 stores that draws 6.5 million shoppers annually.

The Gatlin Brothers—Larry, Rudy, and Steve—perform 250 times a year at the $7.5 million **Gatlin Brothers Theatre** in Fantasy Harbour. The Gatlins' show includes their hit songs, as well as gospel, contemporary, and rock and roll. When the Gatlins are not performing, their celebrity series presents popular artists such as Roy Clark and Mel Tillis for two-week runs. The **Ronnie Milsap Theatre** opened nearby in 1995. Milsap, pianist, songwriter, and singer with more than forty number-one hits, performs six months of the year with guest artists rounding out the schedule. In 1996, additional shows at Fantasy Harbour included *Magic on Ice* and *Medieval Times Dinner and Tournament.* Fantasy Harbour is in the town of Myrtle Beach, west of the Intracoastal on Hwy. 501. For tickets or information about any of the above shows, call (800) 681-5209 or (803) 236-8500.

The supergroup Alabama got its start at The Bowery, a Myrtle Beach nightclub. For nearly a decade, they played six nights a week, six hours at a time, for tips. Now the boys have their own showplace, **The Alabama Theater,** in North Myrtle Beach at Barefoot Landing. Alabama performs sporadically at the 2,000-seat venue. The *American Pride Show,* produced by Opryland U.S.A., is presented six nights a week with traditional and contemporary country, movie hits, nostalgia, comedy, and an Elvis Presley tribute. The seventh night is filled by a celebrity performance. 4750 Hwy. 17 S.; (800) 342-2262 or (803) 272-1111.

Dolly Parton's $7.5 million **Dixie Stampede** dinner attraction in Myrtle Beach duplicates her successful ventures in Pigeon Forge, Tennessee, and Branson, Missouri. The 1800s theme show, performed in an arena, features a slick show with trick-riding, Southern belles in costume, chuckwagon races, and four-course meals eaten by hand. Hwy. 17 and 17 Bypass; (800) 433-4401 or (803) 497-9700.

Another mega-development, called Broadway at the Beach, is going up on 350 acres in Myrtle Beach. The entertainment complex will include the $12 million **Carolina Palace Theatre,** 75 stores, a hotel, aquarium, 25,000-seat amphitheater, and ten restaurants. Mickey Gilley's **Texas Cafe and Cantina** opened here in 1995, with barbecue and Mexican specialties. Hwy. 17 Bypass and 21st Ave. N. (800) FUN-IN-MB or (803) 444-3200.

Myrtle Beach offers a full calendar of special events including the three-day **South Carolina State Bluegrass Festival.** In its third decade, the festival takes place over Thanksgiving weekend.

GETTING THERE: Myrtle Beach is 95 miles north of Charleston. Take I-95 to Hwy. 501 east. Contact the Myrtle Beach Area Chamber of Commerce; (800) 356-3016 or (803) 626-7444.

West Columbia
BILL'S MUSIC SHOP AND PICKIN' PARLOR

After fifteen years on the road with his band, Blue Ridge Mountain Grass, Bill Wells decided to settle down in West Columbia. During the week, **Bill's Music Shop** sells acoustic instruments, song books, and music lessons. On Friday and Saturday nights around 7:30 P.M., the adjoining

Bill Wells hosts bluegrass jam sessions at his Pickin' Parlor. (S. Louise Wells)

250-seat **Pickin' Parlor** starts jumping with lively bluegrass jam sessions. Carolina musicians like Snuffy Jenkins, "Pappy" Sherrill, David Prosser, and Rita Whitson often show up. All are welcome to enjoy the music or join in.

From September to April—the bluegrass festival off-season—Wells also books headline country or bluegrass shows on the second and fourth Saturdays of the month.

GETTING THERE: West Columbia is a suburb of Columbia, a city in the center of South Carolina. Take I-26 to Hwy. 1 east. 710 Meeting St.; (803) 796-6477.

South Dakota

Rapid City Area
COWBOY MUSIC AND CHUCKWAGONS
IN THE BLACK HILLS

The Black Hills region of southwestern South Dakota draws millions of tourists every year for wonderful scenery and wilderness exploration, as well as Old West towns, Mount Rushmore National Monument, and the evolving Crazy Horse Memorial. Badlands National Park and the Black Hills encompass 4,300 square miles of 7,000-foot peaks, forests, canyons, lakes, and streams. Attractions include cave and mine tours, geological and dinosaur sites, tourist museums, amusement parks, and live country-and-western entertainment.

You can't miss **Wall Drug,** with signs posted hundreds and thousands of miles away all over the West. The huge drug store and tourist attraction offers a life-size mechanical cowboy band and chuckwagon quartet, dining rooms serving buffalo burgers and 5¢ coffee, fourteen shops, and Western art galleries. Open year-round. Take I-90/Exit 109 or 110 to Wall; (605) 279-2175.

The **High Plains Heritage Center and Museum** in Spearfish is home of the **National Cowboy Song and Poetry Hall of Fame,** a small exhibit with plaques, pictures, and memorabilia from Patsy Montana, Badger Clark, Jim Bob Tinsley, Roy Rogers and Dale Evans, Red Steagall, and other famous cowboy entertainers. This five-state regional museum offers a fine collection of Western art and sculpture, and outdoor displays of live longhorn steers, a sod dugout, and frontier village. Live cowboy music and poetry are presented on Wednesday nights, Memorial Day through Labor Day. Open daily 9 A.M. to 5 P.M. Take I-90/Exit 14 south. 825 Heritage Drive; (605) 642-WEST.

Larry King's Gold Rush Dinner Show is offered year-round, with a prime-rib dinner followed by a live variety show featuring country classics, in a comfortable new theater south of Rapid City at the Rushmore Inn Resort. Tickets $19.95 (with meal). Take I-90/Exit 57 to Hwy. 16. 5410 Mt. Rushmore Rd.; (800) 654-KING or (605) 343-9186.

At The Fort, three miles north of Custer, the **Dakota Country Family Music Show** features fiddling, harmony, yodeling, and comedy. Shows are nightly, Memorial Day through September. The complex includes three buffet dinners daily, a petting zoo, local crafts, helicopter and trail rides, and live bears. Tickets (show only) $6.50. Take I-90/Exit 57 to Hwy 16-385; (800) 348-FORT (seasonal) or (605) 673-2046.

Entering its third decade, the Dennis family's **Mountain Music Show** presents "hillbilly music and country hokum" nightly at the Flintstones Theme Park, west of Custer. Shows are nightly, Memorial Day through Labor Day. Tickets $6. Take I-90/Exit 57 to Hwy. 16; (605) 673-2405.

Several ranch outfits offer nightly **chuckwagon suppers** accompanied by live Western entertainment. The season is generally mid-May through September, and tickets cost $11 to $13 (including meal and show). Call for reservations. The *Dances with Wolves* film set at **Fort Hayes** offers 99¢ pancake breakfasts every morning and chuckwagon suppers with a Western show every night. The set can be toured for free, 7 A.M. to 9 P.M. Take I-90/Exit 57 to Hwy. 16; (605) 394-9653.

Since 1979, the **Flying T Ranch** has served barbecue beef on tin plates followed by a cowboy show. Take I-90/Exit 57 to Hwy. 16; (605) 342-1905.

In addition to wagon and trail rides, and shoot-outs in a Western town, **Circle B Ranch** offers chuckwagon suppers and a stage show with the Circle B Cowboys. Take 1-90/Exit 57 to Rte. 44 west, to 22735 Hwy. 385 north; (800) 403-7358 or (605) 348-7358.

Numerous festivals and events take place in the Black Hills. The Rapid City Arts Council's **Black Hills Bluegrass Festival** takes place the last full weekend in June with three days of live regional bands, clogging, a Sunday gospel show, and bluegrass picnic. In recent years, the Mystery Mountain resort has hosted the event; camping, swimming, and the odd Mystery Cabin are on-site. Take I-90/Exit 57 to Hwy. 16; (800) 658-2267 or (605) 342-5368.

Michael Martin Murphey usually brings his three-day **WestFest** extravaganza to Deadwood, a town northwest of Rapid City, in mid-June. The festival, modeled after Buffalo Bill's Wild West shows, celebrates the art, music, and culture of the Old and New West with headline concerts, Indian and mountain-man villages, and rodeos. Murphey, a popular cowboy singer, says Deadwood is a true Wild West town where "ghosts of the past walk the streets daily." Take I-90/Exit 17 to Hwy. 85 south; (800) 999-1876 or (605) 578-1876. (*See also:* Colorado—Copper Mountain.)

GETTING THERE: The Black Hills–Rapid City area is in southwestern South Dakota. Take I-90. Contact the Black Hills, Badlands, and Lakes Association; (605) 341-1462.

Tennessee

East Tennessee

The northeast corner of Tennessee is called the **Tri-Cities area** for its three main cities of Johnson City, Kingsport, and Bristol. It covers some awe-inspiring Appalachian territory, with mountains, forests, clear rivers, and lakes. This is where the short-lived state of Franklin took a doomed stand and lost, leading to the establishment of Tennessee. Daniel Boone, Davy Crockett, and Andrew Johnson lived and roamed this wilderness.

The Tri-Cities are fertile territory for country music fans. Bristol, straddling the Tennessee-Virginia border, is known as the birthplace of country music. During July and August 1927, Jimmie Rodgers and the Carter Family were first recorded here, providing millions of people with access to their exciting brand of traditional folk music.

At the Carter Family Fold, just across the border from Kingsport in Hiltons, Virginia, joyous dances are held on Saturday nights. Visiting with the Carters is like stepping back in time, to an era when it was unheard of to mix musical instruments and electricity.

(*See also:* Virginia—Hiltons.)

GETTING THERE: The main thoroughfares through northeast Tennessee are I-81 east-west, and I-181 north-south. Contact Northeast Tennessee Tourism Association; (800) 468-6882, ext. 15 or (423) 753-4188.

Bristol
THE BIRTHPLACE OF COUNTRY MUSIC

In July and August 1927, a scout for the Victor Talking Machine Company of New York City traveled to Bristol to look for "hillbilly musicians." Using new portable recording technology, Ralph Peer made the first recordings of Jimmie Rodgers, the Carter Family, and the Stonemans.

Often hailed as "the Big Bang" of country music, the Bristol Sessions brought Appalachian mountain music to a wide audience, ushering in country music's modern era. Peer, Rodgers, and the Carters have been inducted into the Country Music Hall of Fame; straight lines can be drawn from these seminal artists to all the country music that came after.

People in the area have been working to raise awareness about the Bristol region's crucial role in country music history, and to promote authentic mountain music. "It's a matter of pride," says Fred McClellen of the Birthplace of Country Music Alliance (BCMA). "I've had a serious problem with the identity the mountain people have been given."

Bristol straddles the Tennessee-Virginia border; the state line runs right through the middle of State Street downtown. A railroad center and the largest city in the area in the 1920s, Bristol was a natural destination for Peer to find potentially commercial mountain music.

McClellen explains that the original English, Scottish, and Irish immigrants who came to Appalachia brought little with them except "their instruments and their ballads. Life was limited outside the family for many generations. MTV was not a distraction. If you wanted to have entertainment, you created music."

Mountain music is still very much a living form here, almost taken for granted. "Every family has some member who plays," McClellen says.

The city's prominent role in country music history doesn't end with the Bristol Sessions, though. Tennessee Ernie Ford was born in Bristol and started out as an announcer for local radio station WOPI. He went on to carry "hillbilly music" into the American mainstream, performing around the world and for seven presidents.

Additionally, radio station WCYB was the king of bluegrass radio stations in the late forties and early fifties. The show *Farm and Fun Time* helped launch legendary bluegrass artists Lester Flatt and Earl Scruggs, Ralph and Carter Stanley, Jim and Jesse McReynolds, Mac Wiseman, Jimmy Martin, and the Osborne Brothers.

A **marker** at 408-410 State Street, on the Tennessee side, commemorates the spot where Peer set up his ad hoc recording studio. The original building was torn down in the 1960s. The simple stone marker now sits in a parking lot at the corner of State Street and Edgemont Avenue, catty-corner from the old railroad station. It honors A.P., Sara and Maybelle Carter, and Jimmie Rodgers, "who recorded the first country-and-western music to be distributed in Bristol, Tennessee." In 1997, BCMA plans to host a big party celebrating the seventieth anniversary of the Bristol Sessions.

Down the street at 824 State Street, a three-story **mural** honors the birthplace of country music with portraits of Rodgers, the Carters, Peer, and Ernest "Pop" Stoneman. On Tuesday evenings in good weather, local pickers and singers gather about 7 P.M. for some loose **jamming** underneath the mural. All are welcome.

Tennessee Ernie Ford (1919–1991) was raised in a small white house near downtown, now owned by the Bristol Historical Association. "That house has been through a hard time, and we've restored it to about how it was when he lived there," says the Association's former president, Thomas Fink. The original bathtub is still there.

Fink, who went to school with Tennessee Ernie, says, "He told me that he remembers being scrubbed down in that tub." The Ford family has donated money to fix up **Anderson Street Methodist Church,** which Tennessee Ernie attended. Tours of the church and **Tennessee Ernie Ford's House** can be arranged by calling the Bristol Chamber of Commerce at (423) 989-4850. The Bristol Historical Association plans to open them to the public soon. Anderson Street is off Volunteer Parkway, which intersects State Street. The house is at 1223 Anderson Street; the church is across the street at 1219 Anderson Street.

A sign spanning State Street reads "Bristol VA/TN, A Good Place to Live." At one time Bristol had fierce, even violent border wars. Years ago, the Virginia side was "wet" and the Tennessee side was "dry," meaning that you could order a whiskey on the north side of State Street but not if you crossed the road into Tennessee. "It was a hoppin' little town, with gambling halls, drinking, and brothels," McClellen says. (The two sides still have separate municipal services, including two fire and police departments.)

Things are considerably calmer today. Shops along State Street in downtown Bristol sell Appalachian crafts, antiques, and furniture. The **Trainstation Marketplace,** built in 1902, is a monument to Bristol's heritage as a railroad center. On State Street beside the railroad tracks, the restored station houses shops, restaurants, and a jazz club.

The **Paramount Theatre** is a classic 1931 art-deco movie palace that now hosts theater performances, ballet, choir concerts, and other special events. BCMA hosts country and bluegrass programs here on the last Thursday of every month. 518 State St.; (423) 968-7456.

GETTING THERE: Take I-81 to the Tennessee-Virginia border. Contact Bristol Visitors' Council, 20 Volunteer Parkway; (423) 968-4399.

For information about BCMA, write P.O. Box 216, Bristol TN-VA 37620, or call Fred McClellen (703) 628-1352, Leton Harding (703) 623-2265, or Tim White (423) 323-7829.

THE WORLD'S ONLY GUITAR-SHAPED MUSEUM

The **Grand Guitar Museum** is a 70-foot-long, three-story building shaped like a Martin acoustic guitar, with windows for the fret markers and sound hole. "If you're going to have a music museum and you put up a square building, no one's going to come visit it," explains Joe Morrell, the man who built "The World's Only Guitar-Shaped Music Museum" alongside a highway in Bristol, Tennessee. "I'm sure they won't pass by this building without seeing it," he explains.

It's quite a sight, one of the eccentric wonders that make traveling the roads of America so much fun. Morrell's museum has the exact proportions of a real guitar. The inside is a showcase for his fascinating collection of guitars, lap steels, autoharps, dulcimers, and other unusual instruments gathered over many years running a Bristol music shop. The display includes early American gourd banjos, triple-neck guitars, a violin made out of matchsticks, a one-of-a-kind "harp-o-chord" (combination harmonica/autoharp), and a double-sided mandolin/ukulele.

Morrell has painted a map pinpointing the birthplaces of dozens of nationally known bluegrass and country stars within a 100-mile radius of the museum and Bristol, the Birthplace of Country Music. The map encompasses musically fertile parts of Appalachian Tennessee, Virginia, Kentucky, West Virginia, and North Carolina. "I didn't realize there were that many famous people until I started researching. You can see Chet Atkins, Dolly Parton, Andy Griffith, Tennessee Ernie, the Carter Family, Loretta Lynn, Dwight Yoakam," he says.

The ground floor is current headquarters of **WOPI Radio,** 1490 AM, the first radio station between Knoxville and Roanoke. WOPI began broadcasting from downtown Bristol on June 15, 1929, with much fanfare. A banner headline on the front page of the *Bristol News Bulletin* that day read "Bristol's New

Broadcasting Station to Open Today" and "Residents of Kingsport to Hear WOPI."

Tennessee Ernie Ford got his start as an announcer on WOPI,
and the station broadcast the *WOPI Jamboree* during the thirties
and forties. "Jimmie Rodgers, the Carter Family, and all of them
played music on WOPI in the early days," says deejay Dennis
Wenk, adding that the station now plays traditional country
music and "some real old stuff."

GETTING THERE: Take I-81/Exit 74A. Museum hours vary.
Call Morrell to make an appointment. 3245 West State St.; (423)
968-9575.

Elizabethton

SLAGLE'S PASTURE BARNDANCE

Every Saturday night year-round, Dare and Clayton Slagle hold an
old-fashioned Slagle's Pasture Barndance under a big shelter in the
pasture next to their home. Local and regional bands play bluegrass
and old-time country music, with square-dancing. In the winter, the
sides of the shelter come down and five big heating stoves keep guests
warm. The fun starts at 7:30 P.M. Admission $3.

The second weekend in June, Slagle's Pasture hosts a three-day
bluegrass festival with top-name performers. Camping and RV hookups are available.

GETTING THERE: From Elizabethton, take Old Hwy. 19E north
(*not* the new four-lane Hwy. 19E) for 2½ miles; (423) 542-8615.

Kenny Chesney on the Down Home

(Peter Nash)

"The **Down Home** is kind of a Johnson City version of the Bluebird [Cafe] in Nashville. I like the Down Home a lot better; it's a better room. They have blue-grass music there, a lot of blues, country, and folk singers and song-writers. It's a great place."

GETTING THERE: The Down Home in Johnson City presents headliners Thursday through Saturday nights, and open-mike nights on Wednesdays. The kitchen serves food and beer from 6 P.M. until show-time. Reservations are suggested. From I-181 take Market Street exit. Go four lights to Down Home, on left. 300 W. Main St.; (423) 929-9822.

Bulls Gap

ARCHIE CAMPBELL HOMEPLACE AND MUSEUM

Archie Campbell, a singer and comedian who got his start on WNOX Radio in Knoxville, joined the *Grand Ole Opry* in 1959. In 1969 he helped create *Hee Haw*; he was a popular cast member and one of the show's main writers.

Throughout his long career, Campbell was often introduced as "The Mayor of Bulls Gap." While the title was purely fictional, it might as well have been true. Campbell is a hero to the folks of Bulls Gap, an old east Tennessee railroad town.

Campbell died of a heart attack in 1987. His modest homeplace, which was moved to South Main Street in Bulls Gap, is open to visitors along with several dozen turn-of-the-century structures in a historic district.

Nearby in City Hall, a small museum displays Campbell's original paintings, items from the television show, stage clothing, and other personal items.

GETTING THERE: Bulls Gap is halfway between Knoxville and Johnson City. Volunteers show Campbell's home from May through September. Admission is free. Take I-81/Exit 23. Turn left on Hwy. 11E. At the only stoplight in Bulls Gap, turn left. 139 S. Main St.; (423) 235-5216.

Union County

ROY ACUFF MUSEUM AND MONUMENT

The small but growing **Roy Acuff Union Heritage Museum and Library** is in the King of Country Music's hometown of Maynardville, north of Knoxville in rural Union County. In addition to a fine library of local genealogical information, the museum has memorabilia from famous Union County natives Acuff, Chet Atkins (Luttrell), Kenny Chesney (Luttrell), and Carl Smith (Maynardville). Open Monday and Tuesday 10 A.M. to 4 P.M.; Sunday 1 to 5 P.M.; and by appointment. 3824 Maynardville Hwy; (423) 687-2137.

The Roy Acuff monument, in front of the Union County

Courthouse, is a replica of Acuff's plaque in the Country Music Hall of Fame. From Hwy. 33, go east on Main Street one block. (*See also:* Nashville—Opryland U.S.A.)

GETTING THERE: Union County is 25 miles north of Knoxville. From Knoxville, take I-75 to Hwy. 441 to Hwy. 33 north. For area information, contact the Union County Clerk; (423) 992-3061.

Knoxville
HONORING EAST TENNESSEE'S FINEST PERFORMERS

Knoxville's oldest showplace, the historic Bijou Theatre, first opened as a hotel in 1817. Slated for demolition during the 1970s, it was saved by a citizens' group; since 1980 it has been run as a nonprofit performing-arts center with stage shows, concerts, and special events. Every few years, the Bijou acknowledges achievements in writing, acting, singing, and dancing by inducting new members to its **East Tennessee Hall of Fame for the Performing Arts.**

East Tennesseans honored so far include country music legends Chet Atkins (Luttrell), Tennessee Ernie Ford (Bristol), Archie Campbell (Bulls Gap), Dolly Parton (Sevierville), the McCarter Sisters (Sevierville), and Roy Acuff (rural Union County). Other talented locals in the Hall of Fame include movie actor David Keith, poet and author James Agee, and opera singer Mary Costa, all from Knoxville. Each display case has a portrait, memorabilia, and a summary of the artist's career. (Some cases are mounted high on the lobby walls, making them difficult to read.)

GETTING THERE: Knoxville is 175 miles east of Nashville on I-40. The Hall of Fame is open weekdays and for shows or special events. Free. (Tickets are needed for performances.) 803 S. Gay St.; (800) 738-0832 or (423) 522-0832.

For area information, call Knoxville Visitors' Bureau; (423) 523-2316.

Powell
DAVID'S MUSIC BARN

On Saturday nights at 8:30 P.M, David West and the Cider Mountain Boys perform country, bluegrass, and comedy at David's Music Barn. East Tennessee's oldest country-music show also features visiting artists, guest bands, and door prizes, followed by a dance until 2 A.M.
Ciderville Music Store next door sells string instruments, drums, and P.A. equipment. David's Music Barn is 6 miles north of Knoxville. Take I-640 to Clinton Hwy. 25 west; (423) 945-3595.

Norris
MUSEUM OF APPALACHIA

"I can't imagine any culture anywhere where music was more important," John Rice Irwin says of his native Appalachia. Irwin, executive director of the **Museum of Appalachia** north of Knoxville in Norris, is preserving a culture fast becoming obsolete. The 65-acre park offers thirty authentic Appalachian structures and demonstrations of country living. Every day, members of the Museum of Appalachia Band, including fiddle champion Charlie Acuff (Roy's second cousin), saw out traditional mountain tunes for visitors, urging them to sing along and sharing cornball jokes.

The **Appalachia Hall of Fame,** a large hall on the grounds, contains an extensive exhibit called "A People and Their Music," which highlights the careers of Roy Acuff, Cas Walker, Grandpa Jones, the Carter Family, Uncle Dave Macon, and other famous and less widely known regional musicians. Redd Stewart's original manuscript for the "Tennessee Waltz" is on display, as well as an extensive collection of guitars, dulcimers, banjos, dobros, and fiddles, including several unusual items such as banjos made out of hubcaps and ham cans.

One explanation for the role of music in Appalachian culture can be found in the land itself. The vast Appalachian Mountain range stretches from Canada to Alabama; its rugged geography creates pockets of isolation called "hollows" or "hollers." Life was hard here for early settlers, mostly immigrants from England, Scotland, and Ireland. When they weren't scraping out a living, these new Americans

The annual Museum of Appalachia Tennessee Fair Homecoming features hundreds of old-time musicians and mountain craftspeople. (Museum of Appalachia)

passed the time picking out tunes on homemade instruments and singing songs from home. There wasn't much else to do.

"There are two things you tended to find in isolated, forlorn log cabins and they indicated the things that people valued most," Irwin explains. "One was guns. They always had one hanging over the mantel or the door. If you went out in the afternoon to get the cows, you always took a gun to kill a rabbit or a squirrel for supper. The other was musical instruments. They enjoyed sitting under the big oak tree by the spring, drinking cold water, or maybe moonshine, and picking and singing."

The museum is one of the most authentic nineteenth-century Appalachian towns in existence, with furnished homesteads, barns, hen houses, a whiskey still, grist mill, log church, and schoolhouse. Wild turkeys, goats, cattle, oxen, sheep, and chickens roam the green pastures. Some 250,000 artifacts are on display, most gathered by Irwin himself.

"I had visited some museums where they would have a Victorian organ and right beside it a 1700 flint rock rifle, and no rhyme or reason for it," says Irwin, a former high school superintendent. "My ambition was to have one cabin furnished in an authentic way. One cabin led to another, and before long, we had visitors coming in."

The **Tennessee Fall Homecoming,** held every year in mid-October, showcases the best practitioners of old-time mountain music. Hundreds of musicians perform at the four-day festival, and there are demonstrations of activities and crafts such as pressing apple cider, rail splitting, quilting, and cooking on open fires.

On July Fourth, the museum hosts an **Old Time Anvil Shoot.** The nearly forgotten ritual involves filling an upside-down anvil with gun powder and placing a second anvil on top. After the powder is lit with a fuse, the 125-pound hunk of steel is thrust as high as 75 feet in the air. Early settlers shot anvils to celebrate events such as Independence Day or the election of Davy Crockett, or to scare Indians.

GETTING THERE: Norris is about 15 miles north of Knoxville. Open 8 A.M. to 5 P.M. daily, except Christmas Day. Admission is $6 for adults, $4 for children six to 15. Allow up to three hours. Take I-75/Exit 122 to Hwy. 61 east; (423) 494-0514.

Great Smoky Mountains

Mysterious old mountains with rounded tops, the Great Smoky Mountains are shrouded in a permanent veil of purple fog. Although they're not particularly tall, the Smokies lord over the surrounding valleys like stern fathers towering above respectful children.

The tourist cities of Sevierville, Pigeon Forge, and Gatlinburg, south of Knoxville in Sevier County, are in the shadow of these mountains, making them natural gateways to the Smokies. In recent years they have become travel destinations of their own with a distinctly country flavor. In 1986, Dolly Parton opened the theme park Dollywood in Pigeon Forge, boosting the entire area's country music tourism industry. The three cities are in a row on Hwy. 441—called "Dolly Parton Boulevard" in Sevierville, and "Parkway" in Pigeon Forge and Gatlinburg.

The number of local venues that offer live entertainment continues to grow, with slick new state-of-the-art showplaces, family-run jamborees, and clubs. In a few years, the Pigeon Forge area may be giving Branson, Missouri, some serious competition.

Ticket prices for live country shows generally range from $10 to $20. The theaters and shows listed below are as current as publishing schedules allow. Keep in mind that new venues are opening all the time, while schedules and performers often change. Be sure to call ahead.

Country music aside, outdoor recreation is still the reason most people visit this part of Appalachia. **Great Smoky Mountains National Park** is the most-visited national park in the country, with more than 9 million people annually. Straddling Tennessee and North Carolina, the park offers 800 square miles of wilderness, hundreds of black bears, and a great diversity of plant and animal life. The mountains and surrounding hills offer outstanding hiking, fishing, camping, white-water rafting, horseback riding, tubing, and skiing.

The Smokies have long been a popular spot for **weddings** and honeymoons, in part because Sevier County does not require blood tests or Tennessee residency. In Gatlinburg, the "Honeymoon Capital of the South," starry-eyed newlyweds are everywhere, strolling hand-in-hand or grasping one another on the sky tram. To get married here, you must be 18 or older and show identification. Licenses cost $36, and can be obtained at the Sevier County Courthouse in Sevierville; (423) 453-5502.

Shoppers will find hundreds of factory discount outlets, and other stores selling things like Appalachian crafts, souvenirs, specialty gifts, Western wear, sporting goods, lawn ornaments, knives, and Native American items.

Special events and festivals take place throughout the year. During the **Smoky Mountain Winterfest,** November to February, the region is decorated with millions of lights and many theaters present special Christmas shows.

Food consists mainly of chain restaurants—fast food, cafeterias, or buffets—but a few fine eateries can be found. Liquor and wine cannot be purchased in Pigeon Forge and Sevierville, but packaged beer and wine coolers are permitted. Alcohol is legal in Gatlinburg.

Accommodations are plentiful, with hundreds of motels, inns, bed-and-breakfasts, chalets, and hotels in every price range, in addition to dozens of campgrounds and RV parks.

Discount coupons for nearly all attractions, restaurants, and accommodations in the area are available at visitors' centers.

GETTING THERE: Great Smoky Mountains National Park can be reached from I-40 or I-26. Hwy. 441 runs north-south through the park. When approaching from the north, the Great Smokies Information Station in Sevierville is at 2228 Winfield Dunn Parkway (Hwy. 66 north of 441); (800) 770-4630 or (423) 429-3366.

From the south, stop at Sugarlands Visitors' Center off Hwy. 441, (423) 436-1200; or Gatlinburg Visitors' Center on Hwy. 441; (800) 568-4748 or (423) 430-4148.

Sevierville
YOUR HOMETOWN IN THE SMOKIES

Heading toward the Smokies from Knoxville, the first town you reach is Sevierville. Less intensely touristy than Pigeon Forge or Gatlinburg, Sevierville's motto is "Your Hometown in the Smokies." The town emphasizes its scenery and easy access to hiking, golf, boating, fishing, and swimming. Just 5 miles from Dollywood, Sevierville's hotels, motels, and campgrounds have lower rates than those in Pigeon Forge and provide a less frantic base for a visit to the Smoky Mountains.

Neon signs and billboards are restricted here, and developers are required to landscape their properties and plant trees. At its entrance, Sevierville has posted a sign apologizing for a slew of billboards that the community was legally unable to ban. "Those signs are an eyesore to a lot of people," says Butch Stott, Sevierville's building official. "If it was up to the city, they wouldn't be there."

Plans are in the works for a half-dozen new music theaters in Sevierville, including one for singer B.J. Thomas. Sevierville's first country showplace, the 1,750-seat **Lee Greenwood Theater,** opened in mid-1996 with 250 shows a year between April and December. Grammy award–winner Greenwood is best known for his hit "God

Bless the USA." Parkway at the River Bluff Development; (800) 769-1125 or (423) 453-0777.

The **Dolly Parton statue** in front of the Sevier County Courthouse is one of the honors the superstar is most proud of. The handsome bronze statue shows Dolly sitting on a rock holding a guitar. The graceful courthouse is surrounded by a square of restored buildings, businesses, and storefront wedding chapels. Local attractions include art galleries, caverns, a petting zoo, and the Apple Barn Cider Mill and General Store; 230 Apple Valley Rd.; (423) 453-9319.

GETTING THERE: Sevierville is 30 miles southeast of Knoxville. Take I-40/Exit 407 to Hwy. 441 south (9 miles). Sevierville Welcome Center is at 866 Winfield Dunn Parkway (turn right from Hwy. 441 onto Hwy. 66); (800) 255-6411 or (423) 453-6411.

Pigeon Forge
THE TOWN THAT DOLLY BUILT

The most popular attractions in Pigeon Forge are Dollywood, the Dixie Stampede, live country shows, and shopping at hundreds of brand-name outlet stores. At the north end of town, the section of Hwy. 441 called **Music Road** has been rezoned to encourage new musical theaters. The Dollywood Company opened the $7 million Music Mansion here in 1994, and several new ones are planned.

Then there's "Parkway," the main drag through town along Hwy. 441. For several miles, flashing neon signs hawk go-cart rides, miniature golf, ice cream, video arcades, airbrushed T-shirts, a dinosaur park, Indian jewelry and moccasins, bungee-jumping, pancake houses, motels, water parks, dune-buggy rentals, palm readings, and $5 helicopter trips. Whether you arrive from Sevierville or Gatlinburg, seeing the lush green stretches of the Appalachian foothills give way to this relentlessly gaudy display can be a mind-boggling experience.

Additional Pigeon Forge attractions include hundreds of factory outlet stores, a winery, crafts village, and a number of touristy museums. **Ernest Tubb Record Shop No. 4** features an extensive selection of country recordings, books, and videos. West of Parkway in Settler's Village; (423) 453-3558.

Nothing in Pigeon Forge seems to have an address. In brochures, virtually every attraction is advertised as located "On Parkway." Nonetheless, it's really not hard to find what you're looking for. Detailed maps and brochures are widely available, and there are plenty of big, flashing signs.

Parking is plentiful in Pigeon Forge, but you can avoid the traffic hassles (and help the environment) by taking the city's **Fun Time Trolley.** The trolleys make dozens of convenient stops, looping up and down the length of Parkway, with transfers to Dollywood and Wears Valley Road. The cost is only 25¢ per ride, and discount tokens are available. Simply wait at the red Trolley Stop signs. Trolleys run continuously between 8:30 A.M. and midnight April through October, and 10:30 A.M. to 10 P.M. November and December (except Thanksgiving, December 24, and Christmas Day); (423) 453-6444.

GETTING THERE: Pigeon Forge is 35 miles southeast of Knoxville. Take I-40/Exit 407 to Hwy. 441 south (14 miles). Pigeon Forge Welcome Center is at the north end of Parkway; (800) 251-9100 or (423) 453-8574.

DOLLYWOOD—PARTON'S APPALACHIA-WOOD

Dolly Parton reportedly was inspired to named her theme park Dollywood while gazing at the famous Hollywood Hills sign. Some folks seem to be put off by the name. However, there's absolutely nothing glittery or California-phony about Dollywood. It has all the elements of the typical amusement park: rides, live entertainment, food, and souvenirs. What sets Dollywood apart is its gentle, homespun spirit of Appalachia.

Since becoming an international star, Parton has not forgotten her native east Tennessee. In 1986, she became part owner of Silver Dollar City, a theme park built in the 1960s, renamed it, and began restructuring and adding new attractions. Located in the Smoky Mountain foothills a few miles from where Parton was born, Dollywood has provided thousands of jobs for local residents (including many of her kinfolk), and fueled Pigeon Forge's transformation into a bustling tourist center.

Dollywood is divided into theme areas: Showstreet, Rivertown Junction, Fun Country, The Village, Daydream Ridge, Craftsman's Alley, and Jukebox Junction. The newest is called Dollywood Boulevard, a tribute to movie stars. The park truly has something for everyone, from small children to seniors. One-of-a-kind features include Parton's personal museum, a replica of her home place, and a wonderful eagle sanctuary.

The **Dolly Parton Museum** is one of the best star exhibits anywhere. Large and well organized, it uses memorabilia, music, and videos to tell Parton's rags-to-riches saga. From a very young age, Dolly wanted to be a star. Fortunately, she sang like an angel, and could write beautiful and moving songs. Never doubting her abilities, she worked tirelessly to make them heard.

Items on display include the homemade corncob doll that inspired the song "Little Tiny Tassletop"; her first recording, at age ten, of "Puppy Love," written by her uncle Bill Owens; and photos of young Dolly at school without shoes on her feet. A crowd gathers around the original "Coat of Many Colors," a sweet little jacket constructed from patches of corduroy. In a video, Dolly's mother, Avie Lee, tells the story of how she made the coat for young Dolly and how the ridicule of kids at school inspired her to write the song.

Already a local celebrity on the Cas Walker show in Knoxville, Parton moved to Nashville immediately after her high-school graduation in 1964. Within three years she married the elusive Carl Dean and landed a spot on Porter Wagoner's television show. From there, her career took off like a meteor. All the trappings of stardom are on display, including customized guitars, sparkling stage costumes, big wigs, Dolly Parton dolls, and pinball machines, television and movie clips, and dozens of awards.

Near the museum, you can walk through Dolly's **Tennessee Mountain Home,** a replica of the Parton family's first house in Locust Ridge. It's difficult to visualize 11 kids and two adults in such a tiny shack, but somehow they managed.

The **Heartsong Theatre,** a "multisensory" film/performance, tells how family, faith, and the Smoky Mountains inspired Dolly Parton's music. The movie is incredibly vivid and lively, with an almost 3D effect and some genuine surprises. It is presented in a "forest" theater surrounded by rocks, trees, and hanging vines.

A dozen free shows are presented daily at venues throughout Dollywood, including traditional Appalachian music, contemporary country, gospel, rock and roll, clogging, and comedy. (The **Showcase of Stars,** featuring headline acts, requires a separate admission ticket.) **The Kinfolks Show** at the Backstage Theatre, stars Parton's cousins, aunts, uncles, and other talented musical relatives, many of whom have written songs for or with her.

One of Dollywood's most popular shows is *Wings of America* at the **Eagle Mountain Sanctuary,** featuring live birds of prey. It is not widely known that Dollywood is home to the largest sanctuary for nonreleasable bald eagles in the country, a 30,000-square-foot outdoor aviary. The nonprofit National Foundation to Protect America's Eagles takes care of the endangered birds, which have been critically injured and cannot survive in the wild, and educates visitors about efforts to protect the birds and conserve their habitat. Call (800) 2-EAGLES for more information.

The park is full of pleasant surprises: a working gristmill selling homemade cinnamon rolls and fresh-squeezed lemonade; a fascinating carriageworks that produces wagon wheels; the old-fashioned 1923 Denzel Carousel, which has 48 hand-carved animals and a brass ring.

A relaxing, manageable park, Dollywood is easy to get around and has plenty of restrooms, benches, and shady spots. It's also pretty, decorated with 250,000 flowers. A dozen restaurants and snack bars serve Southern cooking and barbecue. Numerous special events are held throughout the year, like the **National Crafts Festival** in October.

GETTING THERE: Open from mid-April through the end of December, with varying hours and intermittent closures in spring, fall, and winter. Admission up to $25.99 adults (12 and older); $17.99 ages 4 to 11. Allow at least a half day. From Hwy. 441, follow signs to park. Call for current schedules; (800) DOLLYWOOD or (423) 428-9488.

DIXIE STAMPEDE

Few visitors have ever seen a spectacle quite like the Dixie Stampede, Dolly Parton's $5 million dining and entertainment concept. While guests eat vegetable soup, barbecued chicken, and slabs of potato without the aid of utensils, two spandex-clad teams on horseback enact a mock Civil War battle. Conveniently ignoring the issue of slavery, the teams compete for flags in little games, occasionally recruiting members of the audience. While hands and mouths are busy with the food, guests are instructed to stomp on the floorboards to root for their side.

That's not all. The production has Southern belles in lit-up hoop skirts and gallant gentlemen dancing to the "Tennessee Waltz," covered wagons, cowgirls jumping through rings of fire, trick-riding, chicken and pig races, firecrackers, and a 50,000-light parade.

Standing in line with a thousand other people, it's easy to feel manipulated from the beginning. After handing over $30 tickets, visitors are corralled into booths to have $7 pictures taken, herded into the preshow saloon for $3.50 preshow nonalcoholic drinks, then firmly guided to arena seats. Then the forced frivolity begins, with constant commands to stomp, shout, yell, laugh, and have fun.

The waiters run around nonstop, greeting visitors and asking "Where y' all from?", serving course after course, supplying hot towels, enforcing mandatory audience participation, refilling glasses of iced tea, smiling and smiling all the while. Before exiting through the huge gift shop, guests are asked to fill out a comment card rating the staff on "friendliness."

Consider yourself forewarned.

GETTING THERE: Presented year-round, and up to three times daily during the summer season. 3849 Parkway; (800) 356-1676 or (423) 453-4400.

PIGEON FORGE COUNTRY SHOWS

The following shows are listed from north to south on Parkway (Hwy. 441).

The Dollywood Company's **Music Mansion Theater** is currently the largest in the area, a high-tech showplace with 2,000 seats. The show features James Rogers and 25 performers doing traditional and contemporary country, 1950s rock and roll, gospel, comedy, and dancing. 100 Music Road on Parkway; (423) 428-SHOW.

T.G. Sheppard's Theater in the Smokies showcases the popular country singer along with Las Vegas illusionist Sherry Lukas. The 1,500-seat facility opened in 1995. 2249 Parkway; (800) 333-7007 or (423) 428-8000.

Eddie's Heart and Soul Cafe is a 230-seat family restaurant with live entertainment by Eddie Anders, a gospel-country singer and veteran studio musician. Parkway next to T.G. Sheppard's; (423) 453-0833.

Elmer and Faunda Dreyer *Smoky Mountain Jubilee* features a 17-member cast performing country-western, bluegrass, nostalgia, comedy, and gospel. Parkway across from the Pigeon Forge Welcome Center; (423) 428-1836.

Eddie Miles and Ava Barber Country Music Show at the **Rainbow Music Theatre** pairs the former Elvis impersonator with a veteran of the *Lawrence Welk Show.* Parkway across from Music Mansion; (800) 428-5958 or (423) 428-5600.

A Salute to Elvis is at the **Memories Theatre.** Parkway next to the Rainbow Music Theatre; (423) 428-7852.

Stella Parton's Hat House and Coffee Bar is a "country version of a gourmet coffeehouse," run by Dolly Parton's talented sister. It's located away from the bustle of Parkway, in a renovated older building with Stella Parton's personal hat collection decorating the walls. Entertainment is offered nightly on the Pickin' on the Back Porch stage and the Listening Room, often introduced by Parton. In addition to coffee and desserts, sandwiches such as the "Elvis Fit" (peanut butter and banana) and "Dolly's Steak Delight" (bologna and cheese) are served. Show schedules vary. One mile east of Parkway at 725 Wears Valley Rd.; (423) 429-1298.

Comedy and magic are center stage at **The Comedy Barn,** along with juggling, fiddling, and a one-man band. Parkway next to Bell Air Grill; (423) 428-5222.

Gatlinburg
THE HONEYMOON CAPITAL OF THE SOUTH

Gatlinburg sits at the foot of the Great Smoky Mountains, just outside the National Park boundary. While its attractions are similar to Pigeon Forge's, Gatlinburg has taken a bit more care in controlling signs and architecture. The result is a town much easier on the eyes, with the Smokies rising sharply all around and providing a splendid backdrop.

From the downtown, it is possible to hike right into the mountains or join fly-fishermen along the banks of the Little Pigeon River. More than 10,000 couples choose this setting to get married each year, giving Gatlinburg the right to call itself "Honeymoon Capital of the South."

Ronnie Milsap snagged the best location in Gatlinburg for his **Keyboard Cafe**—a central corner across from the Sky Lift. The Cafe is a large restaurant, bar, and dance club on three levels with balconies overlooking the Smokies. It's a stylish wood-and-brick place, decorated with posters of country stars and a selection of Milsap memorabilia and awards, including his "Triple Crown"—three Country Music Association awards received in 1977. Reasonably priced salads, burgers, barbecue, and Italian food are on the menu. Milsap performs here only occasionally, but live music is presented nightly. 812 Parkway; (423) 430-1978.

Helen Cornelius' Nashville South is an intimate dinner club with snapshots of happy customers, baseball caps, and Music City memorabilia lining the walls. Cornelius, known for her duets with Jim Ed Brown, often hosts the variety show, which includes fiddling, country standards, blues, and easy listening. There's no cover charge, but entrées such as steaks and ribs cost between $14 and $20. From Parkway, turn at light #8. 231 Airport Rd.; (423) 430-2191.

Old-time country, bluegrass, gospel, and clogging are featured in Gatlinburg's **Smoky Mountain Jamboree,** a family variety show. Presented nightly, April through October, with some dates in November and December. 517 Parkway, at light #3; (423) 430-3803.

The **Sweet Fanny Adams Theatre** offers original musical comedies, old-time sing-alongs, and vaudeville revues. Shows are presented nightly, except Sundays, April through November; seven days a week in October; and on holiday weekends. 461 Parkway at light #3; (423) 436-4038.

Additional attractions include the 342-foot space needle, miniature golf, and the Gatlinburg Passion Play.

For a spectacular view, take the **Sky Lift** from the heart of town to the top of Crockett Mountain. The chair lift operates April through September and part of November. Parkway at light #7; (423) 436-4307.

Gatlinburg's **Aerial Tramway**, a 120-person gondola, carries passengers to **Ober Gatlinburg All Seasons Amusement Park and Ski Resort** for indoor ice-skating, go-carts, an alpine slide, and bungee-jumping. 1001 Parkway; (423) 436-5423.

Gatlinburg has many crafts and art galleries, specialty stores, and gifts shops. The **Great Smoky Mountain Arts and Crafts Community,** an association founded in 1937, allows visitors to watch more than 80 artists at work and purchase hand-crafted items. From Parkway, take Hwy. 321 three miles north.

Parking is difficult here, but the **Gatlinburg Trolley,** with four routes and more than 100 stops, is convenient and inexpensive. Leave cars at one of the municipal parking lots and hop on. The cost is 25¢ per ride on most routes. The trolley to Dollywood costs 50¢, and $1 buys unlimited access to the Great Smoky Arts and Crafts Community loop; (423) 436-3897.

GETTING THERE: Gatlinburg is 40 miles southeast of Knoxville. Take I-40/Exit 407 to Hwy. 441 south. The Gatlinburg/National Park Welcome Center is on Hwy. 441 at the north end of Gatlinburg. Gatlinburg Visitors and Convention Bureau is at Hwys. 441 and 321; (800) 568-4748 or (423) 430-4148.

East-Central Tennessee

M Y   H O M E T O W N

Mandy Barnett on Crossville

(John Lee Montgomery, III)

"Crossville is kind of small. But when I did the (*Always . . . Patsy Cline*) show my co-star said that she thought there were probably a million people in Crossville because they've all supported me. I don't think there's anyone in Crossville who hasn't seen the show at the Ryman.

"Crossville is beautiful. You're not going to see the pollution, and a lot of the ugly things that you'll see in a city. The trees, the mountains, there's nothing like it. I'll always consider Crossville home."

GETTING THERE: Crossville is about 100 miles east of Nashville, just south of I-40. Contact the Chamber of Commerce; (615) 484-8444.

Crossville

HANK WILLIAMS, JR., GENERAL STORE

Located just north of the interstate near Crossville, Hank Williams, Jr., General Store has rows and rows of fireworks and junky souvenirs including bandannas, key chains, "adult" gag gifts, piggy banks, toothpick holders, tour jackets, and compact discs.

In the back of the store, a small free "museum" displays Hank Jr.'s favorite shirt (a short-sleeved camouflage print), some stage costumes on hangers, and a row of photos. The centerpiece is Hank Jr.'s customized Bocephus pickup truck, a 1986 Dodge souped up with "everything you need for cruisin' with your rowdy friends!!!"—an ice chest, push-button bar, leather captain chairs, hand-tooled woodwork, lowered suspension, and smoked glass etched with "Hank" designs.

GETTING THERE: I-40/Exit 317; (615) 484-4914.

Chattanooga

THE MOUNTAIN OPRY

If there's a bluegrass heaven, the *Mountain Opry* is about as close as you can get on this earth. Bluegrass fans float on a cloud during the three-hour show, performed on top of Signal Mountain in the town of Walden, about 10 miles from downtown Chattanooga. The *Mountain Opry* is held every Friday night at 8 P.M. in the Walden Ridge Civic Center, a comfortable, 225-seat theater in a shady spot next to a park. American flags line the walls, and ceiling fans whirl overhead as the night breeze comes through open windows.

Like the *Grand Ole Opry*, the *Mountain Opry* is broken into half-hour segments with a variety of performers taking the stage during the show. Unlike the *Grand Ole Opry*, there are no flashing cameras, no spangled costumes, and no big stars. What you get is straightforward traditional bluegrass and old-time country music, played by extremely talented local people for the pleasure and joy of it.

According to the brochure, "the music and fun is spontaneous, informal, and set in a wholesome family atmosphere. Everyone is welcomed, including the aged, children, dogs, cats, etc." A small snack bar sells soda, snacks, and inexpensive souvenirs. The Mountain Opry is a non-profit organization dedicated to the preservation of indigenous mountain music; be sure to make a donation before you leave, to help keep the institution alive.

If you're planning to see the *Mountain Opry,* drive out to the **Riverside Catfish House** for a soul-satisfying dinner first. Since 1963, the Massengale family has served fresh fish, flavorful hushpuppies, and homemade coleslaw on a scenic low bluff overlooking the Tennessee River.

The catfish fillets and fingerlings, all-you-can-eat for $8, are deep-fried in peanut oil to soft, not-too-greasy perfection. The buttermilk pie is creamy and mouth-watering, with a thin, lemony crust. Riverside Catfish House is 12 miles northwest of Chattanooga. Open Thursday through Sunday. Call for hours. Take I-24/Exit 174. Turn right on Hwy. 41 and go 8 miles; (615) 821-9214 or 821-2876.

GETTING THERE: Chattanooga is 130 miles southeast of Nashville, on the Georgia border. From downtown Chattanooga, take I-124 across the Tennessee River to Signal Mountain Road. Go to the top of Signal Mountain, through the town of Signal Mountain, and past a large shopping center. Proceed 1.6 miles and turn right on Fairmont Rd. Parking and admission are free; (615) 886-5897.

Lynchburg
JACK DANIEL AND MISS MARY BOBO

The most famous citizens of Lynchburg (about 65 miles south of Nashville) are Jack Daniel and Miss Mary Bobo. The former's whiskey distillery, registered in 1886, is the oldest in the nation; Miss Mary Bobo opened her world-famous boardinghouse in 1908. Moore County is still "dry," meaning that Lynchburg's most famous product cannot be *purchased* here legally. (It can be consumed, however.) There are just two exceptions: the **Jack Daniel's Distillery** sells a souvenir flask, while **Miss Mary Bobo's Boarding House** serves delectable apples and sweet potatoes stewed in the forbidden liquor.

Three things distinguish Jack Daniel's "Tennessee" whiskey from other whiskeys: cave spring water, high-quality grain, and charcoal mellowing. On Jack Daniel's free 70-minute guided walking tour, you will see the cave spring, Jack Daniel's original office, and lots of whiskey in various stages of production. Jack Daniel and nephew Lem Motlow ran the stills here for many years, never varying from their tried-and-true formula. Although Jack Daniel's is now owned by a Louisville company, the Motlows specified that if the recipe is ever altered, ownership of the distillery will revert back to them.

Some tour guides' charming Tennessee accents are so thick that Yankee visitors might miss some of the presentation, but everyone will pick up quite a bit about how Tennessee whiskey is made, a recipe for curing hangovers, and a few laconic drinking jokes. ("Around here, the Baptists *just don't drink . . .* in front of one another.")

At the end of the tour, lemonade and coffee are served in Jack Daniel's original White Rabbit Saloon. As of 1995, by act of the Tennessee legislature, you can purchase a flask of Jack Daniel's whiskey in Moore County for the first time since 1909. The **Jack Daniel's World Championship Invitational Barbecue Contest,** with $13,000 in prize money, clogging, and greased-pig chases, usually takes place the fourth Saturday in October. Free tours daily between 8 A.M. and 4 P.M., except Thanksgiving, Christmas, and New Year's Day. Rte. 55, a ¼ mile north of Lynchburg Square; (615) 759-4221.

Miss Mary Bobo's Boarding House is in one of Lynchburg's oldest buildings, a travelers' hotel built in the mid–nineteenth century. Mrs. Bobo died in 1983, a month shy of her 102nd birthday, during her 75th year of business. A few years later, Lynne Tolley, a fourth-generation Lynchburg resident, reopened the boardinghouse. Every day except Sunday, Tolley summons guests to "dinner" (don't call it lunch!) at 1 P.M. with the clang of a bell.

True to Mrs. Bobo's legacy, the traditional midday meal is served family style. A gracious but firm hostess instructs guests on when to sit and how to pass the many platters of Southern specialties: crispy and tender fried chicken, pot roast, fried okra, creamed corn, baked squash, cold pea salad, little rolled biscuits, preserves, amazing stewed apples, chocolate cream pie, and iced tea—all served with genuine Southern hospitality.

Many of the vegetables are fresh from the garden out back, and the menu changes daily. Be sure to arrive early and take a look around the boardinghouse and grounds. Dinner $11 adults; $5 children under 10. Reservations required. Off the town square, three doors from Moore County Jail; (615) 759-7394.

Moore County Courthouse (built in 1855), in the center of the Lynchburg town square, is surrounded by historic buildings. Whittlers and old-timers hang out in the shade, and fresh lemonade can be purchased from carts. More than twenty establishments are within walking distance of the courthouse, including Moore County Jail and the turn-of-the-century Farmer's Bank. Shops sell espresso, feed, pottery, leather goods, antiques, and local arts and crafts.

Following prohibition, Jack Daniel's nephew Lem Motlow opened the **Lynchburg Hardware & General Store** on the square in 1913. Bragging "All Goods Worth Price Charged," the store is packed with cast-iron cookware, pocketknives, duck decoys, local honey, hand-carved novelties, whittling sticks, and a barrel of marbles. Upstairs is a dizzying array of Jack Daniel's souvenirs: T-shirts, boots, cocktail napkins, shot glasses, bottles of cave spring water, and flasks; (615) 759-4200.

GETTING THERE: Lynchburg is about 75 miles south of Nashville. Take I-24 to Rte. 55 west. For area information, contact the Lynchburg Chamber of Commerce; (615) 759-4111.

Bell Buckle
QUILTS, CRAFTS, AND COUNTRY MUSIC

Bell Buckle's **railroad square** is a charming row of old-fashioned stores selling antiques, quilts, crafts, and books. Margaret Britton Vaughn, Tennessee's poet laureate, even composes verse in a Bell Buckle storefront under a "Poet at Work" sign. A colorful quilt pattern painted on the ground in front invites visitors in. Beneath the covered walkway is a row of rocking chairs and benches, a pleasant spot to sip lemonade, savor an ice-cream cone, pet a lazy dog, and watch a slow freight train go by. Bell Buckle is southeast of Nashville, in the lovely rolling hills of Tennessee walking-horse country.

The **Bell Buckle Cafe,** owned and operated by the Heinike family, regularly hosts live country music on the square. The cafe is decorated with beautiful quilts, overhead fans, and photos of famous visitors including Patty Loveless, Wynonna Judd, Hal Ketchum, Ricky Van Shelton, and Mac Wiseman. Michael Duncan hosts singer/songwriter night on Thursdays and performs on Sunday afternoons. Shows by local and regional artists are presented on Friday and Saturday nights. On Saturday afternoons from 1 to 3 P.M., radio station WLIJ (1580-AM) broadcasts the *J. Gregory Jamboree* live from the restaurant. Hickory-smoked barbecue, burgers, rhubarb upside-down cake, Moon Pies, and hand-squeezed lemonade are served; (615) 389-9693.

Charlie Louvin reopened the **Louvin Brothers Museum,** once in his native Alabama, to a new building near the Bell Buckle square in early 1996. The Louvin Brothers (Charlie and Ira) were a popular bluegrass duet in the forties and fifties, revered for close harmonizing on hits such as "I Don't Believe You've Met My Baby" and "When I Stop Dreaming." Ira, his wife, and two other people died in a car accident in 1965. Charlie pursued a solo career, and continues to perform regularly on the *Grand Ole Opry.*

"I've got to get the [museum] stuff out of storage before the rats eat it," Louvin explains. "My wife saved everything that was ever printed about us, a lot of pictures, magazines that we were on the cover of, and record albums. So many people come to see what's so special about Bell Buckle. I thought it would be a good place to have a museum."

Bell Buckle is also widely known for the **Webb School,** a preparatory academy founded in 1886 that educated ten Rhodes Scholars and three state governors. A small museum is housed in the Junior Room, an original classroom from 1886. Hwy. 82; (615) 389-9322.

Numerous **special events and craft shows** are held throughout the year in Bell Buckle, including the Country Fair the third Saturday in July; the Bar-B-Que Cook-off Labor Day weekend; and the Webb School Arts & Crafts Festival the third weekend in October, one of the biggest crafts shows in the Southeast.

GETTING THERE: Bell Buckle is about 45 miles southeast of Nashville. Take I-24/Exit 97 to Rte. 82 west. Contact Bell Buckle Merchants' Association; (615) 389-6174 or 389-9371.

Smithville

SWINGIN' SMITHVILLE

The annual Smithville Fiddler's Jamboree includes more than twenty competitions in Appalachian music and dance.

Every year, the **Smithville Fiddlers' Jamboree and Crafts Festival** transforms this sleepy town into the vibrant head-quarters for one of the biggest contests anywhere. More than twenty competitions are held in traditional Appalachian music and dance, including bluegrass and fiddle bands, clogging, dulcimer, gospel singing, old-time banjo, the National Championship for Country Music Beginners, and "novelty events" such as spoon-clacking, jug-blowing, washboard, tub, or saws. The two-day festival, always on the weekend closest to July 4, attracts up to 50,000 visitors.

While the contestants vie for modest prize money under an unforgiving sun, sizzling jam sessions go on under shady trees around the courthouse. This is where you can hear fancy picking and see spontaneous buck-dancing on boards. The jammers overlap and compete, going full-tilt right next to each other, resulting in a luscious, overwhelming blend of sounds and voices.

The festival stage is in front of the DeKalb County Courthouse, in the center of Smithville's public square, which is ringed by food concessions run by local service clubs. On side streets are rows and rows of arts and crafts booths. Beyond are residential areas, with pretty Victorian-style homes, trim lawns, and flapping flags. The festival is free.

In 1995, the Smithville town square got a swingin' addition: **John Anderson's Seminole Wind Trading Company.** Anderson's wife, Jamie, often works at the boutique, which doubles as John Anderson's International Fan Club headquarters. (Club membership is free, and has been since it was started in 1991.) The classy shop features Anderson souvenirs, fine women's Western wear, men's hats, Native American blankets, sand paintings, and jewelry. Open Monday through Friday 10 A.M. to 5 P.M.; Saturday 10 A.M. to 4 P.M. 404 Public Square; (615) 597-2828. (Anderson has announced plans to open a family-style restaurant on Hwy. 56 in Smithville in 1996.)

GETTING THERE: Smithville is 65 miles east of Nashville. Take I-40/Exit 273 to Hwy. 56 south. Turn after first stoplight to the public square. For festival or area information, contact the Smithville/ DeKalb County Chamber; (615) 597-4163.

McMinnville
DOTTIE WEST MUSIC FEST

Dottie West's hometown of McMinnville has honored her with a two-day festival in late June since she died in a car crash in 1991. Headline country and gospel stars perform for free on Main Street downtown. A member of the *Grand Ole Opry* since 1963, West had hits with "Paper Mansions," "Rings of Gold," and "Country Sunshine." A section of Hwy. 56 north of McMinnville has been renamed "Dottie West Highway."

GETTING THERE: McMinnville is about 60 miles southeast of Nashville. Take I-24 south to Hwy. 70 east; (615) 473-6611.

Nashville

MUSIC CITY, U.S.A.

With millions of tourists flocking to Branson, Missouri, and Pigeon Forge, Tennessee, Nashville is fighting hard to maintain the title of "Music City, U.S.A." Yet while Branson has the shows and Pigeon Forge has Dollywood and the Smoky Mountains, Nashville is still where the music is made. It's where performers on Branson stages dream of recording and where Dolly Parton lives. For country music fans, Nashville is still a first-class tourist city with a wide variety of museums and attractions, restaurants, and entertainment.

The major areas to visit in Nashville are:

- The District—Nashville's downtown—with the Ryman Auditorium, Tootsie's Orchid Lounge, and historic Broadway and Second Avenue;
- Music Row, home of Nashville's recording and publishing industry, and the Country Music Hall of Fame;
- Opryland, U.S.A., home of the *Grand Ole Opry,* a theme park, the Nashville Network, and the Opryland Hotel;
- Music Valley, a row of museums and theaters adjacent to Opryland; and
- around Nashville are attractions worth special trips such as the Kitty Wells and Jim Reeves Museums.

Additional attractions in Nashville include Andrew Jackson's Hermitage, botanical gardens, a zoo and wildlife park, historic homes, and art museums. The Parthenon in Centennial Park is the world's only full-scale replica of the real one in Athens, Greece. West End Avenue at 25th Ave. N.; (615) 862-8431.

The easiest way get around Nashville is by car. Parking is inexpensive and easy to find at most destinations, and the streets and highways are not difficult to navigate with a good map. The public transportation system is limited to buses and the Nashville Trolley, which runs tourists between downtown Nashville and Music Row, and Music Valley Road and Opryland. Call the Metropolitan Transit Authority at (615) 862-5950 for routes and schedules.

Taxis are not easy to hail, but can be ordered by phone. Check the local Yellow Pages. *River Taxis* run along the Cumberland River between Opryland U.S.A. and downtown Nashville; (615) 889-6611. A variety of bus tours are also available.

GETTING THERE: Nashville is in the center of Tennessee, at I-40 and I-65. The Tourist Information Center, at I-65/Exit 85, is open seven days a week from 8 A.M. to 5 P.M. and can also provide information by phone; (615) 259-4747. Call the Nashville Convention and Visitors' Bureau at (615) 259-4700.

The District

Since the 1980s, downtown Nashville has undergone a nearly miraculous transformation. Second Avenue and Broadway, called "The District," once consisted of sadly boarded-up historic buildings. By the mid-1990s, the area gave birth to a growing number of handsome commercial and entertainment establishments.

For general information about attractions and events in the District, call (615) 244-7835.

A good way to see the District is to follow the Metropolitan Historical Commission's **Nashville City Walk.** The self-guided tour starts at Fort Nashborough on the waterfront at First Ave. N. and Church St., and ends at the Hatch Show Print shop on Broadway. In between are popular attractions such as the Ryman Auditorium and Printer's Alley. Simply follow the blue line on the sidewalk to fifteen historical sites. For a brochure, call (615) 862-7970. The attractions described below follow the City Walk route.

RIVERFRONT PARK—CRUISING THE CUMBERLAND

Riverfront Park at the foot of Broadway is a pleasant place to stroll or sit back and watch the lazy Cumberland River roll by. A replica of **Fort Nashborough,** the area's original frontier settlement, is at the edge of the park. During the summertime free Dancing in the District concerts are held here on Thursday nights. Opryland's **General Jackson** offers river cruises, departing from the park. (*See Opryland entry for details.*)

Tourists can avoid Nashville's freeways by taking **river taxis** between Opryland and Riverfront Park. The catamaran-hulled boats, named *Miss Minnie* and *Mister Roy,* carry about 100 passengers each. The 45-minute, 7-mile ride along the Cumberland River costs $11 round-trip; $8 for ages 4 to 11. The taxis leave frequently from Riverfront Park. Call for schedules; (615) 889-6611.

SECOND AVENUE

Second Avenue, previously known as Market Street, is one of Nashville's oldest streets. Skirting the Cumberland River, it was Nashville's commercial center for most of the city's history. In 1819, the arrival of the steamboat *General Jackson* ushered in a vibrant trade in furniture, tobacco, coffee, cotton, and lumber. The current row of riverside warehouses was built in the late nineteenth century; goods were delivered on First Avenue and sold one floor up on Second Avenue. Most of the warehouses have been renovated and converted into hot new clubs, restaurants, and stores.

You can't miss Nashville's **Hard Rock Cafe** (the 35th worldwide), with a huge 260-foot mural of a black Gibson Les Paul guitar above the restaurant facing Broadway. Inside, the memorabilia is country-tinged, with offerings from Travis Tritt and Marty Stuart in addition to Mick Jagger and U2's Bono. Open 11 A.M. to 1 P.M Sunday through Thursday; 11 A.M. to 2 A.M. Fridays and Saturdays. Second Ave. and Broadway; (615) 742-9900.

Farther down the street, the **Wildhorse Saloon** is tapping into the country dance craze with two-stepping and line dancing on a 3,300-square-foot dance floor. The only country music club in downtown Nashville, the Wildhorse offers live performances, dance lessons, and country videos on a two-story-high screen. Dozens of concerts are also taped here for TNN. To be on the Wildhorse dance show, show up on Tuesday or Wednesday evenings for the tapings. The decor includes full-size papier-mâché horses hanging from the ceiling and caricatures of country stars on the walls. Cover prices vary, depending on the event. Food and drinks are served. 120 Second Ave. N.; (615) 256-WILD.

The Great Escape, Nashville's legendary used-record and comics store, opened its newest branch on Second Avenue. In addition to thousands of used and out-of-print CDs, records and tapes, movie memorabilia and baseball cards, it is the home of the **Marty Party Headquarters.** Hillbilly rocker Marty Stuart souvenirs and fan club applications are available. 112 Second Ave. N; (615) 255-5313. Great Escape branches are also located at 1925 Broadway near Music Row and 111 N. Gallatin Rd. in Madison, near Opryland.

PRINTER'S ALLEY—SPEAKEASY CENTRAL

From the middle of the 1800s until the 1950s, Printer's Alley was home to Nashville's printing and publishing industry. In 1915, thirteen publishers and ten printers had their offices here, as did many furniture manufacturers. The street's entertainment industry grew up around turn-of-the-century saloons that had their back doors to the alley. Prohibition closed the saloons in 1909, but resulted in a proliferation of basement speakeasies.

When Tennessee legalized liquor in 1939, the speakeasies naturally became legitimate nightclubs. Printer's Alley became the center of Nashville's nightlife, with entertainment ranging from "exotic" dancers and comedy to country, jazz, and blues. Performers included Dottie West, Waylon Jennings, Hank Williams, and Barbara Mandrell. In recent years, Tim McGraw got his start singing at a joint called Skull's Rainbow Room. Boots Randolph, a Printer's Alley stalwart for many years, closed his popular nightclub and opened a theater on Music Valley Road in 1995.

Printer's Alley is now home to a disparate collection of honkytonks and restaurants. It has suffered from a somewhat seedy reputation, but close proximity to the flourishing Second Avenue scene may give the street a boost. From Second Ave., walk up Church Street 1½ blocks and turn right into Printer's Alley.

RYMAN AUDITORIUM—THE MOTHER CHURCH OF COUNTRY MUSIC

On March 15, 1974, tears streamed down Minnie Pearl's face as the cast of the *Grand Ole Opry* gave its last performance from the stage of the beloved Ryman Auditorium, a historic 1892 hall in downtown

Nashville. "It's going to be all right," she told an emotional gathering of country stars and *Opry* devotees.

It was all right for the *Opry,* which continues its unassailable streak as the longest running live show in radio history at Opryland. But the Ryman Auditorium, despite its glorious history as Nashville's premiere performance space, was all but abandoned.

"It was not repaired for a number of years," says Mike Hyland of Gaylord Entertainment Company, which owns Opryland and bought the Ryman building during the 1970s. "It became a museum, where people could stand on the stage and look at the tiny dressing rooms. They would sign their names on the walls."

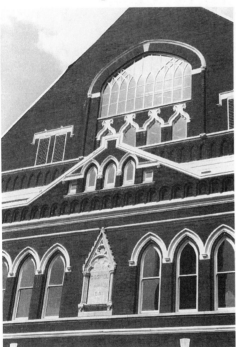

In 1993, Gaylord closed the Ryman and began an $8.5 million renovation. Reopened to the public in 1994, the Ryman once again offers a variety of shows. During the day, visitors can tour the building and a small historical museum.

The Union Gospel Tabernacle, as the building was originally known, was built by Thomas Green Ryman, a prosperous riverboat captain who wanted to move his favorite evangelist, Reverend

The Union Gospel Tabernacle, built by riverboat captain Thomas Green Ryman, later became "The Mother Church": Ryman Auditorium, the original home of the Grand Ole Opry.

Samuel Jones, out of tents and into a more respectable venue. Its intended purpose was as a nondenominational auditorium to promote religion and morality.

A churchlike red-brick structure, the original Ryman had about 3,000 seats, 140 windows (many of them multicolored stained glass), simple Gothic arches, and oak pews arranged in semicircles. In 1897, when the state of Tennessee celebrated its centennial, the Confederate Veterans Association held its national convention at the Ryman and donated funds for construction of the balcony, named the Confederate Gallery.

After Ryman died in 1904 and Reverend Jones in 1906, a promoter named Lula Naff began booking first-rate cultural acts. During the first half of the twentieth century, "the Carnegie Hall of the South" hosted Enrico Caruso, the Ziegfield Follies, Isadora Duncan, Marian Anderson, the Metropolitan Opera, and performances of Shakespeare. The auditorium, renamed for Ryman, was often criticized for its uncomfortable wooden pews, stifling heat, and extremely limited backstage facilities. But Nashvillians kept coming back for their cultural edification.

The *Grand Ole Opry* arrived in 1943. On June 11, 1949, the biggest night in country music's history, Hank Williams received ovation after ovation for his debut performance of "Lovesick Blues" on the Ryman stage. Between sets, Williams and other *Opry* stars would go across the alley to tie one on at Tootsie's Orchid Lounge, the Ryman's unofficial backstage.

For fans of country music, the Ryman inspires an almost religious devotion; many refer to it reverentially as "The Mother Church." On the *Opry*'s last night, after the radio announcer signed off, Johnny Cash and June Carter led the assembled minions in a prayerful sing-along of "Will the Circle Be Unbroken." With the

Martha White Bluegrass Night is one of several summer shows held at the renovated Ryman Auditorium.

renovation and the return of music to its hallowed halls, country's covenant with the Ryman carries on.

During the renovations, Gaylord made the stage more spacious, and added state-of-the-art lighting, television hookups, modern dressing rooms, air-conditioning, and a new lobby. Historic architectural details, including the original oak pews, stage, and floor, were maintained or restored. "Part of the allure of the building is the oak pews," Hyland says. "We never even considered putting in more comfortable seating."

Seeing a show at the Ryman is a special experience. The ghosts of country music's colorful past echo off the 100-foot vaulted ceiling. *Martha White Bluegrass Night at the Ryman* is held on Tuesday nights during the summer. An inspirational music series, *Sam's Place* (named for the Reverend Jones) runs during the summer on Sunday nights. Contact the Ryman for information about special performances.

If you can't get a seat in the front of the Ryman's orchestra, ask for one in the balcony. From the back half of the orchestra, poles and the balcony itself can obstruct views of the stage. Like almost all country music venues, the Ryman is informal. Flash photography is allowed, and you can enjoy a beer and popcorn at your seat.

GETTING THERE: The Ryman Auditorium and Museum are open daily 8:30 A.M. to 4 P.M. Allow one half to one hour for a tour. Admission $5. 116 5th Ave. N.; (615) 889-6611.

TOOTSIE'S ORCHID LOUNGE—WHERE THE MUSIC BEGAN

There really was a Tootsie. Her name was Hattie Louise Bess, and she bought a watering hole named Mom's Place at 422 Broadway in 1960. Mom's Place was a popular haunt for *Grand Ole Opry* performers, including Hank Williams, who used to slip out the back door of the Ryman Auditorium between sets and slide across the alley for a cold one.

Renamed Tootsie's Orchid Lounge by Bess, the bar became the favorite hangout for a generation of classic Nashville singers and songwriters, including Willie Nelson, Kris Kristofferson, Tom T. Hall, and Roger Miller. During this Golden Age of Tootsie's, the "Orchid Lounge Poets" used the bar as their office, where they would sing, collaborate, and generally raise hell. (In a TV special, Harlan Howard blamed Tootsie's for the break-up of two marriages!) Tootsie is fondly remembered as a woman who loved country music and nurtured her starving poets.

Tootsie's death in 1978 and the closure of the Ryman Auditorium nearly killed the bar. However, the 1990s renaissance on Broadway has brought people back, and Tootsie's has taken steps to upgrade its image. A new deck overlooks the world-famous Ryman Alley. Slick souvenirs are for sale, and the exterior was given a fresh coat of purple paint.

Thankfully, the interior hasn't been touched. From the cracked green linoleum floors to the torn bar stools, the place is literally crumbling. The walls are lined with yellowing posters, album covers, and photographs. Every single thing is autographed: walls, tables, chairs, the bar itself. (The bartender will give you a black magic marker to add your name.) All day and well into the night, singers sit in the front window and play for tips, with widely varying levels of talent.

Hank Williams is the patron saint of Tootsie's. The back room was reopened with live entertainment in 1995, and named for the famed honky-tonk singer. A picture of Williams hangs above the front stage, and odds are excellent that you'll hear someone sing "Your Cheatin' Heart" or "Lovesick Blues" if you hang out long enough. One fabled night a few years ago, John Michael Montgomery offered $25 for every Hank Williams song the singer on stage could play; he forked over $600.

Tootsie's is still a dive, no doubt about it. But don't be afraid. Just walk right in and you'll feel welcome. Open 10:30 A.M. to 2 A.M. every day. Admission is free, except during special shows. 422 Broadway; (615) 726-0463.

Once dominated by "adult entertainment" and seedy honky-tonks, the area around Tootsie's is coming alive again. **Robert's Western World** (three doors from Tootsie's), run by a former owner of Tootsie's, is the home of a hip western dance band called BR-549. 416 Broadway; (615) 256-7937.

GRUHN GUITAR

George Gruhn, an authority in fine and vintage instruments, has been selling guitars around the corner from the Ryman Auditorium since

1970. The beautiful new Gruhn Guitar showroom features acoustic and electric guitars, mandolins and banjos, dobros and mobros.

The Gruhn catalogue once featured a 1961 D'Angelico New Yorker Special guitar, purchased by Harold Bradley and used in studio sessions with Elvis Presley, Patsy Cline, and Roy Orbison, for $55,000. If that's out of your price range, Gruhn sells many instruments in the $250 to $2,500 range.

Even if you're not in the market for a stringed instrument, stop in to see the gorgeous guitars displayed in enticingly neat rows along the walls. Open 9 A.M. to 6 P.M. Monday through Saturday. 400 Broadway; (615) 256-2033.

HATCH SHOW PRINT
Advertising without posters is like fishing without worms.
—Hatch Show Print's motto

Perhaps the most famous Hatch Show Print, and the one that Jim Sherraden has cranked out on his decades-old letterpress more times than he'd like to admit, is the poster for Hank Williams's show on New Year's Day 1953. The banner along the top reads: " 'If the Good Lord's Willing and the Creek Don't Rise' . . . I'll See You at Canton Memorial Aud[itorium]."

Hank died on the way to that show, giving the print a permanently lurid appeal. Hatch Show Print restrikes of the poster are among the hottest-selling items at the shop on lower Broadway. "These are authentic reproductions, using the same plates as the original," Sherraden explains.

Since 1879, Hatch Show Print has been creating distinctive advertising posters and handbills for everyone from evangelists, minstrels, and vaudevillians to *Grand Ole Opry* stars and rock stars. The walls are lined with 20,000 photographic plates and carved woodblocks for 500 fonts, one of the largest collections in the world.

Charles and Herbert Hatch, brothers from Wisconsin, founded the print shop. Charles's son William took over in the 1920s and began printing artistic posters for country-music performers; he got the *Grand Ole Opry* account in 1938. New press technologies eventually did in dozens of print shops around Printer's Alley in downtown Nashville, but somehow Hatch survived. The shop is now owned by the Country Music Foundation, which runs it as a nonprofit working museum. Originally located across the street from the Ryman Auditorium on Fourth Avenue, in 1992 South Central Bell paid to move Hatch intact to its present location to make room for a skyscraper.

The printing process Hatch uses, the same as in the Hatch brothers' day, is called letterpress. It involves carving and inking woodblocks, then hand-cranking papers through a heavy roller over and over again for each color. Visitors to Hatch Show Print are encouraged to go behind the counter and watch posters being made, and look through the piles of woodblocks, posters, and artworks.

Hatch has had more jobs in recent years than it can handle. Current clients include Emmylou Harris, ZZ Top, BR-549, Radney Foster, Bill Monroe, Wynonna, Junior Brown, the Mavericks, and dozens of lesser-known bands from all genres from around the country.

Sherraden, who has run Hatch since 1984, also carved the gorgeous prints of Loretta Lynn, Ernest Tubb, Bob Wills, and other classic country artists that appear on the covers of the Country Music Hall of Fame series of recordings. He creates original artwork in the Hatch style for television, radio, books, and commercial ventures.

Jim Sherraden works the presses at Hatch Show Print.

Every Hatch Show Print is different, yet the source is instantly recognizable. "You can come in this place as a seventeen-year-old or a seventy-year-old, a Frenchman or an Alabaman," Sherraden says, "and find something that refers to not only what music you like, but is visually appealing as well."

GETTING THERE: Hatch Show Print is open 9 A.M. to 5:30 P.M. Monday through Friday; 10 A.M. to 5 P.M. Saturdays. Free. 316 Broadway; (615) 256-2805.

To order Hatch Show Prints by mail, call the Country Music Foundation; (800) 255-2357.

ERNEST TUBB RECORD SHOPS

The Texas Troubadour opened the first Ernest Tubb Record Shop on May 3, 1947 in downtown Nashville.

What makes Ernest Tubb Record Shops so great is that if it doesn't have to do with country music, they won't have anything to do with it. The stores carry an excellent selection of country cassettes, CDs, singles, albums, books, videos, and songbooks, including many rare and hard-to-find items.

Ernest Tubb's Midnight Jamboree, still broadcast immediately following the *Grand Ole Opry* on Saturdays, was first performed from the shop. The *Jamboree,* the second-longest continuously running live radio show ever, can now be seen in the Texas Troubadour Theatre next to the Music Valley Road store (*see* Music Valley in this chapter). Ernest Tubb Record Shop also has branches on Nashville's Music Row and in Branson, Missouri; Pigeon Forge, Tennessee; and at the Fort Worth Stockyards in Texas. 417 Broadway; (615) 255-7503; call (800) 229-4288 for mail orders.

COWBOYS LACAGE

Dustin Hoffman, Robin Williams, Patrick Swayze, and Wesley Snipes have all dolled themselves up in major Hollywood feature films, so why can't female impersonators mug for tourists in Music City, U.S.A.? Cross-dressing has become as all-American as, say, Dolly Parton or Reba McEntire. Cowboys LaCage, a happy addition to Nashville's increasingly lively downtown scene, features guys who don wigs, makeup, heels, sequins, and padded bras for outrageous drag send-ups of very impersonate-able country gals such as Dolly, Reba, Minnie Pearl, Loretta Lynn, and Dottie West.

During one recent show, emcee Dennis Russell put his Southern audience at ease by asking them to think of the boys as biscuits and the makeup as gravy. "So what we've got here is a big gravy biscuit," he quipped. One of the few performers who doesn't lip-synch, Russell also does a hilarious Patsy Cline routine singing "Crazy" in voices of everyone from Carol Channing to Elmer Fudd. In addition to country queens, the typical show parodies other popular singers such as Barbra Streisand, Liza Minnelli, and Tina Turner.

Cowboys LaCage is an intimate nightclub with brick walls and red curtains. Appetizers and cocktails are available during the show or in the adjoining bar. Two or three performances are offered nightly Wednesday through Sunday. Admission $15.50. 327 Broadway; (615) COWBOYS (seasonal) or (615) 726-1733.

Music Row
THE REAL MUSIC ROW

If you want to see where all those songs on the radio come from, take a walk around the sleek buildings and funky converted houses of Music Row. This is where would-be country stars "knock on doors," trying to get somebody to listen to their music. Several dozen record companies are based in the ten-block area around 16th Avenue South, including Reba McEntire's Starstruck Entertainment, RCA, and Warner Bros., as are scores of music publishers, recording studios, entertainment lawyers, agents, and other industry-related businesses. Companies often hang banners that advertise their artists' latest hits or awards.

The genesis of today's Music Row can be traced to the mid-1950s, when Harold and Owen Bradley purchased a house on 16th Avenue South and converted it into the Bradley Film and Recording Studio. The Quonset hut they built for the film studio turned out to have remarkable acoustics, and it soon became a preferred recording studio for major labels. Owen produced Loretta Lynn, Patsy Cline, and many other hitmakers here, and Nashville's emerging recording industry took root.

The Country Music Hall of Fame (*see page 226*) is a good place to start a tour of Music Row. (Your admission ticket includes a trolley tour of Music Row and RCA's Studio B.) Or you can simply walk down Music Square East and explore. Souvenir shops in the area sell maps pinpointing various recording companies.

Anchored by the Country Music Hall of Fame, the Music Row known to many tourists is a block-long strip of museums and gift shops on and around Demonbreun Street. Day and night, country music blares from speakers mounted above stores while smiling, enthusiastic street singers belt out hit songs accompanied by prerecorded backup music.

Depending on your perspective, this Music Row is an exciting destination or a big rip-off. The mood is always festive, though, and a few attractions, such as the Hall of Fame and the Hank Williams Museum, are worth special trips.

GETTING THERE: Take I-40 to Exit 209B/Demonbreun St. and follow the signs to Music Row and the Country Music Hall of Fame.

COUNTRY MUSIC HALL OF FAME AND MUSEUM— A CRASH COURSE IN COUNTRY MUSIC

"When I get home, I can tell 'em I sang on the *Grand Ole Opry*," a man remarked with an ear-to-ear grin as he stepped off a section of the original Ryman Auditorium stage in the Country Music Hall of Fame and Museum. The exhibit, which lets you pose in front of a real *Opry* microphone, is one of the museum's crowd pleasers, along with Elvis Presley's solid gold Cadillac, Alan Jackson's "Chattahoochie" water ski, and the guitar Ty England smashed in his infamous television duel with Garth Brooks.

Among the more than 3,000 fascinating items on display is the original pardon signed in 1971 by California governor Ronald Reagan to release Merle Haggard from prison, which reads "the applicant is now a fully rehabilitated member of society"; as well as a letter to songwriter/publisher Fred Rose dated October 31, 1946, that accompanied two songs and reads: "If you can use more at any time, let me know and what type. Let me hear from you. Sincerely, Hank Williams."

However, the Country Music Hall of Fame is much, much more than a collection of cool memorabilia. It's a crash course in country history, and a sincere tribute to the songwriters, musicians, singers, technicians, producers, executives, and fans who make the world of country music tick. Operated by the venerable Country Music Foundation, the museum is a class act. If you can see only one attraction in Nashville, make it the Country Music Hall of Fame.

The museum is especially good for people who don't know much about country, or think they don't like it. A self-guided tour leads visitors from the roots of country and the *Grand Ole Opry*, through the history of Western Swing, bluegrass, Cajun, honky-tonk, the Nashville Sound, and the new traditionalists. Other exhibits feature the art of songwriting using original manuscripts, a hands-on display of instruments, and clips from country movies. A small theater shows rare film clips of Jimmie Rodgers, Hank Williams, Patsy Cline, and other legends. My favorite piece in the museum is Thomas Hart Benton's last painting, *The Sources of Country Music,* a moving tribute to the cultural roots of an American art form.

In 1995, the museum opened a special "Stars and Guitars" exhibit, curated by Chet Atkins. Among the instruments on display is an early Loretta Lynn guitar. She wore out the original pick guard, so her husband Mooney replaced it with Formica.

The best part is the prestigious Hall of Fame itself with bronze plaques featuring a likeness of each artist and a short biography. Since 1961, new members have been selected by an anonymous panel of 200 electors, all heavy hitters in the country music business for at least fifteen years. (The Country Music Association, a separate entity, announces inductees during its annual October awards show.)

Also on site is the invaluable **Country Music Foundation Library and Media Center,** an active research center with more than 160,000 recorded discs; 60,000 historical photographs; 5,000 films and videos; thousands of posters, books, and periodicals; as well as sheet music and hundreds of audio tapes. The reference-desk staff will cheerfully attempt to answer any question, no matter how strange, about country music.

Busting at the seams in its current location, CMF is actively scouting out larger space for the museum and archives. A spokesman said the move likely would not be complete until at least 1998.

Run by Chet Atkins, **RCA's Studio B** was one of the first major recording studios on Music Row (the first was Owen Bradley's studio). Atkins pioneered the smooth, sophisticated "Nashville Sound" that worked so well for Hall of Famers Jim Reeves and Patsy Cline. The formula combined strings, backup vocals by the versatile Jordanaires, and the easygoing "music-by-numbers" style of talented session musicians. Between 1957 and 1977, everyone from Elvis and Dolly Parton to Barbra Streisand and the Beatles recorded here.

GETTING THERE: Open daily 8 A.M. to 6 P.M. Memorial Day through Labor Day, and weekends during May and September; 9 A.M. to 5 P.M. the rest of the year. Admission—which includes, the Hall of Fame, a tour of RCA's Studio B, and a trolley tour of Music Row— $9.95 adults, $4.95 ages 6 to 11. Closed Thanksgiving, Christmas, and New Year's Day. Allow two hours. 4 Music Square East; (800) 816-7652 or (615) 256-1639.

BARBARA MANDRELL COUNTRY

During the seventies and early eighties, Barbara Mandrell was the indisputable Glitter Queen of Country Music, with the number-one hits "I Was Country When Country Wasn't Cool," "Sleeping Single in a Double Bed," and "Till You're Gone." Year after year, she won every country award they gave out: Country Music Association Entertainer of the Year (1980, 1981), Grammy Awards (1982, 1983), and dozens of others. The network variety show *Barbara Mandrell and the Mandrell Sisters* attracted 40 million viewers on Saturday nights during the early eighties.

An unlikely feminist, Mandrell is described, in the excellent book *Finding Her Voice: The Saga of Women in Country Music* by Mary Buffwack and Robert Oermann (New York: Crown, 1993), as "perhaps the toughest soldier in the female army that invaded the country charts in the seventies. Barbara could outwork, outperform, outtalk, and outsmile virtually anyone in show business." Driven more by sheer will and an indefatigable go-getter personality than by any devotion to women's rights, Mandrell nonetheless broke new ground for women.

Sadly, the serious injuries she suffered in a 1984 car accident slowed down Mandrell's career considerably, although she continues to perform and record.

Reflecting her image as a polished, Vegas-style entertainer, Barbara Mandrell Country is one of the slicker establishments on Music Row. You may notice more people in the gift shop than inside the museum, but don't skip the exhibits. The museum feels a little bit stuck in time, but fans won't be disappointed and newcomers will get acquainted with the amazing and appealing Mandrell family.

Barbara Mandrell was a musical prodigy who read music before she could read books, and made her steel-guitar debut in public at age eleven. As a teenager, Mandrell also mastered the banjo, bass guitar, saxophone, accordion, and mandolin. Her sister Louise played bass and fiddle, while Irlene rounded out the trio on drums. As a youngster, Mandrell also toured with Johnny Cash, Patsy Cline, and George Jones. She joined the *Grand Ole Opry* in 1972.

Among the many personal items that are on display at the museum are Mandrell's Chantilly lace wedding dress, sequin-encrusted stage costumes, jewelry, and a Rolls-Royce. Through memorabilia, photographs, and handwritten explanations, the museum shows a very human side of country's Golden Girl, with Mandrell as Christian, wife of Ken Dudney, and mother of Matthew, Jaime, and Nathaniel.

"This is the nightgown I wore on my wedding night," the caption next to her trousseau reads. (Mandrell married Dudney two weeks before her high-school graduation.) "Can you believe I thought it was pretty? I guess it's true that love is blind. The last time I wore this was on May 28, 1993, for our anniversary. I thought it would be a romantic thing to do. I kept asking Ken if he noticed anything special. He didn't have the faintest idea what I was talking about! Men!!!"

In a video at the end of the exhibit, Mandrell shows off "Fontanel," her astounding dream house on 130 acres in the Tennessee hills. The huge log cabin–style mansion has an indoor pool and barbecue pit, soda fountain, hot tub, and the "office," Barbara's elaborate bathroom with a tub constructed to fit her back.

Because Mandrell was born on Christmas Day 1948, her gift shop sells tree ornaments and other Christmas items year-round.

GETTING THERE: Across from the Country Music Hall of Fame. Allow an hour. Admission $6 for adults, free for children under age 12. 1510 Division St.; (615) 242-7800.

HANK WILLIAMS, JR., FAMILY TRADITION MUSEUM—
OLD HANK AND LITTLE BOCEPHUS

I almost didn't visit the Hank Williams, Jr., Family Tradition Museum, simply because it was so hard to find. The gift shop was easy enough to locate, but the museum entrance is hidden in the back of a jewelry shop next door. I'm glad I made the effort; the collection is a good introduction to the Williams family. Gift shops are a Williams "family tradition" anyway: during the height of their fame, Hank Jr.'s parents had a Western-wear shop at 724 Commerce St. in downtown Nashville called Hank and Audrey's Corral.

After seeing the museum, I respect Hank Jr.'s ability to get through an extremely difficult childhood and succeed. Hank Williams, Sr., was the ultimate tough act to follow. In his short but extremely productive career, the elder Williams turned the country music world upside down. According to *The Illustrated History of Country Music,* (New York: Times Books, 1995), "What he did, quite simply, was rise to the top of the business faster than anyone has ever risen, before or since, and became in the process the finest songwriter, one of the finest performers, and the most influential figure that country music has ever produced."

The museum is pretty straightforward about Hank Jr.'s and Hank Sr.'s lives and problems. The displays take you from Hank Sr.'s boyhood in Georgiana, Alabama, where he learned his craft from a black street performer called "Uncle Tee-Tot," to his historic first *Grand Ole Opry* appearance in 1949, to his death in the backseat of a powder-blue Cadillac on New Year's Day 1953; his song "I'll Never Get Out of This World Alive" was at the top of the charts.

Hank Jr. was three years old when his father died. By the time Hank Jr. was eight, Audrey Williams had "Little Bocephus" performing his father's songs onstage, forcing him to parrot Hank Sr.'s singing style, clothing, and mannerisms.

It's no wonder that when Hank Jr. finally broke away, he did so with a vengeance that nearly killed him. According to one of the videos at the museum, by his late teens Hank Jr. was "living out the lyrics of a bad country song." He hit the skids, drinking hard for more than two years and attempting suicide by an overdose of Darvon. When he pulled himself out from under the weight of his father's image, Hank Jr. developed the raucous, rowdy Southern-rock style that has made him an international star.

The museum has some great, albeit lurid, items, such as Hank Sr.'s "death car" and the blue cowboy suit and leather slippers he was wearing when he died. Hank Jr., an avid hunter and fisherman like his dad, shows off some trophies, including a lion bagged in Africa, and a domestic bobcat and wolf.

There's also a display on Merle Kilgore, an important singer and songwriter who is now Hank Jr.'s full-time manager. Predictably, Jett Williams, Hank Jr.'s half sister who was born five days after Hank Sr.'s death, is not mentioned, although her biography is on sale in the gift shop.

Hard-core Hank Sr. fans will find several other points of interest in town. One of his former houses was moved to the top of Music Row years ago. The plain red-brick ranch house failed as a tourist attraction, and is now the Music Machine recording studio. It's up the street from the museum at the corner of 17th Ave. S. and Division. Hank and Audrey's house at 4916 Franklin Rd. is now occupied by Tammy Wynette. It can be viewed from the road, but is not open to tourists.

(*See also:* Tennessee—Crossville; Alabama—Montgomery, Georgiana.)

GETTING THERE: Admission $4. Allow an hour. 1524 Demonbreun; (615) 242-8313.

MORE ON MUSIC ROW

The **Country Music Wax Museum** portrays several dozen stars including Jimmie Rodgers, "The Singing Brakeman," strumming his guitar in front of a railway station; Jim Reeves standing with golf clubs in a wood-paneled office; and Merle Travis and Chet Atkins warming up in a dressing room. Admission $5.50 adults. 118 16th Ave. S.; (615) 256-2490.

The **LeGarde Twins Country Music Theatre** is a charming little showplace attached to the Quality Inn behind the Country Music Hall of Fame. Ted and Tom LeGarde play songs from the forties to the nineties, including their novelty hit "Tie Me Kangaroo Down Sport," with a bit of gospel, bluegrass, and comedy thrown in. Dinner and drinks are served in the adjoining restaurant. 1407 Division St.; (615) 251-7007.

George Jones is the greatest. Unfortunately, the **George Jones Gift Shop and Mini-Museum** is not. "Mini" is the operative word. In the back of a big gift shop, in which most items have nothing to do with Jones, a single case displays a disorganized smattering of Jones's gold records, photos, and stage costumes. The most interesting item is the pair of boxing gloves worn by Jones to spar with George Foreman in the "I Don't Need Your Rocking Chair" video. Admission is free. 27 Music Circle East (across the street from the Hank Williams, Jr., Museum); (615) 255-9119. If you really want to learn about "the Possum," visit the *Grand Ole Opry* Museum at Opryland.

The **Car Collector's Hall of Fame** displays some fun Cars of the Stars, including Roy Acuff's last road car and Marty Robbins's 1934 Packard. Admission $5 adults, $3 children. 1534 Demonbreun; (615) 255-6804.

The **Ernest Tubb Record Shop No. 3** has a terrific selection of country recordings and books. 1516 Demonbreun; (615) 244-2845. **Conway's Twitty Bird Record Shop** also sells recordings and souvenirs. 1530 Demonbreun; (615) 242-2466.

HOUNDOGS ARE KING

Loud music blasts from the speakers above Houndogs, the hippest hillbilly hot-dog hut in Music City. Sure, it's just a little trailer in a parking lot across the street from Barbara Mandrell Country, but as far as hot-dog stands go, this is about as cool as they come. Owner "Flash" Flanigan sells hot dogs, corn dogs, fries, and fresh lemonade. And like any respectable country eating establishment, signed photos of star patrons, like Tim McGraw ("Gimme that dog!"), Kenny Chesney ("Thanks for all the dogs!"), and Johnny Paycheck ("The best hot dogs in the world.") flank the trailer's windows. Ain't no doubt about it, Houndogs are King. (Photo by Anne Paine)

Opryland U.S.A.

Opryland U.S.A., owned by Gaylord Entertainment, encompasses 750 acres and numerous attractions, including Opryland Theme Park, the *Grand Ole Opry,* WSM Radio, several museums, the Opryland Hotel, Springhouse Golf Course, the **General Jackson River-**

boat. Gaylord, the dominant force in Nashville's tourist industry, also owns the Ryman Auditorium, Wildhorse Saloon and River Taxis, the Nashville Network, Country Music Television, and Z Music. If Nashville succeeds in luring a professional sports team to their new arena at 5th and Broadway, Gaylord will probably own it, too.

Opryland U.S.A. offers several different packages, bundling together attractions. Before purchasing separate admission tickets to Opryland attractions, call ahead or check at the ticket booth to see if a package will save you money. If you'd prefer to let someone else do the driving, **Grand Ole Opry Sightseeing Tours** will take you by bus to historical sites, Music City attractions, or tours of the stars' homes.

GETTING THERE: Opryland U.S.A. is 9 miles northeast of downtown Nashville between I-40 and I-65 off Briley Parkway/Exit 11. For information about all Opryland attractions including the theme park, the *Grand Ole Opry,* Nashville on Stage, and the *General Jackson,* call (615) 889-6611.

PARKING AT OPRYLAND

Unless you're staying at the Opryland Hotel or in Music Valley, Opryland U.S.A. is not convenient. There are few ways to get there except by car. (River taxis run from downtown Nashville to Opryland but they cost $9.95 round-trip.) Otherwise, there's no way to avoid Opryland's $4 parking fee. If you plan to visit Opryland four or more times during your stay, you can save money by purchasing a season parking pass for $15.

Be aware that the parking lot does not have numbered rows or spaces. To avoid spending a half-hour in the hot sun trying to locate your car in one of 8,800 spots, park on the aisle or write down precise directions.

OPRYLAND THEME PARK

Opryland has everything other theme parks have: roller coasters, a flume ride that will get you drenched, plenty of gift shops and snack stands, long, sweaty lines, boisterous teenagers, and excited children.

What sets Opryland apart from the other amusement parks is the musical entertainment. The shows at Opryland are uniformly terrific. On any given day, there are a dozen different shows to choose from featuring country, bluegrass, rock, popular music, and comedy, in addition to magic and special entertainment for kids.

Opryland conducts annual talent searches in 40 cities and recruits hundreds of enthusiastic young singers, dancers, musicians, and production staff. Graduates of Opryland include Chely Wright, Jon Randall, members of Little Texas and Diamond Rio, and "literally scores of people making their livings on Broadway," spokesman Tom Adkinson says.

The performers work hard, and if doing four shows a day is getting to them, no one can tell. There are no weak links in Opryland's entertainment chain; everyone on both sides of the stage smiles and enjoys himself.

Try to see as many shows as possible. Pick up a schedule at the turnstile and plan your day around the ones you want to see. If so inclined, you could spend a whole day or more being entertained and never set foot on a ride.

Opryland's headline concert series, **Nashville on Stage,** presents more than 700 performances over 150 days. George Jones and Tammy Wynette, Patty Loveless, Lorrie Morgan, Sammy Kershaw, and 25 others perform throughout the summer in the 4,000-seat Chevrolet/GEO Celebrity Theater. Admission to Opryland theme park is not required. Prices range from $14.95 to $21.95.

Opryland has five "theme" areas: New Orleans, State Fair, American West, Doo Wah Diddy City, and Opry Village. There are more than twenty rides, ranging from a tame gondola ride above the park, to the Hangman, an $8 million inverted roller coaster with four 360-degree loops, and the Skycoaster, a 152-foot swing akin to bungee-jumping.

Benches and shady spots are plentiful, and in my experience, the Opryland staff is unfailingly courteous and helpful.

Food choices range from frozen lemonade and corn dogs at snack bars to large Southern-style meals at Jeanne Pruett's Feedin' Friends, Cafe Mardi Gras, and Riverside Plantation restaurants. Candy, music, souvenirs, and gifts also are for sale. As an added bonus, *Grand Ole Opry* stars often sign autographs at a booth inside the park.

Opryland stages **special events** throughout the year, including celebrations for Easter, Independence Day, "Howl-O-Ween," and Christmas; Gospel Jubilees on Memorial Day and Labor Day weekends; the BellSouth Senior Classic at Springhouse Golf Club in early June; the TNN Salute to Motorsports in late August; and the *Grand Ole Opry* Birthday Celebration in mid-October.

GETTING THERE: Opryland Theme Park is open weekends mid-March through April; Fridays, Saturdays, and Sundays in early May, mid-September, and October; and daily late May through Labor Day. The park opens at 10 A.M. Closing times vary throughout the year. One-day admission $26.95; $16.95 for ages 4 to 11. Allow up to a full day. Call (615) 889-6611.

THE NASHVILLE NETWORK

For cable television's The Nashville Network (TNN), one of the perks of being located at Opryland is a built-in studio audience. For people at the park, it's an opportunity to relax in an air-conditioned studio, see how a real television show is made, and perhaps be on the air themselves.

The TNN studio at Opryland hosts tapings of an evening variety show year-round, *The Statler Brothers Show* in the winter, and numerous specials throughout the year. A TNN taping is a lot of fun for the studio audience. In addition to the thrill of seeing big stars up close, you get to watch a working television studio in action, with moving sets, scrambling technicians, and a guy whose job is to make sure the audience claps at the right times.

Audiences are always needed, and most tapings are free. The TNN studio is inside the Opryland turnstiles, but you do not need to purchase park admission to see a taping. Schedules and tickets are available by calling Opryland's main number a few weeks in advance (615) 889-6611. (You may want to bring a sweater; the studio is air-conditioned to the hilt.)

Ralph Emery's popular talk show is taped live in the mornings at the Opryland Hotel. On Tuesday and Wednesday evenings, TNN also tapes a dance show from the floor of the Wildhorse Saloon in downtown Nashville. (*See the District—this chapter.*)

THE GENERAL JACKSON

The *General Jackson,* a paddle-wheel riverboat said to be the largest in the world, offers sightseeing, dining, and entertainment cruises. The $12 million showboat is 300 feet long with four decks, and its on-board Victorian Theater seats 1,000 people. The typical cruise offers beautiful scenery, food, stage shows, strolling musicians, and comedians.

Steve Hall and his popular puppet, Shotgun Red, perform on the midday cruise. Specialty cruises vary from month to month, and include evening and midnight cruises, tours of Old Hickory Lake, holiday events, and a New Year's Eve extravaganza. As many as five cruises per day leave from Opryland year-round. Morning and day cruises, $16.95; evening outings with dinner, $44.95 ($33.95 for children). Call (615) 889-6611.

THE GRAND OLE OPRY—SIMPLE AS SUNSHINE

The *Grand Ole Opry,* the longest-running radio show in history, has been broadcast live over WSM (650-AM) ("We Shield Millions") since 1925. After outgrowing several spaces in downtown Nashville, the *Opry* settled into the Ryman Auditorium at Fourth and Broadway. From 1943 through 1974, happy audiences watched the show from hard wooden pews in the un-air-conditioned tabernacle.

In 1974, the show moved to swankier digs at Opryland, several miles east of the city. The new Opry House is bigger, more comfortable, and climate-controlled, with better backstage facilities. Still, many people felt that leaving the Ryman behind tore the heart out of the *Grand Ole Opry.*

However, the *Opry* has always been a commercial venture, run by corporate executives to make money. Although the Ryman will always be its spiritual home, the *Opry* did not sell its soul by moving to Opryland. The show maintained its down-home charm; the formula is exactly the same.

There are no rehearsals, and the lineup isn't determined until a day or two before the show. Performances are broken into half-hour segments, each sponsored by an advertiser and hosted by an *Opry* star. For example, during Hank Snow's segment, a slide for Kraft macaroni and cheese is projected onto the familiar red barn. Snow will do a number, then introduce Skeeter Davis, who will do several songs. After introducing Jim Ed Brown and Charlie Walker for a few songs each, Snow will close out the set as the heavy red curtain comes down. Since the *Opry* is a live radio show, announcers on the side of the stage prompt the audience to applaud. During short breaks they record commercials.

About 25 different acts take the stage during a typical three-hour performance. A premium is placed on variety; the *Opry* is a mix of individual singers, groups, instrumentals, comedians, and cloggers. In addition to the *Opry* "cast" (more than 70 are on the roster), talented newcomers and guest artists often perform. Regulars include Bill Anderson, Little Jimmy Dickens, Jim and Jesse, Grandpa Jones, Bill Monroe, the Whites, and Jeannie Seely. Although you're most likely to see old favorites, there's always a chance that popular stars such as Holly Dunn, Hal Ketchum, Garth Brooks, Marty Stuart, or Randy Travis will appear.

Like most country shows, the *Opry* allows members of the audience to walk up to the front of the stage and photograph the performers. Most performers eat it up, waving and mugging for the cameras.

If you ever have the opportunity to go backstage at the *Opry*, don't miss it. Passes aren't that hard to come by, if you're persistent and ply all your contacts. Fan clubs and friends in the business are a good place to start. Once backstage, you can wander around among the performers, peering into Porter's dressing room, drinking lemonade with Grandpa Jones in the waiting room, taking pictures from the sidelines, and watching the show from one of the relocated Ryman pews at the back of the stage.

George D. Hay, known as the Solemn Old Judge, was the original announcer for the *Opry* and gave the show its name. Before his death in 1968, Hay described the *Opry* as "simple as sunshine. It has universal appeal because it is built upon goodwill, and with folk music it expresses the heartbeat of a large percentage of Americans who labor for a living." His words are still true today.

(*See also: Grand Ole Opry* Museum [*see page 240*]; Ryman Auditorium—this chapter; Arkansas—Mammoth Spring.)

GETTING THERE: Shows take place on Friday and Saturday nights, with matinees on Tuesdays during the summer. Tickets $18 at night, $16 for matinees. You do not need to purchase admission to Opryland to attend the *Grand Ole Opry.* Call (615) 889-6611.

G E T   Y E R   G O O   G O O !

Ten steps for obtaining nourishment during the *Grand Ole Opry:*
1) Walk to snack bar. 2) Pick up pretty silver package with bright red letters. Notice how perfectly it fits in your palm. Purchase **Goo Goo Cluster.** Return to seat. 3) Rip open package and remove Goo Goo Cluster. Admire the hefty, lumpy, creamy-brown blob of chocolate, caramel, marshmallow, and nuts. 4) Take a large bite. 5) Chew. Chew. Chew. 6) Chew. Chew. Chew. 7) Swallow. 8) Repeat steps 4 through 7. 9) When no more Goo Goo Cluster remains, lick fingers. 10) Repeat steps 1 through 9.

It's a common misperception that "Goo Goo," as in Goo Goo Cluster, stands for *Grand Ole Opry,* perhaps because the item is a staple in any respectable *Opry*-goer's diet. Well, fans, it's not true.

According to the official *Goo Goo History* published by Nashville's Standard Candy Company, the world's first-ever combination candy bar was concocted in 1912, more than a decade before the Solemn Ole Judge announced the first *WSM Barn Dance* in 1925 (renamed the *Grand Ole Opry* two years later). Standard candy-maker Howell Campbell, Sr., and plant superintendent Porter Moore mixed up the first batch in a copper kettle. The candy was a hit; the recipe has not changed for more than eighty years.

Among the many stories about how the candy was named, two prevail. One version refers to the first thing a baby says. The other, more plausible, story, related by Mr. Campbell's son, is that the inventor discussed the dilemma with fellow passengers on the streetcar he took to work. The name Goo Goo was simply suggested one morning by a schoolteacher and stuck, like caramel on the roof of the mouth.

Wherever the name comes from, it certainly is right for this perfect candy. You can find Goo Goos at the *Grand Ole Opry*, stores in Nashville, and throughout the South. Everyone else must order by mail. A box of six Goo Goos costs about $3.50. Call (800) 231-3402 or (615) 889-6360 for a mail-order catalogue of Standard candies.

GRAND OLE OPRY, MINNIE PEARL, AND ROY ACUFF MUSEUMS—OPRYLAND ON A BUDGET

Unfortunately, too few among the hordes that visit Opryland's theme park every year take the time to visit the *Grand Ole Opry* Museum, Minnie Pearl Museum, or Roy Acuff's Museum and Musical Instruments. All three are excellent, and they're free. If you can't afford or aren't in the mood for the theme park, it's well worth a trip out to Opryland to see them, as well as the amazing Opryland Hotel and the Starwalk.

My favorite is the **Grand Ole Opry Museum,** to the right of the ticket booths at Opryland's main entrance. The museum is designed in the style of the Ryman Auditorium, with red-brick alleys and tabernacle-style stained-glass windows. The museum is entered through a Ryman-esque doorway onto a mock *Opry* stage. Later on, visitors walk through a back alley into a model of Tootsie's Orchid Lounge, just as *Opry* stars did on Saturday nights between sets. The Ryman theme unifies the exhibits and shows proper reverence for the *Opry*'s traditions and past.

The museum itself is actually a series of mini-museums devoted to major *Opry* figures: Hank Snow, Patsy Cline, Marty Robbins, Jim Reeves, Little Jimmie Dickens, and George Jones. In addition to memorabilia and chronologies of the stars' lives and careers, interactive screens show videos of Snow singing "I'm Movin' On," or discuss how the Possum earned his prior reputation as "No-Show" Jones. Displays include a re-creation of Patsy Cline's den, with "Patsy and Charlie" written in brass studs on a red leatherette bar; Marty Robbins's race car; and the original equipment used by

The Grand Ole Opry *Museum features exhibits on past and present Opry stars. (Gaylord Entertainment)*

Reeves in Henderson, Texas. A whole room is devoted to contemporary *Opry* stars such as Reba McEntire, Vince Gill, Patty Loveless, and Garth Brooks.

For more than half a century, Minnie Pearl and pal Roy Acuff embodied the heart and spirit of the *Grand Ole Opry,* happy ambassadors for country music all over America and the world. The **Minnie Pearl Museum,** across a plaza from the *Grand Ole Opry* Museum, is as touching, sweet, and funny as the *Opry* comedienne herself. In 1990, Pearl (her real name is Sarah Colley Cannon, but even close friends called her Minnie) celebrated fifty years of entertaining with stories of Brother and all the folks from Grinder's Switch, Tennessee. About a year later, she suffered a severe stroke that kept her out of the public's loving eye. She died in early 1996.

The homey museum features a carefully selected collection of awards, memorabilia, and photographs, with charming hand-lettered explanations. Also on display is a diorama of Grinder's Switch, and a 15-foot model of Pearl's famous flower-festooned straw hat. Hilarious videos play constantly on a large video screen. (*See also:* Centerville—*this chapter.*)

Roy Acuff's Museum and Musical Instruments, next door to Minnie Pearl's museum, houses his wonderful collection of stringed instruments. The "King of Country Music," whose reign ended with his death in 1992 at the age of eighty-nine, was enormously popular during the forties and fifties. As cofounder of Acuff-Rose, he pioneered Nashville's music-publishing industry and became a rich man. In 1962, Acuff was the first living person elected to the Country Music Hall of Fame.

Dozens of rare and unusual dobros, mandolins, banjos, dulcimers, guitars, fiddles, Russian balalaikas, and African instruments are displayed in cases and along the walls. The tasteful museum was renovated in 1994, and now includes a display on making stringed instruments. Acuff memorabilia is scattered throughout, including his coin and yo-yo collections and gifts from fans. (*See also:* Union County—*this chapter.*)

In the plaza between the *Grand Ole Opry* Museum and the Opry House itself, Opry stars leave hand- and footprints on the **Starwalk,** blocks of cement on pedestals with personal messages from Garth Brooks, Mary Chapin Carpenter, Loretta Lynn, and others.

GETTING THERE: The museums are open daily year-round, even when Opryland theme park isn't. They are also open on evenings of *Grand Ole Opry* performances. Allow up to three hours for all three. Free. Call Opryland for specific hours; (615) 889-6611.

OPRYLAND HOTEL—GARDEN PARTY

The largest hotel property in Tennessee, Opryland Hotel has 1,900 rooms, two swimming pools, a golf course, convention facilities, shops and boutiques, restaurants, bars, and clubs. A major expansion will add nearly 1,000 new rooms, a theme restaurant, and a huge amphitheater.

Opryland Hotel is not impressive merely because of its sheer size. What makes the place so awesome are the incredible, one-of-a-kind indoor gardens, complete with rushing water and thousands of lush green plants.

The showpiece is the Conservatory, a two-acre greenhouse flanked by six stories of New Orleans–style iron balconies and topped by a one-acre skylight. The Conservatory is a horticulturist's paradise, with hundreds of plant species and banana, palm, and orange trees. A crystal gazebo lights up at night.

A second enormous garden called the Cascades features three waterfalls crashing into a 12,500-square-foot lake. In the center of the Cascades is "Dancing Waters," a water display once part of Liberace's act. All day and well into the night, hundreds of jets of water shoot into the air, synchronized to music in wild, colorful rhythms. The rotating Cascades Terrace restaurant provides patrons with optimum views of the spectacular scene. (Remember, this is all indoors!)

A multimillion-dollar expansion, scheduled for completion in the summer of 1996, will add a third, even larger, interior landscape called the Delta, which will cover more than four acres with gardens, a 560-foot-long moving sidewalk, 85-foot fountain, and 110-foot-wide waterfall.

The studios of **WSM Radio,** broadcaster of the *Grand Ole Opry,* are located just off the Magnolia Lobby. Tall windows allow you to observe a real radio station in action, and see live interviews with the stars. The **Country Music Disc Jockey's Hall of Fame** is next to WSM, with several rows of plaques honoring Ralph Emery, Grant Turner, Tom Perryman, and others.

Places to eat include Rhett's, a restaurant with a *Gone with the Wind* theme; Rachel's Kitchen, named for Andrew Jackson's gracious wife; and Old Hickory Restaurant, which serves elegant Continental fare. For entertainment, try the Stagedoor Lounge, featuring live country bands and a large dance floor, or Jack Daniel's Saloon, a bar with snacks and live music.

Opryland Hotel is as exciting as any Vegas showplace, but is splendid instead of garish. By all means, stay there if you can afford it. (Standard double rooms cost $179 per night.) If you can't, there's no excuse not to check it out. Viewing the gardens at night, lit by twinkling multicolored lights, is a terrific way to complete the evening after the *Opry* or a show on Music Valley Road.

GETTING THERE: From I-40 or I-65, take Briley Parkway/Exit 12 to McGavock Pike. Allow an hour. 2800 Opryland Drive; (615) 889-1000.

Music Valley

Capitalizing on the traffic from Opryland, Music Valley is a slicker version of Music Row featuring hotels, restaurants, museums, and gifts shops. The best attractions are Willie Nelson's museum, Bobby's Bare Trap gift shop, and E.T.'s *Green Hornet* tour bus inside the Ernest Tubb Record Shop. Live entertainment is plentiful at Nashville Palace, Nashville Breakfast Theater, and two new country-music venues, the Texas Troubadour and Stardust Theatres. Music Valley Road and the Music Valley Village are within walking distance of Opryland Hotel. **Shotgun Red's Collection,** featuring the "Shotmobile," is next door to the **Music Valley Car Museum.** The latter includes 45 vehicles, such as Hank Williams, Jr.'s Cadillac, George Jones's DeLorean, and Randy Travis's Mustang. Open 8 A.M. to 8:30 P.M. Admission $5 for both museums, $2 for ages 6 to 12. 2611 McGavock Pike; (615) 885-7400.

In front of the **Music Valley Wax Museum of the Stars,** the "Sidewalk of the Stars" features large blocks of cement with hand- and footprints of the famous and not-so-famous. It's fun to see which parts of their bodies stars commit to concrete and what they decide to write. Inside are more than fifty full-size wax figures of stars such as Crystal Gayle, Eddy Arnold, Merle Haggard, Stringbean, Grandpa Jones, Tom T. Hall, and Ronnie Milsap. Admission $3.50. 2515 McGavock Pike; (615) 883-3612.

Music Valley Village is a mall with the Stardust and Texas Troubadour Theatres (*see below*) and stores selling souvenirs, clothing, and gifts. Among them is the **Alabama** shop, peddling the supergroup's souvenirs; (615) 883-3415. **Bobby's Bare Trap** is an adorable shop filled with hundreds of teddy bears of every size and shape. The "largest teddy bear in the world" is a ten-by-ten-foot brown monster with a huge red bow, nicknamed "Big T." The star advertises "free bare hugs" when he's in town; (615) 872-8440.

GETTING THERE: Music Valley is across the street from the Opryland Hotel. Take Briley Parkway to Exit 12/McGavock Pike.

WILLIE NELSON AND FRIENDS FAMILY MUSEUM

Willie Nelson and Friends Family Museum is a tribute to all the people Willie admires and loves. Anyone who knows anything about Willie knows he's usually surrounded by plenty of people and lots of love.

Willie's second wife, Shirley, from whom he split in 1969, wrote in 1988: "I have never come close to remarrying. I can't make a commitment to anyone, because I love Willie. I'm happy with that. At last, I can handle knowing there's nobody else for me."

And Biff Collie, a record executive and disc jockey who was married to Shirley when she met Willie, wrote: "If there's any man I'd like to have run off with my wife, it would be Willie Nelson. . . . People would phone and say, 'Don't you know that S.O.B. stole your wife? Why do you keep playing his records on your show?' I'd say, 'Hell, it's my job to play the best music, and Willie is one of the best no matter whose wife he's with.' "

That's the kind of love Willie inspires.

Other tried-and-true members of the "I Love Willie" Society: the Country Music Hall of Fame, which inducted him in 1993; millions of fans who buy his records and concert tickets year after year; critics, who love his ability to experiment with new styles and musical accomplices (in 1994 he recorded and toured with a 100-string orchestra); and America's family farmers, whose plight Willie has tirelessly championed.

The museum is located at the back of the **Music Valley Gift Emporium,** billed as "Nashville's Largest Gift Shop." Enter through the swinging doors, and you're in the completely lovable world of Willie. A series of large rooms are filled with memorabilia. Willie has assembled tribute cases for his idols and the people he loves, including Webb Pierce; "Tootsie" Bess of Tootsie's Orchid Lounge; Faron Young; and Lloyd Lindroth, the flamboyant Opryland harpist who died in 1994.

Prized pieces include Marty Robbins's piano, the silver watch Patsy Cline was wearing when she died, and an Indian headdress presented by an Oklahoma tribe in 1987. A Seeburg Selectomatic 100 jukebox plays songs by Elvis, Mel Tillis, and Bobby Bare for 25¢. Sitting on an overstuffed couch, you can watch videos of Willie singing "Valentine" and "On the Road Again," as well as clips from his movies.

GETTING THERE: Open daily 8 A.M. to 9 P.M. Allow an hour. Admission $2. 2613A McGavock Pike; (615) 885-1515.

NASHVILLE PALACE: "YOU MIGHT SEE THE NEXT RANDY TRAVIS"

Nashville Palace is a dark, woodsy restaurant with a small stage, tiled dance floor, and walls covered with signed photographs. The biggest one is of Randy Travis, who got his start here on the Wednesday-night employee showcase.

The ghosts of prospective Randy Travises haunt the place. On a Tuesday night during the summer, Nashville Palace is nearly packed for "New Talent Night." The emcee reminds the itchy crowd, "You never know. You might see the next Randy Travis or Lorrie Morgan up here." The air is thick with promise and possibility.

The staff hands out ballots to the audience before the showcase gets under way. The singers are all earnest, and in most cases, talented but unpracticed as they plow through their two songs onstage. Each performs an up-tempo number and a ballad. The house band, fronted by Steve Hill, does an energetic job backing them up.

In this city of dreams, where nine out of ten times your cab driver is pursuing a career in country music, it's thrilling and heartbreaking to watch.

On other nights, the live entertainment features Hill, Granny Johnson, Dianne Sherrill, and the Nashville Palace Band. During the summer, *Grand Ole Opry* stars play on Monday nights. The restaurant is known for prime rib and catfish. The bar has a happy hour in the early evening, with hot and cold snacks.

GETTING THERE: Shows begin at 8 P.M. Cover charge $5 most nights. 2400 Music Valley Rd.; (615) 885-1540.

ERNEST TUBB RECORD SHOP NO. 2, TEXAS TROUBADOUR THEATRE, AND THE *GREEN HORNET*

Nashville has lagged behind other cities in offering inexpensive country shows in small venues. The Texas Troubadour Theatre, a 600-seat showplace adjoining the renovated Ernest Tubb Record Shop No. 2 in Music Valley Village, opened in April 1995 and music

Kitty Wells and family perform at the Texas Troubadour Theatre soon after its opening in 1995.

fans felt it was about time. "This is long overdue for Nashville," manager Lloyd Pearson says. "We feel that once this catches on, bigger theaters will come in and the whole scene will take off."

In its first season, the theater showcased Kitty Wells, her husband Johnny Wright, and their son, Bobby Wright. Bobby is energetic, Johnny is earnest and endearing, and Kitty's voice is clear and sweet. Onstage, the family's routine is to poke and annoy each other for the amusement of the audience.

Ernest Tubb's Midnight Jamboree has moved to the Texas Troubadour from its longtime Broadway location. The second-longest continuously running radio show in America after the *Grand Ole Opry,* the *Jamboree* features new and established country talent. It's performed live between midnight and 1 A.M. on Saturday nights and is broadcast over WSM (650-AM). There is no charge to watch the *Jamboree.*

Along with an outstanding selection of country recordings, the record shop displays E.T. memorabilia and photos, along with the *Green Hornet* tour bus used by Tubb and the Texas Troubadours from 1971 to 1979. The bus is outfitted with gold- and black-tooled leather, a reel-to-reel tape player, six stacked cots with brown covers, and six lockers. Tubb had a private room in the back, with a sign on the door that read, "The boss may not always be right, but he's always the boss."

"We feel we're keeping the tradition of Ernest Tubb alive," says Wayne Chandler, marketing director for the Texas Troubadour Theatre. "He was so dear to people's hearts. I've seen some folks walk on the *Green Hornet* and have to step right off because it's so emotional for them."

GETTING THERE: Texas Troubadour Theatre shows are about $12 adults, $5 children. Call for schedules and times. 2416 Music Valley Dr., #108; (615) 885-0028.

STARDUST THEATRE

It wasn't long after Boots Randolph shut down his nightclub on Printer's Alley that the "Yakety Sax Man" caught the performing bug again. Less than a year later, he invested in the 614-seat Stardust Theatre in Music Valley Village. Opened in May 1995, the Stardust is another exciting showplace for Nashville.

Since his first hit with "Yakety Sax" in 1963, Randolph has recorded more than 40 albums and collaborated with Elvis Presley, Chet Atkins, and Johnny Cash. Randolph performs regularly with veteran band leader Danny Davis and the Nashville Brass.

GETTING THERE: Shows Monday through Saturday, 8 P.M. Tickets $15; $5 children under age 12. 2416 Music Valley Dr., #140; (615) 889-2992.

NASHVILLE BREAKFAST THEATER

Jeannie Seely, Del Reeves, and other *Grand Ole Opry* stars perform regularly at the Nashville Breakfast Theater, accompanied by Katherine Kay, Linda Juma, and Willie Rainsford and the Early Times Band. The show is upbeat and entertaining, a fine way to start the day. The all-you-can-eat breakfast, served at 8 A.M., includes ham, eggs, sausage, grits, biscuits, gravy, and cereal. Tickets $17.95. 2620 Music Valley Dr. in Nashville Nightlife Building (formerly Gilley's); (615) 329-2091.

Around Nashville

JIM REEVES MUSEUM—REMEMBERING GENTLEMAN JIM

Unfortunately, many museums bearing stars' names are little more than glorified gift shops. The star throws together a few personal mementos, some stage costumes and gold records, and surrounds them with T-shirts, compact discs, and souvenir mugs. On the other hand, a *good* star museum respectfully satisfies the fan's thirst for background and personal information about their hero. The best star museums make fans out of people who didn't know much about the star to begin with.

The Jim Reeves Museum is one of the latter. After Reeves's death in a 1964 plane crash, his widow, Mary Reeves Davis, bought a historic 1794 plantation at Evergreen Place, which Reeves had often admired. "It was a farmhouse and he grew up on a farm," Davis explains. "He'd say, 'That would be a nice place to retire, to sit on the porch and swing on the swing.' " Davis fulfilled Reeves's wish by converting the white-brick manor into a museum. It sits on five quiet, shady acres off Briley Parkway, a few miles north of Opryland.

"Gentleman Jim" was the consummate country crooner and practitioner of the Nashville Sound. Chet Atkins produced all of Reeves's 400 recordings at RCA's Studio B, including "He'll Have to Go," "Distant Drums," and "Am I Losing You." Reeves joined the *Grand Ole Opry* in 1955 and was elected to the Country Music Hall of Fame in 1967 after his death at age thirty-nine.

Visitors get a guided tour through Reeves's professional and personal life. "To me the saddest thing in the museum are his boots," tour guide Joan Morrissey says. "You can tell he just lived in them." Of Reeves's famous red jacket, Morrissey explains, "He wore red a lot because he felt like it looked better onstage. But his favorite color was blue." According to Morrissey, the young Elvis idolized Reeves, and, nervous before his first performance on the *Louisiana Hayride,* begged Reeves to push him onstage so he wouldn't chicken out.

The museum displays memorabilia from Reeves's early days as a minor-league baseball player and disc jockey for KGRI in Henderson, Texas; plenty of gold records and awards; and replicas of his and Mary's den and bedroom. A somewhat morbid exhibit shows the circumstances of the plane crash, along with the billfold in Reeves's pocket and the diamond ring he was wearing at the time. The bodies of Reeves and band member Dean Manuel weren't discovered for three days.

Outside the museum, visitors can wander around the lovely grounds, look over Reeves's 1960 Cadillac El Dorado, and peer into his and Mary's bunk on his tour bus. A short walk from the house is a stream and a small stone structure which housed one of Nashville's first schools. (Reeves is buried with his dog Shepherd in a small park near Carthage, Texas, where he was born.)

Davis, who lives nearby in Madison, runs Jim Reeves Enterprises on the premises and often drops by the gift shop to greet tourists. "Most of the visitors know about Jim and enjoy seeing personal items," Davis says. "That's just a pleasure people have." She explains that the museum is as relaxed and enjoyable as Reeves's music: "There's nothing frantic about it."

(*See also:* Texas—Carthage.)

GETTING THERE: Open daily 9 A.M. to 5 P.M. Allow an hour. Admission $5. From Briley Parkway, take Exit 14B/Gallatin Rd. south and turn right on Joyce Lane. 1023 Joyce Lane; (615) 226-2062.

KITTY WELLS AND JOHNNY WRIGHT FAMILY COUNTRY JUNCTION

With her sensational 1952 hit, "It Wasn't God Who Made Honky-Tonk Angels," Kitty Wells blazed a trail for female artists in the male-dominated world of country music. Wells (born Muriel Deason) was named the top female artist by trade magazines every year from 1952 to 1965, and was elected to the Country Music Hall of Fame in 1976.

She has been married to singer Johnny Wright since 1939; their son, Bobby, is a singer/songwriter and former television star.

Despite her incredible career, Wells is an unlikely Queen of Country Music, an unpretentious woman who never got caught up in the glitter and glamour. When Wells was inducted into the Country Music Hall of Fame, Minnie Pearl had this to say about her: "She came into the world of country music bringing with her a quiet manner, a deeply religious nature, and a sense of dignity and integrity apparent to everyone who has known her. Her unique talent lies in the fact that she is a *pure* country singer. She sings from the heart, and her voice is the sound of the hills. . . . She has never acted like a star. She has never needed to. Kitty Wells *is* a star!"

Kitty Wells and Johnny Wright Family Country Junction is a modest little museum opened by the couple in 1983 in Madison, just north of Nashville. It has the welcoming feeling of a wood-paneled family room lined with bowling trophies and the kids' football and cheerleading awards. Posters and family photos are tacked up on walls with hand-lettered labels; a worn video plays clips of various performances. There are even model trains, a homage to Wells's father Cary Deason, who was a brakeman for 33 years.

At the back of the gift shop is a "country kitchen," in deference to Wells's reputation as a first-class country cook. Kitty and Johnny greet fans from the kitchen table when they're in town. Miss Kitty's cookbooks and homemade grape jelly, onion relish, and pear preserves are for sale.

The museum also houses the Junction, an active 24-track recording studio, which can be rented for $45 an hour with an engineer. Kitty and Johnny's staff of musicians will demo a song for $125, and enhance it free of charge. According to a recent price list, a custom album with "five musicians, two background singers, engineer, studio time, and tape" costs $4,500.

GETTING THERE: Open 9 A.M. to 5 P.M. Monday through Friday; 10 A.M. to 4 P.M. Saturday. Closed January through March. Allow an hour. Free. From Nashville, take Briley Parkway to Gallatin Rd. north. Turn right on Old Hickory Blvd. 240 Old Hickory Blvd. (Kitty Wells Boulevard) in Madison; (615) 865-6543.

Homes of the Stars

For the price of a tank of gas and a cheap map (available for about $2 at area gift shops), you can cruise by the homes of dozens of famous Nashville residents. The highlight of my jaunt was seeing Jessi Colter walk out to the mailbox in front of the home in Brentwood she shares with Waylon Jennings, then get into a black Mercedes and drive away. After she left, I had my picture taken in front of the entrance, which is framed with a tall black wrought-iron archway that reads "Southern Comfort."

I also saw Ronnie Milsap's yellow Colonial-style mansion behind a tall brick fence, Minnie Pearl's white-brick house with brown trim at the top of a long, tailored lawn, and Tammy Wynette's tour bus being cleaned in front of Hank and Audrey Williams's former home on Franklin Pike. (Wynette and her husband, George Richey, live in Hank's former palace.) Webb Pierce's house, famous for the guitar-shaped pool, has a distinctive mailbox with a sign that reads "Wandering Acres" sitting on top of a black guitar.

Several companies offer drive-by tours of the stars' homes, but if you have the time and inclination, mapping out your own course can be an adventure. Don't forget your camera, bring along a friend to help navigate, and drive carefully.

Nashville Cemeteries

Don't be hesitant about poking around Nashville cemeteries in search of stars' graves. For example, the **Spring Hill Cemetery** office staff will happily provide you with a map featuring "Entertainment Celebrity Estates" and "Historical Personalities and Sites."

Established in 1785, Spring Hill got its name from a huge spring that flowed out of a cave under what is now the Jim Reeves Museum. Dean Manuel, who died in the same plane crash as Reeves, is buried here, as are Roy Acuff, Keith Whitley, and Beth Slater-Whitson, who wrote "Let Me Call You Sweetheart."

Acuff's simple grave, with a fiddle engraved on the monument, is straight ahead and just to the right as you drive in. During a recent Fan Fair, Whitley's grave was covered with wreaths left by his fan club. A space beside his grave is reserved for his widow, Lorrie Mor-

A marker commemorating one of the Opry's first stars, harmonica wizard DeFord Bailey, is at the corner of 12th Ave. South and Edgehill Ave.

gan. The original Spring Hill Meeting House, a rough-hewn stone structure, stands in a historic part of the cemetery. 5110 Gallatin Rd., off Briley Parkway in Nashville; (615) 865-1101.

Songwriter, publisher, and impresario Fred Rose, one of the first inductees to the Country Music Hall of Fame, is buried in **Mt. Olivet Cemetery,** as are Captain Tom Ryman, members of the Stoneman Family, and many prominent Nashvillians and people of historic significance. Members of Bill Monroe's family also rest here. Stop by the office to obtain a map with a walking tour of burial sites. Take I-40/65 to Lebanon Pike/Hwy. 70 exit, going east. 1101 Lebanon Rd.; (615) 255-4193.

DeFord Bailey, the first black performer on the *Grand Ole Opry,* is buried in **Greenwood Cemetery,** along with other notable black Nashville citizens including Cornelia Shephard of the original Fisk Jubilee Singers. Bailey's monument is just to the left inside the front gate. His tombstone reads "Harmonica Wizard," followed by "Musician, Composer, Entertainer—Early Star of *Grand Ole Opry.*" From I-24, take Fessler's Lane exit. Go right on Fessler's then left on Elm Hill. 1428 Elm Hill Pike; (615) 256-4395.

HOUSE OF CASH

Late, Great Star Site

Johnny Cash closed the House of Cash in Hendersonville a few months before this book went to press. His publicist hinted that the Man in Black might move his collection to someplace more accessible. It would be a shame to keep it from the public.

Johnny Cash's museum was an interesting, eclectic collection packed with a lifetime of items: tin cups and shackles from Folsom and San Quentin prisons, John Wayne's Colt Peacemaker, Buddy Holly's motorcycle, a small dresser made by Cash as a boy, Audrey Williams's stage costume, Mother Maybelle Carter's banjo lute, antique furniture, and bronze cowboy statues by Frederic Remington.

In addition to awards, photos, and gold records, some odd, inexplicable stuff was thrown in, like the box of "peanuts grown in Mississippi" and Al Capone's chair. Johnny and June's first bedroom set, with a 1620 European bed and desk that belonged to Chang Kai-Shek, were also on display.

Maybe if all his fans write a letter (700 Johnny Cash Parkway, Hendersonville, TN 37075), Johnny Cash could be persuaded to relocate his museum.

Note: The *real* house of Cash is near the former museum on Old Hickory Lake. Friendly but armed guards are on duty; visitors are allowed to take pictures from the driveway. To get there, take I-65 north to Briley Parkway east, to Gallatin Pike (Hwy. 31E) north. Pass Trinity Music City U.S.A. (formerly Twitty City) on the right, then turn right on Caudill Rd. The Cash compound is #200 on the right behind a long stone fence.

CONWAY TWITTY'S HOME

Until his untimely death in 1993, Conway Twitty lived in a house on the grounds of Twitty City in Hendersonville. In the aftermath, reported family disputes over Twitty's property resulted in the auctioning of his personal items and the sale of Twitty City to Trinity Broadcasting Network. The Christian-themed complex, now called **Trinity Music City U.S.A.,** has reopened Conway's original estate and a memorial garden. Tours of the Church Auditorium, WPGD Studios, and the Laverne Tripp Ministries Studio are offered, as well as movies in the Virtual Reality Theater, live televangelist broadcasts, and a model of Jerusalem.

GETTING THERE: Open 9 A.M. to 6 P.M. Monday through Friday; 9 A.M. to 9 P.M. Saturday; noon to 6 P.M. Sundays. From I-65, take Hwy. 386 (Vietnam Veterans Parkway) Exit 8 and follow the signs. Free. Call (615) 822-8333 or 826-9191 for a recorded schedule of events.

Entertainment in Nashville

Dozens of venues, from hotel lounges to intimate clubs and concert halls, offer live performances throughout the year. Check the *Tennessean*'s "Hot Ticket" supplement, the Nashville *Banner,* or the weekly *Nashville Scene* for listings. A few favorites are noted here, but this is by no means a comprehensive listing of entertainment options in Nashville.

Bluegrass musicians of all ages jam on Sunday nights at The Station Inn.

The **Station Inn** is serious about bluegrass music. Shows take place every night except Monday in a funky bar with Formica tables and mismatched plastic-and-metal chairs. The wood-paneled walls are lined with bluegrass festival posters. The menu features cheap pitchers of beer, pizza, and bar snacks.

Sundays are reserved for free-form bluegrass jams with no cover charge. The Station Inn fills up slowly as musicians of all ages, from kids barely into their teens to old-timers, wander in carrying fiddles, guitars, banjos, stand-up bass, mandolins, and harmonicas. As the circle of musicians expands, the music grows richer and more resonant. Some nights, many more people are in the jam than watching from the sidelines, but no one minds. Such stars as Ricky Skaggs, Vince Gill, Emmylou Harris, and the Father of Bluegrass himself, Bill Monroe, drop in from time to time. 402 12th Ave. S., a block from Broadway; (615) 255-3307.

The esteemed **Bluebird Cafe** is an intimate and professional showcase for established and up-and-coming singers and songwriters. A modest storefront venue with round tables and a row of wood pews in the back, the Bluebird has a knack for attracting polished and talented artists seven nights a week to its somewhat remote location. (Leroy Parnell, Kathy Mattea, and Garth Brooks all played here early in their careers.) Food and drinks are served. Take I-440/Exit 3 to Hillsboro Road south, then drive 1½ miles. Watch for the Bluebird on the left. 4104 Hillsboro Road; (615) 383-1461.

Twenty miles northeast of Nashville in rural Goodletsville, **The Long Hollow Jamboree** caters to aficionados of square-dancing, buck-dancing, and the two-step. On Tuesday nights, the stage is open to beginner and professional singers and dancers. The house band performs Friday and Saturday nights, and pit-barbecue and fried-chicken dinners are served from 5 to 11 P.M. Take I-65 north/Exit 97. Turn right on Long Hollow Pike for 4½ miles; (615) 824-4445.

Shopping in Nashville

Crystal's for Fine Gifts and Jewelry in Bell Meade Plaza is Crystal Gayle's "dream come true." In her brochure, the elegant singer explains, "For years I have loved and collected crystal, porcelain, and jewelry. And for years I have wanted to create a store that combined the widest selection of gifts with a comfortable atmosphere and a friendly, helpful staff." The unique shop, located in a tony suburban auto mall, sells watches, jewelry, clocks, music boxes, fine porcelain, and lots of crystal. The shop also sells Crystal Gayle recordings and T-shirts. 4500 Harding Rd.; (615) 292-4300.

South of Nashville in Franklin, a boutique called **Gill and Arnold** is owned and operated by the Sweethearts of the Rodeo. The sweet-sounding duo, which gets its name from the 1968 Byrds album of the same name, consists of sisters Janice Gill and Kristine Arnold, who also are country musicians.

Gill and Arnold specialize in classic updated clothing with a contemporary feel, and a wide range of accessories. The boutique is reasonably priced, Gill says, and provides "personal assistance in putting a look together. We wanted to make sure that a woman of any means could walk out with something she's proud of." Gill and Arnold also carry a small selection of Sweethearts of the Rodeo recordings and souvenirs. 214 E. Main St. in Franklin; (615) 791-1207.

We can't all be stars, but for the right price we can look like one. Celebrities can often be spotted outfitting themselves at trendy Nashville shops such as **Manuel Exclusive Clothier,** which fits stars with expensive, handmade stage costumes. 1922 Broadway; (615) 321-5444, and **Dangerous Threads,** serving rock-and-rollers and country artists—105 Second Ave. N.; (615) 256-1033, and 2201 Elliston Place; (615) 320-5890.

Where to Eat

Nashville offers a variety of good restaurants, mostly Southern-style, American, or Continental. (Few of the city's ethnic restaurants are worth mentioning.) New cafes, bagel stores, and microbreweries, as well as lively eateries in the downtown area, are opening all the time.

When stars want some Southern cooking to remind them of home, they go to the **Loveless Motel** restaurant. This dining room in a small motel in the country, about 15 miles southwest of the city, has been serving big plates of fried chicken and thick rib-eye steaks since 1951. The breakfast specialty is little rolled biscuits served with bowls of tart homemade peach and blackberry preserves and a slab of butter. Omelets come with thick slices of ripe red tomato. The dining room has wood floors and paneling, and tables decked out with red-checked oilcloth and heavy white linen napkins. Photos of country stars line the entryway and walls. It's a bit overpriced, but you can't help loving the Loveless. 8400 Hwy. 100; (615) 646-9700. From downtown, take West End Ave. south, which turns into Hwy. 100.

Celebrities are often spotted at **Pancake Pantry** in Hillsboro Village. Established in 1961, the restaurant serves waffles, French toast, sandwiches, steaks, salads, and—surprise!—pancakes, day and night. Varieties include wild blueberry, Caribbean, Swiss chocolate chip, apricot lemon, and Smoky Mountain buckwheat. The silver-dollar pancakes are sold in quantities of eight or fifteen. 1796 21st Ave. S.; (615) 383-9333.

Buddy Killen's Stock-Yard Restaurant and Bull Pen Lounge is in the historic Nashville Union Stock-Yard building, which housed the city's livestock market from 1921 to 1974. The elegant dining rooms are in former offices, with the ranchers' names still posted above the doors. Large portions of seafood, grilled chicken, fresh lobster, and all cuts of beef are served with beef-vegetable soup, salad, and a hot loaf of bread. A strolling guitar player takes requests and live country music is performed downstairs in the Bull Pen Lounge. (The Stock-Yard places ads in local papers listing celebrities "seen this week" in the restaurant.)

Don't walk here at night; park in the well-lit lots right next to the restaurant. Open daily for lunch and dinner. Second Ave. and Stockyard Blvd.; (615) 255-6464.

For a quick lunch or dinner in Nashville, try **Hog Heaven,** next to Centennial Park. A take-out joint with picnic tables in front, Hog Heaven serves spectacular barbecue by the pound, plate, or in sandwiches. The pulled-chicken sandwich on *cornbread* (ask for it, or you'll get a roll) with an unusual spicy white BBQ sauce is especially good. Hog Heaven also serves hand-pulled pork, beef brisket, turkey, quarter or half chickens, and ribs. 115 27th Ave. N., off Broadway; (615) 329-1234.

Special Events
INTERNATIONAL COUNTRY MUSIC FAN FAIR

The International Country Music Fan Fair is an action-packed, non-stop orgy of entertainment and star worship in Music City, U.S.A. It's also the absolute best vacation value for country-minded travelers. There's no other way to see so many stars, so close, for so little money.

There are three basic elements to Fan Fair, held in mid-June at the Tennessee State Fairgrounds since 1972. First, there's live music performed all day at the fairgrounds stadium by big shots and rising stars. Monday night is a bluegrass festival-within-a-festival, with performances by current artists and legends. These contemporary shows begin on Tuesday morning and continue through Friday evening. Music showcases are sponsored by various record companies, with a series of performers doing two or three songs each.

Second are the exhibit halls, where stars hold court in their booths, patiently signing autographs and mugging for photos.

Last, there's the rest of Nashville: For an admission price of just $90, Fan Fair attendees get three passes to Opryland (worth about $80), free tickets to the Country Music Hall of Fame and the Ryman Auditorium (worth $13), and discounts on many other attractions around town. Admission also includes two barbecue lunches, served with spirit by the Oddessa Chuck Wagon Gang.

Worlds collide at Fan Fair. In the exhibit halls, the hottest new videos play continuously on monitors above the Country Music Television booth, competing with old-timers at the *Grand Ole Opry* booth. In 1995, a mellow Eddy Arnold signed autographs amiably at his record company's booth, while Marty Stuart's appearance caused a near riot across the hall. Tom T. Hall's wife Dixie kept a book for his fans to write messages because Fan Fair "isn't his style," while Maureen McCormick (Marcia from *The Brady Bunch*), attempting to launch a singing career, attracted a gawking crowd. No matter what brings you to Fan Fair, the festival will expand your knowledge and appreciation for different kinds of country music.

Fan Fair week events include the TNN/Music City News Country Awards, the International Fan Club Organization's Fun Fest show, "Super-

Junior Brown takes the stage at International Country Music Fan Fair 1995.

star Spectacular" shows, celebrity golf tournaments and fashion shows, and events organized by individual fan clubs. Most require separate admission tickets. Tower Records holds free in-store performances and autograph sessions in the evenings. 2400 West End Ave.; (615) 327-3722.

The art of fiddling is showcased during the prestigious **Grand Master Fiddler Championship,** held on the last Saturday of Fan Fair week at Opryland. Fiddlers perform a waltz, breakdown, and one song. Trick-fiddling and show tunes are prohibited from the competition, as are "Orange Blossom Special" and "Black Mountain Rag." The winner, considered the best in the country, gets to wear the traditional blue sports jacket and take home a tall trophy.

Although the 24,000 Fan Fair tickets generally sell out by February, a few weeks after they go on sale, it's a myth that you can't get one. Most people obtain their tickets by lottery, mailing in their checks in early January. In recent years, bus tour companies have also purchased blocks of tickets. If you miss the lottery, you can book your trip through a travel agent. In recent years, Fan Fair has also been selling one-day passes to the fairgrounds on Friday.

It's often possible to buy cut-rate tickets, usually leftovers from oversold bus tours or cancellations. If you buy a ticket from a scalper, make sure that the bag contains the following items: the correct color plastic wrist bracelet (Fan Fair attendees must show their bracelets to get into the fairgrounds), and a small booklet of coupons with free passes to Opryland and other attractions (check the dates).

If you're going to Fan Fair for the first time, a good strategy is to "graze." Wander up and down the exhibit-hall aisles, and jump on an autograph line if someone interests you. Catch the grandstand morning show, spend the afternoon on the rides at Opryland, and see a show at the Ryman Auditorium at night. The trick is not to let the fair overwhelm you. Do as much as you can handle; there's always next year!

GETTING THERE: Call the Fan Fair office at (615) 889-7503 or write 2804 Opryland Dr., Nashville, TN 37214 to get on the mailing list. In late December or early January you will receive an application. Send your check back promptly. Take I-440 to Exit 6/Nolensville Rd. and follow the signs to the Tennessee State Fairgrounds. Parking is free.

SURVIVAL TIPS FOR FAN FAIR

- Wear comfortable shoes, light clothing, and a hat.
- Drink plenty of water or soft drinks.
- Carry as little as possible.
- Consider buying the official program, very helpful for three dollars. It includes the concert schedule, a directory of booths, profiles of new artists, and information on restaurants, attractions, and other Fan Fair week events.
- Use the valuable coupon booklet that comes with every Fan Fair admission, and keep an eye out for additional discounts on attractions, entertainment, restaurants, and stores.
- Don't bring video cameras into the grandstand. (Cameras are permitted everywhere else at the Fairgrounds, including the exhibit halls.)

OLD-FASHIONED CHRISTMAS AT FOX HOLLOW WITH DIXIE AND TOM T. HALL

For nearly two decades, singer/songwriter Tom T. Hall and his wife, Dixie, have opened up their home to friends for three weeks around Christmastime. Their mansion, **Fox Hollow**, sits on 63 acres in Franklin, south of Nashville. "I'm there the whole time," says Dixie, who organizes the event with her friends. "Tom T. isn't. There's no way I can tie him down for 22 days."

Visitors can tour Fox Hollow, mod-

Dixie Hall hosts an old-fashioned Christmas at Fox Hollow.

eled after Rosedown Plantation in St. Francisville, Louisiana, and enjoy continuous entertainment. "A lot of our celebrity friends will come over and pick and sing," Dixie explains. "Once I came in and there was a group around the piano and Glen Campbell was singing 'Blue Christmas.' " This event is a fund-raiser for Animaland, a humane shelter that does not put animals to sleep. Crafts and baked goods are also for sale. "We have a huge gift tent where we sell jellies and pickles and so forth that I make throughout the year," Dixie adds.

GETTING THERE: Franklin is about 15 miles south of Nashville. Open 10 A.M. to 7 P.M. from the Friday after Thanksgiving until the Thursday before Christmas. From Nashville, take I-65 south to Hwy. 96 west. Turn right on Franklin Rd., then left on South Berry's Chapel Rd. Fox Hollow is on the right. Admission $5; (615) 790-1883.

Oprys
MURFREESBORO—*LEANNA OPRY*

For forty years, Carl and Sophie Tipton were partners on- and off-stage. A bluegrass artist, Carl was also a disc jockey and hosted a television show in Nashville for twenty years. After Carl died in the late 1980s, Sophie says she and sister Louise Tomberlain "couldn't just stop singing."

In Carl's memory, they started the *Leanna Opry* near Murfreesboro. The idea was to give old-time and bluegrass performers a place to go during the winter, when it's too cold for outdoor festivals. Every second and fourth Saturday night, October through March, the 250-seat Leanna Community Center comes alive with the sound of bluegrass bands.

Marty Stuart, Ferlin Husky, the Stonemans, and Bashful Brother Oswald have stopped by, but the evening is primarily a showcase for amateur bluegrass musicians. "These aren't professionals. They have their day jobs, but they love their music," explains Tipton, who hosts the show and sings tight harmonies with Tomberlain.

In recognition of their dedication to bluegrass, Tipton and Tomberlain received the prestigious Uncle Dave Macon Days Heritage Award in 1995. The sisters were on Garrison Keillor's *Prairie Home Companion,* and performed with the "Sisters of the South" tour produced by the Southern Arts Federation in 1994.

The *Leanna Opry* begins at 6 P.M. Bands play for thirty minutes each, and the show isn't over until everyone who wants to take the stage gets a chance. Sophie says there's no admission charge, but "we pass the hat to pay the light bill."

The **Carl Tipton Memorial Bluegrass Festival** takes place here the last Saturday in September.

GETTING THERE: Murfreesboro is 30 miles southeast of Nashville. Take I-24 south/Exit 78B. Turn left on Thompson Lane, then left on Sulphur Springs Rd. Drive four miles to the Leanna Community Center; (615) 896-0623.

MILTON—CAJUN L'OPÉRA

On Friday and Saturday nights, the only road in Milton, Tennessee, comes alive with "fais do do." Folks set their lawn chairs up around 6 P.M. in front of **Manuel's Cajun Country Store,** while a small stage on the side of the porch is unveiled. When the musicians are tuned up and ready, they launch into a string of Cajun and country favorites. Kids and cats scamper underfoot; people have been known to dance. The fun continues until 8 or 9, or whenever.

Inside the store, housed in a converted red barn, the Manuel family serves up "true Cajun cooking, not hot or spicy!" The menu also explains a few useful Cajun terms, such as *"Pooh-yi!"* ("Everything is great!") and *"Allons!"* ("Let's go!").

The atmosphere is down-home, with long tables with red-and-white-checked plastic tablecloths and folding chairs. Catfish, shrimp, frog legs, and gator (in season), oysters, and shrimp or crawfish étouffée are served with slaw, fries, and hushpuppies, or rice, beans, and potato salad. The crawfish is flown in from Baton Rouge, and excellent shrimp-okra gumbo is prepared in a tasty broth.

GETTING THERE: Milton is about 40 miles southeast of Nashville. Open for lunch and dinner, Wednesday through Saturday (lunch only Wednesday and Thursday during the winter). *Cajun L'Opéra* is free on Friday and Saturday nights, from roughly 6 to 9 P.M. From I-24 in Murfreesboro, take Hwy. 96 east 15 miles to Milton Street (the turn is easy to miss if you're not paying attention); (615) 273-2312.

Nashville Area Festivals

Old-time music and dance, including fiddling and buck-dancing, are highlights of Uncle Dave Macon Days in Murfreesboro.

The first week in June, downtown Nashville bustles with **Summer Lights in Music City,** a huge arts-and-crafts fair and music festival. Entertainers perform everything from country and bluegrass to blues, big band, classical, and swing. The festival takes place between Riverfront Park and Sixth Avenue, and Union and Charlotte Avenues; (615) 726-1875. Named for one of the *Grand Ole Opry's* first stars, **Uncle Dave Macon Days** is a wonderful music and dance festival with national competitions in old-time banjo, buck-dancing, and clogging. A highlight is the "motorless parade," featuring horses, mules, goats, dogs, wagons, and bicycles. The three-day festival takes place the second weekend in July at Murfreesboro's Cannonsburgh Pioneer Village, a historic preservation park about 30 miles southeast of Nashville. Free. Take I-24 south to Exit 78B/Old Fort Parkway. Turn right on Broad St., then right on S. Front; (800) 716-7560 or (615) 893-2371.

Centerville
MINNIE PEARL'S GRINDERS SWITCH

For more than fifty years, comedienne Minnie Pearl regaled *Grand Ole Opry* audiences with hilarious and heartwarming tales from Grinders Switch. Pearl, whose real name was Sarah Ophelia Colley, was born west of Nashville in Centerville. (Sadly, she died in 1996, several years after suffering a stroke.) A well-educated Southern woman, young Sarah developed the Minnie Pearl persona from rural folks she met while staging dramatic productions in small towns. A railroad switching station near Centerville became the locale for Miss Minnie's (mis)adventures.

The real **Grinders Switch** is a few miles from downtown Centerville in rural Hickman County. Unlike the lively community in Minnie Pearl's world, visitors will see a decaying station building, abandoned house, and an old barn behind a barbed-wire fence. A wood sign reading "Grinders Switch 1940" marks the spot. Don't expect too much, and you won't be disappointed. Regardless, it's a nice drive out to the quiet, shady spot. From Rte. 48/Exit 100 (Linden Rd.), take Rte. 50 west for 1½ miles. Turn right on Grinders Switch Rd. Drive about 1½ miles along the railroad tracks to Grinders Switch.

Hickman County displays its growing collection of Minnie Pearl memorabilia in its offices on the Centerville Courthouse Square, weekdays. 117 N. Central Ave.; (615) 729-5774. **Breece's Cafe,** on the square since 1939, is a wonderful, family-run restaurant. The specialty is "meat and four": customers choose one meat dish (turkey, meatloaf, fried chicken, etc.), and four side dishes, for an unbeatable $3. Homemade pies, including apple, lemon icebox, and a killer chocolate fudge with pecans, cost 95¢ a slice. 111 S. Public Square; (615) 729-3481.

Grinders Switch Inn, a friendly little motel with a covered porch and rockers, is on Hwy. 100, which used to be the main road between Nashville and Memphis before the interstate. The proprietor says that Elvis Presley slept here in the late 1950s, and drove his pink Cadillac around the square the wrong way to get attention. 107 N. Central Ave. (Hwy. 100); (615) 729-5195.

(*See also:* Opryland, Minnie Pearl Museum [*this chapter*].)

GETTING THERE: Centerville is about 50 miles southwest of Nashville. Take I-40/Exit 163 to Rte. 48 south. Contact the Hickman County Chamber of Commerce; (615) 729-5774.

Hurricane Mills
LORETTA LYNN'S DUDE RANCH

In the mid-1960s, Doolittle (Mooney) and Loretta Lynn stumbled on their dream house while driving around middle Tennessee. It was love at first sight for Loretta; the plantation mansion reminded her of "Tara" from *Gone with the Wind.* The house was in deplorable condition, but they bought it anyway. Their $220,000 also purchased the whole town of Hurricane Mills: a post office, gristmill, general store, and cattle ranch. While Loretta toured, Mooney put in many long hours fixing the place up for her.

Over the years, the Lynns trans-fomed Hurricane Mills into a down-home tourist attraction called Loretta Lynn's Dude Ranch. Family-run and appropriately dubbed the Double L, the ranch has grown to more than 6,500 acres, and is

Loretta Lynn's "Double L" dude ranch in Hurricane Mills spans more than 6,500 acres.

equipped with an RV park, campground, rodeo arena, riding stables, hiking trails, miniature golf, petting zoo, swimming pool, and concert pavilion.

The plantation house, which the Lynn family lived in for 22 years, was opened for tours in 1988. (To protect their privacy, Loretta and Mooney moved to a secret one-bedroom house somewhere in the vicinity.) A guided-tour package includes the house, a simulated coal mine like the one Loretta's father worked in in Van Lear, Kentucky, a replica of her Butcher Hollow birthplace, and Loretta's personal museum.

Built in the early 1800s, the house has 14 large rooms, eight fireplaces, and 48 nine-foot windows. Loretta's tour buses are out front, as well as Mooney's gold Cadillac and the Golden Eagle Jeep driven by Tommy Lee Jones in the movie *Coal Miner's Daughter*.

Inside, Loretta and Doolittle did all the decorating themselves. To settle a dispute over the den, Mooney did his wall "cowboy" style and Loretta did hers "Indian." (She is one-quarter Cherokee.) Loretta did all the wallpapering herself, and filmed most of her Crisco commercials in the kitchen. The pink-and-green ground-floor bedroom is filled with gifts from fans. Fifty-seven record covers line the "Stairway of Albums" to the second floor, which is off-limits to the public, à la Graceland.

Back in the old mill, the small museum offers Astroturf-lined display cases filled with awards, personal items, and memorabilia, accompanied by Loretta's hand-scribbled explanations. "Patsy [Cline] gave me this nightgown about three days before she was taken from us," reads one. "The sexiest little nightgown she ever had, she said, when she gave it to me. We had a big laugh together."

Loretta also has gifts from Ernest Tubb and Tex Ritter, bars of soap from the New York City hotel where Jimmie Rodgers died, the dress she wore for her first *Grand Ole Opry* performance, Marty Robbins's suede jacket, scrip from the Van Lear coal-mine store, her parents' stern wedding photo, and a letter from Frank Sinatra, written after the two toured together in 1977.

The guided tour is fun, but is not required to visit Loretta Lynn's ranch. It's possible to spend an hour or a week here, hiking or riding the trails, fishing in Hurricane Creek, or puttering around the shops in Western Town. One store sells handicrafts made by Loretta, as well as pieces of her clothing and personal items. Loretta and Mooney visit with fans when they can.

For overnight guests, there are campfire sing-alongs nightly, and hoedowns on Saturday evenings. Annual special events include two Loretta Lynn concerts, the National Motorcross Championship, pow-wows, trail rides, and a talent search. If you can't make it to the dude ranch, **Loretta Lynn Kitchen,** a buffet restaurant and gift shop, is north of I-40 on Hwy. 13.

(*See also:* Kentucky—Van Lear.)

GETTING THERE: Loretta Lynn's Dude Ranch is 63 miles west of Nashville and 122 miles east of Memphis. Tours available March through December, except Thanksgiving Day, Christmas Eve, and Christmas Day. Guided tours $10.50. Allow two hours. Reservations requested for overnight stays. Take I-40/Exit 143 to Hwy. 13 north (Loretta Lynn Parkway). Go 8 miles to the ranch; (615) 296-7700.

Camden
PATSY CLINE MEMORIAL MARKER

On March 5, 1963, the small plane carrying Patsy Cline, Hawkshaw Hawkins, Cowboy Copas, and Cline's manager, Randy Hughes, crashed in a storm, and all were killed. The crash site is in Camden, less than 30 miles from Loretta Lynn's ranch at Hurricane Mills. In 1995, Bill and Linda Culver of Battle Creek, Michigan, members of the Always Patsy Cline Fan Club, put up a memorial plaque at the crash site in a wooded area west of Camden. They also placed a mailbox for fans to leave notes, and a guest book.

Officials in Camden reportedly have plans to build a new road to the site, with a monument and pavilion.

GETTING THERE: Take I-40/Exit 126 to Hwy. 641 north. After crossing Hwy. 70, make the first left (at the Shell station) onto Mt. Carmel Road. Bear right past the American Shell Company. You will then see two trailers on the right. A path into the woods next to the second trailer leads to the crash site. The Culvers recommend that you stop at the trailer to ask for permission. For a map and fan club information, write to the Culvers: 10257 Crase Rd., Battle Creek, MI 49017.

For area information, contact Benton County Chamber of Commerce; (901) 584-8395.

West Tennessee

Tamarack
CHARLIE LOUVIN BLUEGRASS FESTIVAL

The first weekend in August, Henry Harrison holds a four-day Charlie Louvin Bluegrass Festival at Tamarack campground. The festival is in a 2,700-seat amphitheater, with RV hookups and tent camping. Headliners, including Louvin, perform on Thursday and Friday. On Saturday, the Jackson Area Plectral Society hosts a playing contest of traditional instruments with $2,000 in prize money. New artists have an opportunity to perform on Sunday afternoon. Tamarack is south of Jackson, on Hwy. 100 between Hwys. 45 and 18; (901) 427-8521.

(*See also:* Bell Buckle [*this chapter*].)

Jackson
CARL PERKINS'S SUEDE'S RESTAURANT

Rockabilly icon Carl Perkins's restaurant, Suede's, is run by his daughter and son-in-law. Inspired by his megahit "Blue Suede Shoes" (also recorded by Elvis Presley), the restaurant is a tasteful, upbeat place decorated all in blue with stained-glass "blue suede shoes" dividing the booths.

On the menu, in a note to customers, Perkins explains that he grew up a sharecropper's son in Lake County, Tennessee, about two hours north of Jackson. "In case you're wondering, a sharecropper does the work while the land owner makes the money. Having enough to eat was hard to come by," Perkins writes. "Maybe those days in the cotton fields made me aware of just how special a restaurant really is."

Perkins's memorabilia and awards are displayed in several tall cases and along the walls, including his birth certificate reading "Carl Perkings" (*sic*), a handwritten Christmas card from fan Paul McCartney, and the original lyrics for Perkins's compositions "Pink Pedal Pushers" and "Daddy Sang Bass," a big hit for Johnny Cash.

The menu is reasonably priced, and features things like "Boppin' to the Blues Bar-B-Q," "Rockabilly Sandwiches," and "A Whole Lotta Steakin' Going On." Prices range from $4.99 for a burger and fries to $11.99 for a porterhouse steak supper. Lunch specials cost less than $5. Stop by for a meal, or feel free to look around without buying anything. A small selection of souvenirs is sold at the front counter.

Perkins lives a few blocks away, in what once was the biggest house in Jackson. From the restaurant, go north on Highland, then left on Country Club Lane. His red-brick house is #459, on the right, with the big wrought-iron guitars on the front.

(*See also:* Tiptonville [*this chapter*].)

GETTING THERE: Jackson is 85 miles east of Memphis and 125 miles west of Nashville. Open daily 11 A.M. to 9 P.M. Take I-40/Exit 82A. Suede's is two blocks on the right. 2263 N. Highland; (901) 664-1956.

Dyersburg
WEST TENNESSEE OPRY

"I've been beatin' on an old guitar since I was eight years old," says Otha B. Mallard, owner and star of the *West Tennessee Opry*. "I thought I'd give this a try, an' it just kind of took off." Since Mallard opened his 450-seat hall in 1987, local country bands have performed three nights a week year-round. He has a 36-foot lighted stage, concessions, and two dance floors, one for two-stepping and one for line-dancing. "It's strictly straight country, family entertainment," Mallard says.

The music begins at 7 P.M. on Thursdays; 7:30 P.M. on Fridays and Saturdays. Admission $3 adults, $1.50 children. South of Dyersburg, about 75 miles north of Memphis, on Rte. 51; (901) 285-1934.

Tiptonville
HOMETOWN OF CARL PERKINS

Carl Perkins was born in 1932 in the northwest corner of Tennessee near Reelfoot Lake. His family moved to Jackson when he was fourteen years old. While revered as a rock and roll pioneer, his sound has its roots in the bluegrass music he grew up on and the blues he heard around Jackson. He had numerous hits on the country charts, and toured with the Johnny Cash show for many years.

Today, Carl's first cousins, Hubert and Laverne Perkins, show **Carl Perkins's Boyhood Home** by appointment during the summer months. In 1988, the four-room house, one of several that Perkins lived in as a boy, was moved to Hwy. 78 (Carl Perkins Parkway). Unable to insure their collection of Perkins memorabilia, the Lake County Historical Society instead fixed up the house to look as it did when Perkins lived here in the 1930s. "We put in stuff like they had back then," Laverne says. She leads the tour, talking about Carl's childhood and pointing out Depression-era artifacts

Marcia Mills (right) and her mother, Laverne Perkins, welcome guests to Sweet Dreams Cottage Bed and Breakfast in Carl Perkins's hometown.

such as a wood-burning stove, butter churn, washstand, and chamber pot.

While getting a feel for Perkins's humble beginnings, visitors have the pleasure of talking to Laverne and Hubert, who are full of anecdotes about their famous cousin. Laverne proudly shows albums of family photos, and a book she helped write about Lake County history. Hubert tells a touching story about the time his father lay in a Memphis hospital suffering from cancer. Perkins would drive 80 miles from Jackson to give him a shave. "Carl still does not realize that he's a star," he says earnestly. "He's just a good old country boy as far as I'm concerned," Laverne adds.

Hubert and Laverne's daughter Marcia Mills runs **Sweet Dreams Cottage Bed-and-Breakfast** in Tiptonville with her husband, Calvin. The charming, fully equipped cottage is next to their Queen Anne Victorian house, which they meticulously restored over five years. It is now on the National Register of Historic Places. 431 Winn St.; (901) 253-7203.

Reelfoot Lake, the largest natural lake in Tennessee, was formed by the New Madrid earthquakes of 1811 and 1812, when the Mississippi River actually switched directions. Surrounded by giant cypress forests and marshes, the 13,000-acre lake is a paradise for bird watchers, hunters, and anglers. Hundreds of bald eagles winter here; viewing tours can be arranged through the **Reelfoot Lake State Resort Park.** A huge arts-and-crafts festival takes place the first weekend in October. Hwys. 22 and 78; (901) 253-7756.

(*See also:* Jackson [*this chapter*].)

GETTING THERE: Tiptonville is about 100 miles north of Memphis and 70 miles north of Jackson. Admission $1. Allow an hour. You *must* make an appointment in advance to see Carl Perkins's Boyhood Home. Take I-155/Exit 13 to Rte. 78 north. (Carl Perkins Highway). Call Perkins Tire, (901) 253-7653, or Lake County Historical Society, (901) 253-6650 or 253-6219.

For area information, contact the Reelfoot Lake Area Chamber of Commerce; (901) 253-8144.

Memphis

BLUES YOU CAN USE

Since it opened in 1982, Graceland has become the cornerstone of Memphis' growing tourism industry. Approximately 700,000 people visit Elvis Presley's mansion every year (*see page 277*), including many who would not have considered traveling here otherwise.

Taking advantage of these new visitors, Memphis has developed several new attractions in recent years, making the city an increasingly attractive destination in its own right. The downtown and Beale Street, home of the blues, are undergoing a renaissance. Sam Phillips's legendary Sun Studios is open for tours. Memphis is also touting itself as an attractive base for exploring a dozen new casinos south of the city in Mississippi.

Among the city's attractions are several art and history museums, botanical gardens, a children's museum, planetarium, and IMAX theater. Following are attractions notably unique to Memphis.

- The powerful **National Civil Rights Museum** is located at the Lorraine Motel, where Dr. Martin Luther King, Jr., was shot and killed. 450 Mulberry St.; (901) 521-9699.
- **Mud Island,** in the middle of the Mississippi River, offers recreation, museums, an amphitheater, and **River Walk,** a five-block model of the lower Mississippi ending in a public pool shaped like the Gulf of Mexico. 125 North Front St.; (800) 507-6507 or (901) 576-7241.
- No trip to Memphis is complete without a visit to the Peabody ducks, in the elegant lobby of the Peabody Hotel. Every day at precisely 11 A.M., a small troop of mallards take the elevator down from their "penthouse" on the roof, and waddle on a red carpet to their fountain in the center of the lobby as John Philip Sousa's "King Cotton March" plays. At 5 P.M., the reluctant ducks repeat the ritual in reverse. 149 Union Ave.; (800) PEABODY or (901) 529-4000.

Memphis is a terrific town for barbecue, especially pork ribs. Award-winning **Corky's** serves succulent dry ribs that pull right off the bone. Year after year, Corky's is voted Best Barbecue in Memphis. 5259 Poplar Ave.; (901) 685-9744. Elvis Presley was a fan of **Leon-**

ard's pit-cooked ribs and shoulders, slow-cooked over hickory and charcoal. 5465 Fox Plaza Drive; (901) 360-1963.

(*See also:* Mississippi—Nesbit.)

GETTING THERE: Memphis is in the southwest corner of Tennessee, on the Mississippi River. Take I-40 or I-55. Memphis Visitors' Information Center is at 340 Beale St.; (901) 543-5333.

HARVESTER LANE BLUEGRASS

Every Friday night, Joe Taylor and Ken Bingham lead a bluegrass jam session in a union hall across from the old International Harvester plant in the Frayser area of northwest Memphis. "We're not in it for the money. We're just trying to promote bluegrass in Memphis," Taylor says, urging bluegrass lovers and players to come on down. "If you can pitch your foot and grin, you're welcome."

Formerly known as the Lucy Opry, Harvester Lane Bluegrass hasn't missed a week since it began in the late 1960s. The show is free and begins at 8 P.M. Once or twice a month, professional bluegrass artists perform and $5 admission is charged. Take I-40/Exit 12A, to I-240 north/Exit 2A, to Hwy. 51 (Thomas Blvd.) north. Turn left on Whitney Ave., then right to 2984 Harvester Lane; (901) 357-6432.

BLUES ON BEALE STREET

Memphis is world-famous as home of the blues; legendary Beale Street is where the blues live. Early in the twentieth century, W.C. Handy published the first commercial blues here, songs like "Memphis Blues," "Beale Street Blues," and "St. Louis Blues." Largely dormant after the devastating riots following the assassination of Dr. Martin Luther King, Beale Street is coming back to life again in the 1990s.

Day and night, the sounds of live music pour out of B.B. King's Blues Club and Restaurant, the Rum Boogie Cafe, and King's Palace, while restaurants serve traditional Southern cooking and barbecue. The atmosphere is like the French Quarter in New Orleans, on a smaller scale.

The historic district begins a few blocks from the Mississippi River, marked by a statue of Elvis Presley at Second and Beale streets. Attractions include the Center for Southern Folklore (*see page 275*) and

Beale Street Blues Museum, which takes a look at the early Memphis music scene. 329 Beale St.; (901) 527-6008. Around the corner, the **Memphis Music Hall of Fame** chronicles the city's contributions with costumes, recordings, memorabilia, and an exhibit on record labels such as Sun and Stax. 97 S. Second St.; (901) 525-4007.

A. Schwab's Dry Goods, open since 1876, stocks thousands of items. The general store's motto: "If you can't find it at Schwab's, you're better off without it." 163 Beale St.; (901) 523-9782.

GETTING THERE: The Beale Street historic district runs from Second to Fourth Streets in downtown Memphis. Contact the Beale Street Merchants' Association; (901) 529-0999.

CENTER FOR SOUTHERN FOLKLORE— CELEBRATING "PEOPLE ART"

Since 1972 the Center for Southern Folklore has celebrated what executive director Judy Peiser calls "people art—not high arts," by documenting and showcasing the Memphis/Delta area's diverse musicians, cooks, artists, quilters, storytellers, and dancers. The vibrant center offers rotating photo and art exhibits, videos, live music, and a gift shop full of eclectic and colorful Southern folk arts, music, and books. Visitors can get a feel for the flavor and intensity of Memphis in its heyday while exploring the current folk-arts revival.

The Center is on Beale Street in the old Lansky Brothers Clothing Store, which occupies its own special place in Memphis music history. Bernard Lansky proudly called himself "Clothier to the King." His tall three-way mirror, used to suit up Presley and other stars, is on permanent display at the Center. A plaque in the corner dedicates the reflecting glass to Presley. "Elvis used this very mirror many times. His first suit was fitted here," it reads. "Here he was fitted for his *Ed Sullivan* appearance. Lansky made and fitted the first glitter-and-glitz show suits he became famous for, using this very mirror."

The Center's annual three-day **Memphis Music and Heritage Festival,** usually in mid-July, draws up to 100,000 people. Three stages hop with free blues, jazz, country, rock, and folk music.

GETTING THERE: Open 10 A.M. to 8 P.M. Monday through Thursday; 10 A.M. to 10 P.M. Friday and Saturday; 11 A.M. to 8 P.M. Sundays. Free, but donations are encouraged. 130 Beale St.; (901) 525-FOLK.

SUN STUDIOS—ROCKABILLY ROUNDUP

In 1950, a mortician from Florence, Alabama, named Sam Phillips opened a recording studio near downtown Memphis at 706 Union Avenue. Sun Records, perhaps the most famous recording studio in the world, nurtured the high-energy fusion of country and blues sounds which came to be known first as rockabilly, later called rock and roll.

Elvis Presley, Johnny Cash, Carl Perkins, and Jerry Lee Lewis (the "Million Dollar Quartet") got their starts here, as did Roy Orbison and Charlie Rich. Sun's first million-seller was Perkins's "Blue Suede Shoes," which was later recorded by Presley. Sun's biggest hits were Lewis's "Whole Lotta Shakin' Goin' On" and "Great Balls of Fire." Phillips put famed bluesmen Howlin' Wolf and B.B. King on tape, and recorded "Rocket 88" with Ike Turner on piano, often considered the first rock and roll song.

After Phillips shut the doors at 706 Union Avenue in 1960, the studio was occupied by a barber and a scuba-diving shop, and various unsuccessful tour companies before it become a viable tourist attraction in the late 1980s.

The fascinating half-hour guided tour of Sun Studios takes visitors back in time, playing music clips on an old reel-to-reel to illustrate the Sun story, demonstrating the period's recording techniques, and discussing Phillips's crucial role in the birth of rock and roll.

"Sam Phillips never really got rich from the music business. He was always pumping the money back into the product," tour guide Michael Conway says. "But don't feel bad for Sam. He's doing just fine. He was one of the first investors in another little Memphis company you may have heard of, Holiday Inn."

Next door, the **Sun Studio Cafe** serves plate dinners, burgers, shakes, and "Dixie Fried Banana Pie." Upstairs, a shop sells Sun recordings and souvenirs with the label's distinctive yellow sunburst logo. A small gallery displays additional memorabilia, including the original "706" aluminum door grill and the mike used to record Elvis's first on-air interview. The recording studio is again fully operational, available for rent in the evenings.

Getting there: Tours daily, every hour on the half-hour, 9:30 A.M. to 6:30 P.M. Admission $7.50; children under 12 free. 706 Union Ave.; (901) 521-0664.

GRACELAND—ONLY IN AMERICA

The pilgrimage to Graceland is virtually a rite of passage for many Americans, a civic duty akin to climbing the Statue of Liberty or touring the White House. (In surveys, it is the most famous home in America, after the president's place.) Built in 1939 by the Moores, a prominent Memphis family, the mansion was named for their female relative, Grace.

Twenty-two-year-old Elvis, flush with new fame, bought the 23-room, red-brick house and grounds in 1957 for $100,000 and moved in with his beloved parents, Vernon and Gladys, and grandmother, Minnie Mae. Shown exactly as it was when Presley died in 1977, the house is an historic relic from the era of shag rugs, lava lamps, and bell bottoms.

The Graceland experience reveals Presley as a poor rural boy who came of age in the big city, the perennial kid let loose in the candy store, who embodied the brightest and darkest aspects of the American Dream. Raised in the humblest of circumstances in Tupelo, Mississippi, he harnessed his musical creativity and made a million dollars long before he reached 30.

Adhering to core American values, Presley took his career seriously, recording hundreds of songs, starring in dozens of movies, and touring constantly. He was generous almost to a fault, showering friends and family with expensive gifts, donating regularly to charities, and doing benefit concerts. Yet most of his philanthropic endeavors went unpublicized. He would quietly pay hospital bills, support needy families, and fulfill sick children's wishes. One of Presley's proudest moments was being named "One of the Ten Outstanding Young Men of the Nation for 1970" by the Junior Chamber of Commerce (Jaycees).

But Presley was no choirboy. His downfall was a fatal obsession with the excesses of life in America: drug abuse, conspicuous consumption, gluttony, sexism, a bad temper, intolerance for people who disagreed with him, the need for instant gratification. A Graceland press release says that while playing billiards, he would "move a ball on the table to his advantage and wait to see if his opponent had the wherewithal to call him on it."

It is such competing aspects of Elvis's personality that make a visit to Graceland so interesting. While remembered as the King of Rock and Roll, many people don't realize how country his origins were. Presley's first single for Sam Phillips's Sun Records was a hyperactive version of Bill Monroe's "Blue Moon of Kentucky," and he had numerous hits on the country charts throughout his career.

In 1970, Presley recorded a successful album in Nashville called *Elvis Country*. On Graceland's audio tour, Presley casually tells a reporter, "I think it's fantastic. You see, country music was always a part of the influence on my type of music anyway. It's a combination of country music, gospel, and rhythm and blues, is what it really was. I was influenced by all of that."

Although Presley's lifestyle was by no means a model for "family values," he was nonetheless extremely religious and a devoted family man. Elvis, Vernon, Gladys, and Minnie Mae Presley are buried in a small mediation garden next to the kidney-shaped swimming pool. There is a marker for Jesse Garon, Presley's twin brother, who died at birth and is buried at an undisclosed location in Tupelo. Elvis's marker reads, "God saw that he needed some rest and called him home to be with Him."

The audio tour of Graceland ends at the gravesite where Elvis, Vernon, Gladys, and Minnie Mae Presley are buried. (© 1996, Elvis Presley Enterprises, Inc.)

To do Graceland right, allow a whole day to tour the **Graceland Mansion,** and everything in **Grace-**

land Plaza across the street: the Elvis Presley Automobile Museum, "Sincerely Elvis" personal museum, and Lisa Marie Jet and Hound Dog II airplanes. Watch the free 20-minute film of Presley's career highlights, *Walk a Mile in My Shoes*. Don't deny yourself any part of the total Graceland experience.

Graceland hosts the **Elvis Presley Birthday Tribute** around January 8, and **Elvis International Tribute Week** during the week that includes August 16. Dozens of special events are held in Memphis, while Graceland hosts an Elvis art exhibit and contest, a reunion concert of performers from Elvis's band, bus tours to Tupelo, and a candlelight memorial vigil.

(*See also:* Mississippi—Tupelo.)

GETTING THERE: Graceland is open daily 8 A.M. to 8 P.M. Memorial Day through Labor Day, and 9 A.M. to 5 P.M. the rest of the year. Closed Tuesdays, November through February, and Thanksgiving, Christmas, and New Year's Day. Admission $17 for the Platinum Tour, which includes the mansion and all attractions in Graceland Plaza; $9 for the mansion only, with separate tickets available for the museums and planes. Allow two hours for the mansion, and up to six hours for the Platinum tour.

Graceland is 15 minutes from downtown Memphis. Take I-55/Exit 5B to Hwy. 51. 3734 Elvis Presley Boulevard; (800) 238-2000 or (901) 332-3322.

Texas

Northeast Texas

Jefferson
HOMETOWN OF VERNON DALHART

Country music's first recording star was a fellow from Jefferson, Texas, named Marion Try Slaughter II. Taking his stage name from two small towns in west Texas where he apparently worked as a cowboy, Vernon Dalhart went on to record a remarkable 5,000 songs under more than 135 pseudonyms during the twenties and thirties. He is best known for his 1924 Victor recordings of "Prisoner's Song" and "The Wreck of the Old 97." These records, widely considered the first hillbilly songs on 78 rpm, sold millions.

Dalhart's voice was an operatic tenor that generally doesn't appeal to today's country fans. But his terrific success, at a time when recording technology was new, convinced highbrow executives in New York that there was gold in them there hillbillies. (In 1927, Victor's Ralph Peer found Jimmie Rodgers and the Carter Family on a scouting trip in Bristol, Tennessee/Virginia.)

Unfortunately, Dalhart was dogged by bad luck. He lost a fortune when the stock market crashed in 1929, just as more "authentic" hillbilly singers like Rodgers and the Carters found their audiences. His recording career was over by the late 1930s. Quickly forgotten, he ended up working as a night watchman in Bridgeport, Connecticut.

Dalhart's hometown in northeast Texas began celebrating **Vernon Dalhart Days** in the mid-1990s. The Labor Day weekend **Country Music Celebration** features a headline act, songwriters' showcase, and local bands. Jack Palmer of Battle Creek, Michigan, the nation's (and probably the world's) most dedicated Dalhart fan, displays items from his collection. Since 1974, Palmer has collected more than 1,300 recordings. "What interested me was that he was supposed to be this seminal figure in country music history, but I didn't know a thing about him," Palmer says. "My mother used to sing 'The Prisoner's Song' to me, but she didn't know who he was, either.

"The thing is, I like his music," he adds. "I make tapes and listen to them on my car radio. To me he sounds better than Jimmie Rodgers, because he doesn't have that backwoods effect."

In downtown Jefferson, a restaurant called the **Cotton Gin** is where young Marion first sang as a boy. The place was called Kahn's Saloon then, and was owned by Marion's uncle, who is said to have killed Marion's father in the saloon. Two historical markers about Dalhart are outside the Cotton Gin, and photographs of Dalhart hang on the walls inside. 123 W. Austin St.; (903) 665-1153.

Kathy Johnson, who used to own the Cotton Gin and helps organize the festival, says the town would like to build a Vernon Dalhart Museum but is having trouble gathering enough items to display. Dalhart died in 1948, and most of his relatives are dead or difficult to find.

Jefferson is among the most historic small towns in Texas. In the late nineteenth century, it was the state's largest inland shipping port; 226 steamboats landed at Jefferson's port on Big Cypress River in 1872. Now known as the "Bed-and-Breakfast Capital of Texas," the city has dozens of inns, cottages, and converted Victorian mansions where guests are graciously received. The well-preserved community offers several small museums, antique shopping, outdoor recreation, restaurants, and several old-fashioned soda fountains.

Tours of homes, plantations, the downtown, and the Big Cypress bayou are available by foot, mule, boat, carriage, trolley, or train. Contact Jefferson's Tour Headquarters. 222 E. Austin St.; (903) 665-1665.

(A marker in Danville, Virginia, 65 miles south of Lynchburg, shows the site of the actual wreck of the Old '97; (804) 793-5422.)

GETTING THERE: Jefferson is about 60 miles south of Texarkana and 10 miles from the Louisiana border. Take I-20 to Hwy. 59 north. Contact the Marion County Chamber of Commerce; (903) 665-2672.

Carthage

HOMETOWN OF TEX RITTER AND JIM REEVES

Carthage, in Panola County, Texas, nurtured not one, but two members of the Country Music Hall of Fame: Tex Ritter (in 1964) and Jim Reeves (in 1967). Ritter was born in 1905 in Murvaul, while Reeves was born nearly twenty years later in Galloway. Tributes to both can be seen in Carthage, the county seat. (Contemporary singer Linda Davis is also from Panola County.)

A star on Shreveport's *Louisiana Hayride* early in his career, Reeves was a velvety-smooth crooner in a red suit jacket. After his death in a plane crash, his widow, Mary, built the **Jim Reeves Memorial** on Highway 79, in a private park about 2 miles north of Carthage. "I had a monument designed and built by an artisan from North Carolina, out of granite," says Davis, who is from the nearby town of Marshall. "He did a nice job."

The walkway to the Reeves monument is imbedded with a marble guitar. In the center where the sound hole should be is a 45 single that reads: "Gentleman Jim. Time: August 20, 1924 to July 31, 1964. Producer: God."

A statue stands atop a 15-foot-high monument, with Reeves tall in his trademark jacket and bow tie, hands folded over his guitar and eyes set in a kindly straightforward gaze. "If I, a lowly singer, dry one tear, or soothe one humble heart in pain," the inscription reads, "then my homely verse to God is clear and not one stanza has been sung in vain."

A little marker behind the monument shows the spot where Reeves's dog Chey-

At the Tex Ritter Museum, visitors can learn why Ritter is known as America's Favorite Cowboy.

enne was buried in 1967. The park is a peaceful, fitting memorial to Reeves.

Tex Ritter, a matinee idol in more than 80 motion pictures, got his start on Broadway and the radio. He recorded the theme song to *High Noon,* joined the *Grand Ole Opry,* served as president of the Country Music Association, and ran for U.S. Senator in Tennessee.

The **Tex Ritter Museum** begins in a small screening room with a short video narrated by John Ritter, who became a television star after his father's death in 1974. Rooms of the house are devoted to various stages of Ritter's career: Texas, New York, California, Nashville, as well as Trail's End, a re-creation of his Western-style living room. There are movie posters, costumes, campaign memorabilia, and personal items, including mementos from his sidekick, Lloyd "Arkansas Slim" Andrews, and his wife, the actress Dorothy Fay Southworth. All the top country stars backed Ritter's unsuccessful political campaign, including Roy Acuff, chair of Citizens for Tex; Johnny Cash, chair of the Ritter Finance Committee; and Chet Atkins, a member of Celebrities for Tex.

In a *Dallas News* article on display, longtime fan Jim Cooper of the Tex Ritter Fan Club movingly speaks of the singer's "humility, honesty, and willingness to lend others a helping hand." It's this aspect of Ritter's personality that the museum puts across beautifully—a sense of the man's charm, humor, and humanity, the reasons why he is known as America's Most Beloved Cowboy. Says John Ritter, "No man respected personal and professional integrity more than my father." Open weekdays 9 A.M. to 4:30 P.M.; 10:30 A.M. to 4:30 P.M. Saturdays; and 1 to 4:30 P.M. Sundays. Admission $2. Allow an hour. 300 W. Panola; (903) 693-6634.

Surrounded by tall pines, rolling hills, and clear lakes, Carthage is a relaxing place to spend a half-day or more. A shady central square anchors the downtown. On one side is the **Panola County Heritage Museum,** in the restored 1903 Bank of Carthage. The museum displays memorabilia about Reeves and Ritter, as well as famous Panola County residents Walter Prescott Webb, Margie Neal, and Milton Holland. The Texas Tea Room downstairs serves sandwiches and salads for lunch, and afternoon tea. 100 E. Sabine; (903) 693-8689.

The *Country Music Hayride* is staged in a storefront across the square. Free shows take place Saturday nights at 7 P.M., with local musicians performing for free.

(*See also:* Tennessee—Nashville; Texas—Beaumont Area.)

GETTING THERE: Carthage is on Hwy. 79 in northeast Texas near the Louisiana border, about 170 miles from Dallas and 40 miles from Shreveport. Take I-20 to Hwy. 59 or Hwy. 149 south. Contact the Panola County Chamber of Commerce; (903) 693-6634.

Dallas–Fort Worth
TEXAX METROPLEX

The Dallas–Fort Worth region, known as "the Texas Metroplex," is a sprawling cosmopolitan area encompassing two large cities and many smaller communities, with tall buildings, crisscrossing highways, and millions of people.

Willie Nelson's hometown of Abbott, a tiny community between Waco and Dallas, is just east of I-40/Exit 358. For information, contact City Hall; (817) 582-3911.

The Dallas–Fort Worth Area Tourism Council brags that the Texas Metroplex has "more music than Nashville," with at least a hundred nightly live performances of rock, classical music, blues, and jazz. For country fans, there are saloons and the world-famous Billy Bob's Texas at the Fort Worth Stockyards (*see below*). More than a dozen country music shows and Oprys are presented within a hundred miles of Metroplex (*see page 288*).

All the attractions expected of major American cities are here: science and art museums, historic sites, zoos, amusement parks, professional sports, performing arts, and dozens of shopping malls. The best way to avoid being overwhelmed by all Metroplex has to offer is to explore one unique neighborhood at a time. For example, you could spend a whole day in historic downtown Grapevine or Dallas's State Fair Park.

GETTING THERE: Texas Metroplex is 185 miles west of Shreveport, 250 miles north of Houston, and 210 miles south of Oklahoma City. Take I-20, I-30, I-35, or I-45. Contact The Dallas–Fort Worth Area Tourism Council; (800) METROPLEX or (214) 680-8580.

MY HOMETOWN

Jon Randall on Billy Bob's

"I always loved **Billy Bob's.** It's like the ultimate honky-tonk. Sometimes we just go hang out there, just to get our fill of honky-tonk. It's a bit touristy, but mostly it's people from around, a lot of your true Texas cowboys. They come in from the surrounding areas to two-step and drink and fight and whatever else. But it's really safe." (*See below.*)

Fort Worth Stockyards
COWTOWN, U.S.A.

Fort Worth, a central stop on the famed Chisholm Trail, has been known as Cowtown since the 1860s. During its heyday, the Fort Worth Stockyards handled more than 100 million head of livestock, many bound for the city's large meat-packing plants. During the mid–twentieth century, the packing houses closed one by one; by the 1960s the stockyards had seriously deteriorated.

The community rallied and launched a major redevelopment effort. Today, the cow population has been replaced by thousands of happy tourists who amble along gas-lit cobblestone streets in the 150-acre **Fort Worth Stockyards Historic District.** The Stockyards are lively, with a variety of activities: tours, museums, restaurants, saloons, shopping, rodeos, entertainment, and live country music day and night. (Weekly hog auctions and special cattle sales still take place in the auction arena.)

A good place to get started is the **Stockyards Visitors' Center,** where advice, maps, and brochures are dispensed by friendly volunteers. A free film is shown at regular intervals. The Center is also the starting point for historical walking tours of the Livestock Exchange Building (built in 1902), hog and sheep pens, cattlemen's catwalk, and mule alley. Tours cost $7 and leave on the hour, seven days a week. 130 E. Exchange Ave.; (817) 625-9715.

Billy Bob's Texas, "the world's largest honky-tonk," is 100,000 square feet (2.5 acres) of pure country, with 40 bar areas, 600 feet of bar rails, and two stages and dance floors. The sprawling place has an indoor bull-riding arena, barbecue restaurant, rows of pool tables, and video games. One section of wall is devoted to celebrity handprints, another to photographs. There's live entertainment every night, dance lessons, and headline acts on weekends. Admission $1 during the day; $5 to $15 for evening shows. Children are permitted at all times. 2520 Rodeo Plaza; (817) 624-7117.

Cowtown Coliseum, built in 1908, was the site of the first indoor rodeo. Every Saturday night late April through September, Cowtown Coliseum Rodeo showcases the original sport of Texas with bull riding, calf roping, and steer wrestling. On Saturday afternoons, *Pawnee Bill's Wild West Show* features singing cowboys, trick roping and shooting, live buffalo, and Texas longhorns. 121 E. Exchange Ave.; (817) 654-1148.

On Sunday afternoons Memorial Day through September, *Cowtown Opry* is presented for free, outdoors in front of the Livestock Exchange Building. The Cowtown Opry Bovine Band plays Texas traditional music and backs up local performers, 131 E. Exchange Ave.; (817) 366-9675.

Inside the Exchange, the **Stockyards Collection and Museum** displays historical exhibits, artifacts, and old photographs. Open 10 A.M. to 5 P.M. Monday through Saturday year-round, 131 E. Exchange Ave.; (817) 625-5082.

The Stockyards are a shopper's paradise, with unique stores selling Western wear, collectibles, antiques, gifts, original art, and Indian jewelry. **Ernest Tubb Record Shop No. 6** stocks country music recordings, books, and videos, including rare and hard-to-find items. 140 E. Exchange Ave.; (817) 624-8449.

In addition to steak and barbecue restaurants, there are more than a dozen saloons in the Stockyards with names like Filthy McNasty's, the Watering Trough, the White Elephant, and the Booger Red Saloon, where live music, dancing, and drinking take place every night.

Annual events at the Stockyards include Chisholm Trail Roundup in late June, Pioneer Days in late August, and Red Steagall's Cowboy Gathering the fourth weekend in October.

GETTING THERE: The Stockyards are just north of downtown Fort Worth at N. Main St. and Exchange Ave. Take Bus. Hwy. 287, I-35W, or Rte. 183, and follow the signs; (800) 433-5747 or (817) 336-8791.

COWGIRL CONNECTION

The **National Cowgirl Hall of Fame and Western Heritage Center,** based in Hereford, Texas, since 1975, is in the process of relocating to downtown Fort Worth. The Hall of Fame honors more than 130 wonderful women of the West, including Annie Oakley, Betty Gayle Cooper Ratliff (an Oklahoma rodeo star), Laura Ingalls Wilder, and Georgia O'Keefe. Musical honorees include Louise Massey, Patsy Montana, and Dale Evans.

The new museum, expected to open around 1998, will feature professionally designed exhibits of memorabilia, photographs, and biographical information. The Center's library and archives are currently open to the public in downtown Fort Worth, in addition to a gift shop and small preview showcase. Four new members are inducted annually (two real cowgirls, two western heritage) at the annual **Rhinestone Roundup** festival, timed to coincide with the **Women's Rodeo Finals** in early November.

The center also provides quarterly exhibits to the Cowgirl Hall of Fame restaurants in New York City and Santa Fe, New Mexico.

GETTING THERE: Call for current information on the Cowgirl Hall of Fame museum's status. The offices are open 9 A.M. to 5 P.M. weekdays. 111 W. 4th St., Suite 300; (800) 476-FAME.

Country Shows
METROPLEX MUSIC MADNESS

Oprys in the Texas Metroplex area usually take place on Saturday nights year-round, and feature a house band, a regular cast of singers, and special guests. Most of these shows cost between $4 and $10. Call ahead to confirm schedules and times. When estimating driving times, remember that Dallas and Fort Worth are 40 miles apart.

I am indebted to a wonderful magazine called *Metroplex Entertainment News,* edited by "DottyB," which provides detailed information on the area's country music scene. For a sample issue or subscription, contact DottyB at 1620 Hillcrest St., Mesquite, TX 75149; (214) 329-5035.

Following is a partial listing of Metroplex area shows:

Johnnie High's Country Music Review in Arlington has been going strong since 1975. A country-and-variety show is presented on Saturday afternoons and evenings, and a gospel show on the first and third Friday nights of each month. Arlington is midway between Fort Worth and Dallas. Take I-20/Exit 30B (Hwy. 80 east). 224 N. Center; (817) 577-8287.

The **Grapevine Opry,** in the city's historic Palace Theatre, offers a new show every Saturday night. The *Opry*'s monthly "special theme" shows are scripted productions with scenery and props. A gospel show is presented on the fourth Friday of every month. Grapevine is midway between Dallas and Fort Worth; Grapevine Lake is just north, Dallas–Fort Worth Airport to the south. Take Hwy. 121 or Hwy. 114. 308 S. Main St.; (817) 481-8733.

Downtown Grapevine has more than 50 restored turn-of-the-century buildings, numerous shops, and restaurants. Numerous special events take place year-round, including **Historic Main Street Days** the third weekend in May and **Grapefest** the second week in September; (800) 457-6338 or (817) 481-0454.

In Stephenville, 60 miles southwest of Fort Worth, Carroll Parham's *Cross Timbers Opry* is a year-round Saturday-night show with a variety of guests, Nashville performers, and specialty acts such as cowboy poets. Milton Brown Day, a tribute to the Western Swing pioneer, takes place the third Saturday in March, featuring the Light Crust Doughboys. Take Hwy. 377 bypass, 1 mile east of Stephenville; (817) 965-5582 or 965-4575.

Country Love in Granbury, 35 miles southwest of Fort Worth, presents a gospel show on Friday nights and a country show on Saturday nights. Bob and Mel Smith are featured artists, along with the Country Love Band and special guests. Take Hwy. 377 to Granbury, then north on Hwy. 51. 404 N. Houston; (800) 950-2212 or (817) 573-5548.

About 10 miles south of Fort Worth, *Burleson Jamboree* is a Saturday-night Opry with a house band and talented regional performers. Take I-35W/Exit 37 (Hwy. 174) to Burleson. 306 N.E. Wilshire; (817) 295-3512.

One of the premier shows on the Texas circuit is *Wylie Opry,* just north of Dallas. The Texas Legend Band puts on a fast-paced show and makes their guest artists feel welcome. Headline acts are booked from time to time. Take I-635/Exit 12 to Rte. 78 north through Garland to Wylie. 111 N. Ballard; (214) 442-3047.

Garland Opry features the band Silverado and new performers each Saturday night. Garland is a large city in the northeast corner of Dallas County. Take I-635/Exit 12 to Rte. 78 north. 605 W. State St. (on downtown square); (214) 494-3835.

A few miles north of Dallas in Carrollton, Plaza Theatre/Music on the Square presents *Carrollton Country Opry* on Saturday nights and bluegrass, jazz, or gospel performers on Friday nights. The theater is located in an historic district surrounded by shops and restaurants. Take I-35/Exit 443A. 1115 Fourth St.; (214) 242-2775.

Corsicana

LEFTY FRIZZELL MEMORIAL

Honky-tonk hero Lefty Frizzell was born in Corsicana, south of Dallas, on March 31, 1928. Achieving stardom in the early 1950s with "I Love You a Thousand Ways" and "If You've Got the Money, I've Got the Time," Frizzell had dozens of hits in a hard-driving, Texas dance-hall style. He died in Nashville in 1975, and was inducted into the Country Music Hall of Fame in 1982.

Several years later, Frizzell was honored in Corsicana with a monument. At its base is a quote from Merle Haggard: "There is really no way I can describe the effect Lefty had on audiences back in those days. He had the soul of Hank Williams, the appeal of Johnny Cash, and the charisma of Elvis Presley. He had it all—brilliance and clarity!"

Tim Steely's mural in Corsicana's Jester Park commemorates Lefty Frizzell's hits, awards, and honors.

The Lefty Frizzell Memorial in Corsicana's Jester Park features a statue with Frizzell standing on a marble pedestal, strumming his guitar and tapping a toe. It stands in the center of a guitar-shaped walkway surrounded by benches and yellow marigolds.

A small mural by Tim Steely, dedicated in 1993, commemorates Frizzell's Top Ten hits, awards, and honors, his star on Hollywood's Walk of Fame, and his 25-year Columbia recording contract. Haggard, Hank Williams, Jr., Merle Kilgore, Floyd Tillman, and Johnny Duncan contributed to erecting the monument, as did Lefty's brothers David and Allen Frizzell and KAND Radio. It's a moving tribute to one of country's most influential artists. (N. 19th St. and W. Park Ave.)

Adjacent to the memorial in Pioneer Village, a small **Lefty Frizzell Museum** displays country music memorabilia and items donated by the Frizzell family. Open 9 A.M. to 5 P.M. Monday through Saturday; 1 to 5 P.M. Sundays. Admission $1. 912 W. Park Ave; (903) 654-4846. Lefty Frizzell festivals take place some years. Call for information.

Corsicana's historic downtown is being restored through the Texas Main Street Program. Local attractions include **Collin Street Bakery,** world-famous for Deluxe Fruitcakes. 401 W. Seventh Ave.; (903) 874-7477. **Hat Brands** manufactures Stetson, Resistol, and George Strait hats. I-45 Bus; (903) 874-7446. The second-largest pecan sheller in the world, **Navarro Pecan Company,** cracks about 35 million nuts a year in Corsicana. I-45 and Hwy. 31; (903) 872-5641.

GETTING THERE: Corsicana is about 50 miles south of Dallas. Take I-45/Exit 228 to Hwy. 31; Contact the Corsicana Area Chamber of Commerce; (903) 874-4731.

Meridian
REMEMBERING THE BALLAD HUNTER, JOHN LOMAX

John A. Lomax was a reknowned scholar of American folklore who collected cowboy ballads and songs out on the range in Bosque County, along one of the Chisholm trails. Known as the Ballad Hunter, Lomax preserved cowboy folk culture that had been passed along solely by word of mouth. Working with his son, Alan, Lomax documented cowboy culture and made the first recordings of Woody Guthrie and Huddy Ledbetter (Leadbelly).

Lomax's hometown of Meridian honors him the last Saturday in May with the **John A. Lomax Gathering and Music Festival,** featuring American folk music, cowboy poetry, blues, barbecue, and crafts exhibits. Everyone is urged to dress in clothing styles of the 1860s to early 1900s. Lomax's daughter Shirley, in her nineties, has sung and told stories at several gatherings.

GETTING THERE: Meridian is about 60 miles southwest of Fort Worth. Take I-35/Exit 368A (Hillsboro) to Rte. 22 west; (817) 435-2966.

Salado

COUNTRY MUSIC ASSOCIATION OF TEXAS HALL OF FAME

Father and son Bud and Lee Fisher, entertainers and ex–radio announcers, formed the Country Music Association of Texas in 1989 to promote new artists and to recognize established Texas artists. "We decided that there's a lot of people trying to get off the ground who might need our help, as well as old-time and traditional country artists who are not on major labels," Bud Fisher says.

Their Country Music Association of Texas Hall of Fame is in Salado, south of Waco. The museum displays a modest collection of memorabilia. Mostly "old-timers" are inducted into the Hall of Fame each year, such as Vernon Dalhart and Floyd Tillman. The awards show takes place at a different location every year, usually around October 28, "Country Music Day in Texas."

GETTING THERE: Salado is about 45 miles south of Waco. The museum is on the interstate access road, next to the Howard Johnson Inn. Take I-35/Exit 283. Call for hours or appointment; (817) 947-0018.

For area information, contact the Salado Chamber of Commerce; (817) 947-5040.

Abilene Area Festivals

Abilene's **Western Heritage Classic,** the second weekend in May, celebrates the ranching life with a rodeo, cowboy poets, nightly dances, and the world's largest bit-and-spur show. Abilene Expo Center, 1700 Hwy. 36; (915) 677-4376.

Stamford, 40 miles north of Abilene, has hosted the annual **Texas Cowboy Reunion** since 1930. The famous four-day event, over the July Fourth weekend, draws more than 15,000 people for chuckwagon dinners, parades, and the world's largest amateur rodeo. Local attractions include the **Cowboy Country Museum** and **Old-Timers' Association Museum.** Take I-20/Exit 286 (Abilene) to Hwy. 273/83 north; (915) 773-2411.

Thirty-five miles northwest of Abilene in Hamlin, the two-day **Back to Rath's Trail** festival takes place the first weekend in June, and features living history camps, Western crafts, and much more. Take Hwy. 277 to Hwy. 83 north; (915) 576-3501.

The *Fort Griffin Fandangle* in Albany is an outdoor musical that tells the frontier history of the area with a "unique blend of hoedown and ballet, laughter, and solemnity." Performances are the last two weekends in June at the Prairie Theatre in Albany, about 35 miles northeast of Abilene. From Abilene, take Rte. 351 north and follow signs; (915) 762-3642.

Southeast Texas

Beaumont Area
EAST TEXAS HEROES

Mark Chesnutt, Tracy Byrd, and Clay Walker all got their starts in the clubs around Beaumont, a center for oil, agriculture, and industry in Texas' southeastern corner. (Spindletop, the world's first oil gusher, blew here at 10 A.M. on January 10, 1901, creating a boomtown.) For country fans, however, Beaumont can only mean one thing: George Jones. "The Possum," considered by many to be the greatest country singer ever, was born in Saratoga, a small town northwest of the city, on September 12, 1931.

Beaumont held its first **George Jones Day** on October 1, 1995, and renamed the 300 block of Fannin Street "George Jones Place." The I-10 bridge spanning the Neches River in Beaumont was also renamed for Jones. The 1927 Jefferson Theater, where Jones did his first show, is on the block. The *Charlie Pruitt Country Music Show* is presented here monthly, as well as community theater and special events. 345 Fannin; (409) 832-6649.

Attractions in Beaumont include industrial, agricultural, and crawfish farm tours, restored Beaux Arts mansions, the Melody Maids Museum, Texas's official Fire Museum, the Old Town district, and Spindletop. A good place to start is the **Babe Didrikson Zaharias Museum and Visitors' Center,** which honors the world's greatest woman athlete and provides travel information. 1750 I-10E/Exit 854; (409) 833-4622.

Ten miles south of Beaumont in Nederland, a small **Tex Ritter Museum** is housed in a Dutch windmill. The beloved country-and-western star lived near Nederland, and his family donated a suit, boots, and other mementos. Free; hours are limited—call for times and appointments. Take Rte. 347 (Twin Cities Hwy.); (409) 722-0279. (*See also:* Carthage [*this chapter*].)

In Port Arthur, the **Museum of the Gulf Coast** offers exhibits on the region's musical heritage, including Tex Ritter, George Jones, Janis Joplin, and J.P. Richardson (The Big Bopper). Take I-10 to Hwy. 287 into Port Arthur. Beaumont and 4th St.; (409) 982-7000.

GETTING THERE: Beaumont is 90 miles east of Houston on I-10. For information, call the Beaumont Visitors' Bureau; (800) 392-4401 or (409) 880-3749.

Houston Area Music Shows

Rosenberg Opry, which calls itself the "Biggest Little Show in Texas," is located in the 1919 Cole Theater in downtown Rosenberg, 20 miles southwest of Houston. Performances are every Friday night at 8 P.M., with a five-piece house band, a regular cast of entertainers, and special guests performing country, gospel, and polka music. Kitchen opens at 6:30 P.M. Tickets $6. Rosenberg is at Hwy. 59 and Rte. 36. 930 Third St.; (713) 342-3827 or (409) 732-9322.

Columbus Opry is located in Columbus, about 65 miles west of Houston. The show offers live music every Saturday night at the Oaks Theater, two blocks west of Columbus town square. Take I-10/Exit 696. 715 Walnut St.; (409) 732-9210.

In Magnolia, about 15 miles north of Houston, **Country Music Jamboree** is a Saturday-night variety show with country, gospel, clogging, comedy, and guest singers. There's a talent showcase on the first Friday and a gospel show on the last Friday of every month. Take Rte. 249. 37937 Rte. 1774; (713) 356-3737.

Texas Hill Country

Ever since Jimmie Rodgers built his "Blue Yodeler's Paradise" mansion in Kerrville, the Texas Hill Country has had a special place in the heart of country music. From Kerrville to Luckenbach, to Austin to San Antonio, southeast Texas jumps and swings in dozens of dance halls, country clubs, roadhouses, and honky-tonks. It also happens to be beautiful territory, lush with rivers, forests, hills, lakes, and streams. Following is only a sampling of the live country music waiting for you in the Hill Country.

GETTING THERE: The Hill Country is in south-central Texas. Contact the Hill Country Tourism Association; (210) 895-5505.

Austin
LIVE-MUSIC CAPITAL OF THE WORLD

Austin lives up to its motto, the "Live-Music Capital of the World." Willie Nelson, Kelly Willis, Nanci Griffith, Jerry Jeff Walker, and Robert Earl Keen are among the many artists who live and perform around the city.

Downtown on **Sixth Street** (Old Pecan Street) the sounds of alternative rock, country, folk, Tejano, and blues pour out of dozens of nightclubs. The Sixth Street entertainment district is seven blocks long, between Congress Avenue and I-35. Other clubs around the city offer live music, and free outdoor concerts are offered year-round. Check the *Austin-American Stateman* or the *Austin Chronicle* for listings.

One of Texas' most famous dance halls is **The Broken Spoke,** a classic honky-tonk that books dance bands. Its museum displays old guitars and unusual mementos left by performers. 3201 S. Lamar Blvd.; (512) 442-6189.

Jerry Jeff Walker's Birthday Celebration the last weekend in March draws more than 5,000 fans to Austin every year for a three-day bash. The festival includes rodeos, dances, golf tournaments, and a Saturday-night concert at the Paramount Theater; (512) 477-0036.

Since 1975, the popular PBS series *Austin City Limits* has brought the city's unique brand of country and folk music into millions of American homes. Performances, taped live, are scheduled irregularly. Tickets are difficult to obtain, but it's well worth a try; (512) 471-4811.

Austin area **attractions** include the state capitol, historic sites and tours, museums, parks, the excellent Lyndon B. Johnson Presidential Museum and Library, and the Dallas Cowboys' training camp. More than 1.5 million bats, the nation's largest urban colony, hang out beneath the Congress Avenue Bridge on Town Lake, emerging nightly March through November in a spectacular display. The city also boasts more restaurants and bars per capita than any city in the nation.

Willie Nelson's Pedernales Golf Course, about 25 miles west of Austin in Briarcliff, is often open to the public, and the pro-shop displays memorabilia and gold records. Call for directions; (512) 264-1489.

GETTING THERE: Austin is 85 miles north of San Antonio on I-35. Contact the Visitors' Bureau; (800) 926-2282 or (512) 474-5171.

¡Viva Luckenbach!

There really is a Luckenbach, Texas, about 70 miles west of Austin. Waylon Jennings immortalized this tiny hamlet with his 1977 hit "Luckenbach, Texas (Back to the Basics of Life)." Jerry Jeff Walker recorded his classic 1973 album, *¡Viva Terlingua!,* here, and returned in 1993 for a sequel, *¡Viva Luckenbach!* Walker even got married here.

Luckenbach has 25 residents, a general store that doubles as a tavern, and that's about it. On Sunday afternoons, fiddlers, banjo players, and other musicians often perform in spontaneous "happenings" under huge live oaks. **Luckenbach Hall,** a weather-worn place that dates back to the 1880s, books concerts once or twice a month.

GETTING THERE: Luckenbach is 70 miles west of Austin. Take I-10 to Hwy. 87. At Fredricksburg, go east on Hwy. 290, then south on Rte. 1376. Call for schedules; (210) 997-3224.

Kerrville
BLUE YODELER'S PARADISE

The small city of **Kerrville** is west of San Antonio. Living high in 1929, Jimmie Rodgers built his "Blue Yodeler's Paradise," a large red-brick home at 617 West Main Street for $50,000, overlooking the downtown. It is privately owned, but can be viewed from the road. From downtown, take Hwy. 27 west to West Main, to the top of the hill. The house is on the left. Local attractions include the **Cowboy Artists of America Museum,** open daily. 1550 Bandera Hwy. (Rte. 173); (210) 896-2553. The **Texas Heritage Music Celebration** features traditional country music and cowboy culture the third weekend of September at Schreiner College. The festival includes Texas's only tribute to Jimmie Rodgers. Hwy. 27; (210) 896-3339.

Begun in 1972, the **Kerrville Folk Festival** has grown into eighteen full days of folk concerts, workshops, and bike rides in the hills surrounding Quiet Valley Ranch. In the campgrounds, groups gather under trees to write songs, sing ballads, and jam. Campfires burn all night long. The festival begins the Thursday before Memorial Day. Nine miles south of Kerrville on Rte. 16; (800) 435-8429 or (210) 257-3600.

GETTING THERE: Kerrville is 65 miles west of San Antonio on I-10. Contact the Visitors' Bureau; (210) 792-3535.

Bandera
COWBOY CAPITAL

Bandera County, the "Cowboy Capital of the World," received its title from the days when it was a staging area for the great cattle drives of yesteryear. Fifty miles northwest of San Antonio, Bandera is the place for dude ranches, rodeos, ranch tours, horseback riding, and chuckwagon cookouts in the Hill Country. The music of choice is country, of course, at clubs like the world-famous **Silver Dollar** and **Arkey Blue's Silver Dollar Saloon** on Main Street downtown.

GETTING THERE: Take I-10 to Rte. 46 west, to Rte. 16 north. Contact the Bandera Visitors' Bureau; (800) 364-3833.

New Braunfels
GRUENE HALL

The oldest continuously operating dance hall in Texas is Gruene Hall, built in 1878 in New Braunfels, an historic town between Austin and San Antonio. George Strait played Gruene Hall for six years before he became a star; David Ball says he started writing "Thinkin' Problem" while on its stage. Jerry Jeff Walker, Joe Ely, John Hiatt, and Guy Clark are regulars. Take I-35/Exit 187. 1281 Gruene Rd.; (210) 606-1281. For New Braunfels information, call (210) 625-2385.

MY HOMETOWN

Ray Benson on Texas Dance Halls

"**John T. Floore Country Store,** that's where I first played with Willie Nelson, years ago. That was Willie's home place. It's in Helotes. It's got to be over 60 years old. They serve sausage sandwiches and beer. He's got an outdoor dance patio that holds two or three thousand, and an indoors that's pretty small, holds about three or four hundred. John T. Floore, he's dead now, he was as tall as I am, six foot seven. Back then, that was a big man. Floore's is outside San Antonio, about 40 or 50 miles. It's still cooking.

"Dance halls in Texas are a world unto itself. First of all, there's certain songs that you play that you play nowhere else. There are many Germans and Prussians and Czechs and Bohemians all over Texas, and they've kept the traditions of polkas and schottisches alive. You have to do the cotton-eyed Joe and as soon as you're done with it you play the schottische. That's the routine.

(Photo by Brenda Ladd)

"They also do waltzes and the famous Texas two-step. It's all based on Johnny Bush, Ray Price, Western Swing. Bob Wills's music. 'Faded Love.' You have to do 'Faded Love.'

"They used to do a thing in Texas called the Paul Jones dance. Part of being a bandleader was that you had to have a whistle. There were two circles, men on the outside, women on the inside. The circles went around, and when the band leader blows the whistle, wherever it stopped, that's who you danced with. So there were a lot of fights, usually, after the Paul Jones dance. That's what a real Texas dance hall is about."

GETTING THERE: John T. Floore's Country Store is in Helotes, about 15 miles northwest of San Antonio. Take I-410 to Rte. 16. 14464 Old Bandera Hwy.; (210) 695-8827.

San Antonio
CORNUCOPIA OF CULTURES

San Antonio, the tenth largest city in the United States, describes itself in brochures as "part Old South, part Wild West." Mix in some Mexican, Spanish, and German culture, and you've got a truly eclectic American city. Local attractions include cultural arts venues, botanical gardens, crafts and fine-arts museums, centuries-old neighborhoods, and historic sites. (Remember the Alamo!) In downtown San Antonio, **Riverwalk** is a charming district of restaurants, hotels, shops, and clubs.

The **Institute of Texan Cultures** lets visitors get acquainted with the twenty-six different ethnic and cultural groups that make up the state—their food, clothing, music, and festivals. Open daily 9 A.M. to 5 P.M. (except Monday). Free. 801 S. Bowie; (210) 558-2300.

The theme park **Fiesta Texas** celebrates Texas music and culture in areas called Los Festivales (Hispanic), Crackaxle Canyon (Western boomtown), Spassburg (German village), and Rockville (1950s nostalgia). Developed by La Cantera Group and a subsidiary of Nashville's Opryland, Fiesta Texas offers professional music shows in the Opryland style, roving performers, and concerts by well-known performers. There's also a water park, pyrotechnic displays, rides and roller coasters, and a 90-foot Ferris wheel.

Open mid-March through December, with varying hours and seasonal closures. Admission $27.95 adults, $18.95 children. The park is 15 miles northwest of San Antonio, at I-10 and Loop 1604/Exit 555; (800) 473-4378 or (210) 697-5050.

On the grounds of the Lone Star Brewery, the **Buckhorn Hall of Horns Museum** displays an incredible taxidermy collection: horns (including a 78-point deer antler), feathers, fins, rattlesnake artwork, and more. Admission $5. 600 Lone Star Blvd.; (210) 270-9467.

When the urge to two-step hits, try **Farmer's Daughter,** a classic dance hall with a large collection of Texas country-music photos and memorabilia. 542 N. W.W. White; (210) 333-7391.

San Antonio offers numerous **festivals** throughout the year, including George Strait's Labor Day Country Music Festival at the Alamodome. The Tejano Conjunto Festival in mid-May celebrates this unusual mix of Mexican and German music.

GETTING THERE: San Antonio is in south-central Texas, at I-10, I-35, and I-37. Contact the Visitors' Bureau; (800) 447-3372 or (210) 270-8700.

Palo Duro Canyon
THERE'S A LITTLE BIT OF EVERYTHING IN *TEXAS*

TEXAS: A Musical Romance of Panhandle History has been performed in an outdoor theater under the big Texas sky for more than four decades. The story, written by Pulitzer Prize–winning dramatist Paul Green, is about the settling of a Texas Panhandle town by feisty pioneers in the 1890s. The play is first-rate entertainment, but what makes *TEXAS* so special is the setting: Palo Duro Canyon State Park, a dramatic gorge south of Amarillo carved into the north Texas plains by the Red River.

The 1,740-seat Pioneer Amphitheater, with its 40- by-80-foot stage on the canyon floor faces a 600-foot red-clay cliff. The entire canyon comes alive with cowboys and Indians on horseback, farm animals, brightly colored flags, stagecoaches and trains, colored lights, and campfires. There's a re-creation of a thunderstorm sweeping in across the plains, and a brilliant fireworks show. A barbecue dinner can be purchased before the show, just outside the amphitheater.

The 110-mile canyon is a beautiful place to spend a day or more, camping, hiking, biking, and horseback riding.

Nearby, covered wagons take visitors to Creekwood Ranch for an **Old West Show and Chuckwagon Dinner** with cowboy poetry, singing, and rope tricks. Trips leave Thursday through Saturday evenings, May through October. Take I-40 to Washington St. south. Reservations required; (800) 658-6673 or (806) 356-9256.

Michael Martin Murphey brings his **WestFest** to Palo Duro Canyon the weekend after Labor Day. Modeled after Buffalo Bill's Wild West show, Murphey's two-day festival celebrates the art, music, and culture of the Old and New West. It features top-name country stars, Western artists, an Indian village, and Red Steagall's cow camp. Before the festival, Murphey and Steagall usually lead a three-day trail ride through the canyon; (806) 378-3096. (*See also:* Colorado—Copper Mountain.)

Texas Panhandle

All Gonna Meet Down at the Cadillac Ranch

In 1974, an eccentric millionaire named Stanley Marsh III gave three young idealistic architects from San Francisco the money to upend ten Cadillacs in a cornfield west of Amarillo. The graffiti-covered cars, models from 1949 to 1964, can be seen from I-40. They stand in a row, noses down, leaning at the same 52-degree angle as the Egyptian pyramids. The artists sought to memorialize the tail fin, a symbol of the Route 66 car culture that was destroyed by the interstate highway system.

"Cadillac Ranch is the greatest expression of American art," Marsh once said. "It is better than Mount Rushmore or the Statue of Liberty, which was actually made by a Frenchman so it really doesn't count."

Whether it's great art or not is debatable, but the Cadillac Ranch has definitely become a cultural icon, immortalized in song by Chris LeDoux and Bruce Springsteen. A steady stream of visitors stop by to gawk daily.

East of Amarillo, the **Big Texan Opry** is a country dinner show performed on Tuesday nights at the Big Texan Steak House, accompanied by live Western entertainment. Take I-40/Lakeside exit; (800) 657-7177 or (806) 372-6000.

GETTING THERE: Amarillo is in the center of the Texas panhandle. There is no sign, no gate, and no admission charge to Cadillac Ranch. Look for the Cadillacs on the south side of I-40 between Exits 62 and 64, a few miles west of Amarillo. Park on the service road and walk through the fence opening into the field. Contact the Amarillo Visitors' Bureau; (800) 654-1902 or (806) 374-1497.

GETTING THERE: Palo Duro Canyon State Park is 25 miles southeast of Amarillo. Park admission is free after 5:30 P.M. for those attending *TEXAS.* The show is presented mid-June through August. Tickets $3.50 to $16. Take I-27 south to Hwy. 217; (806) 655-2181.

For camping and park information, contact Palo Duro State Park; (806) 488-2227.

Lubbock Area
WEST TEXAS HEROES

In a career spanning just 18 months, Buddy Holly (born Charles Hardin Holley) had seven Top Ten hits including "That'll Be the Day" and "Peggy Sue." Considered a pioneer of rock and roll, he was one of the first to rely almost exclusively on his own songs and to overdub guitar and voice. Waylon Jennings, from nearby Littlefield, was bassist for Holly's band, the Crickets. (In turn, Holly played guitar on Waylon's first record.)

On a tour of the Midwest, the charter plane carrying Holly, Ritchie Valens, J.P. Richardson ("The Big Bopper"), and pilot Roger Peterson crashed on February 3, 1959, killing all on board. As the story goes, Jennings and Richardson flipped a coin for the last seat on the plane; Jennings lost and boarded the bus instead.

The **Buddy Holly Statue and Walk of Fame** in downtown Lubbock honors the rich musical heritage of west Texas. Surrounding a life-size statue of Holly in a stark Civic Center plaza, bronze plaques pay tribute to Jennings, Jimmy Dean, Mac Davis, Tanya Tucker, Bob Wills, Roy Orbison, Joe Ely, the Gatlin Brothers, and others. Avenue Q (Hwy. 84) and 8th Street.

The Lubbock Chamber of Commerce publishes a guide to a **driving tour** of eleven Buddy Holly places of interest, including his birthplace, high school, Baptist church, and home. Fans leave guitar picks on Holly's grave at the **City of Lubbock Cemetery,** a gesture symbolizing that his music continues on. The cemetery entrance is at 2011 East 31st Street. Take the right fork to the gravesite.

City brochures show Holly's trademark thick glasses as the "OO" in their slogan "LOOK TO LUBBOCK"; the city's minor-league baseball team is even called the Crickets. Twenty-six items of Holly memorabilia were purchased in 1995, including his Fender Stratocaster guitar, personal notebook, and recording contract, which will anchor a future museum honoring west Texas musicians.

The second weekend in September, Lubbock hosts the four-day **National Cowboy Symposium, Celebration, and Chuckwagon Cook-off.** This tribute to the American cowboy features live performances by poets, singers, musicians, and storytellers, as well as a chuck-wagon cook-off and a trade show. Free. Lubbock Memorial Civic Center; (806) 742-2498.

Littlefield, **hometown of Waylon Jennings,** is 40 miles northwest of Lubbock. The town built a stage for him on Route 385, with a big "W" at the top. There's now a Waylon Jennings RV park, a Waylon Jennings horseshoe court, and Waylon Jennings Boulevard. Tall black letters on the water tower, visible for miles, declare Littlefield the "Hometown of Waylon Jennings." The town's Denim Festival, during Labor Day weekend, features a concert by Jennings and friends. Littlefield is at Hwys. 84 and 385. Contact the Chamber of Commerce; (806) 385-5331.

In O'Donnell, 45 miles south of Lubbock on Hwy. 87, a bust of **Dan Blocker** stands in the central square. Blocker, an O'Donnell native, played Hoss Cartwright on the television show *Bonanza.*

(*See also:* Iowa—Clear Lake; New Mexico—Clovis.)

GETTING THERE: Lubbock is in the center of the Texas Panhandle, 120 miles south of Amarillo at I-27 and Hwys. 82, 84, and 87. Contact the Visitors' Bureau; (800) 692-4035 or (806) 747-5232.

Turkey
HOME OF BOB WILLS

Turkey, Texas (pop. 507), is in the middle of a flat stretch of the Texas Panhandle that seems to go on forever. There really is nothing else for miles and miles around; the closest cities are Amarillo and Lubbock, about 100 miles away.

Yet that's exactly what gives Turkey its unexpected grace and charm. You are welcomed to "Turkey, Texas, Home of Bob Wills" by a lovely black wrought-iron sign with silhouettes of cowboys, bulls, windmills, a fiddle, and dancing musical notes. Street markers in the same style line the dusty downtown. A marble Wills monument sits at one end of Main Street, a small museum at the other. The classic Hotel Turkey, where Wills played his first gigs, wouldn't be surprising in the downtown of a small Texan city, yet it's a delightful surprise in this tiny town.

Bob Wills, the King of Western Swing, was born near Kosse, south of Dallas. He moved to Turkey as a young man and cut hair at Ham's Barber Shop on Main Street. In 1929, he angrily left town after being jailed for rowdiness, and eventually became a wildly popular fiddler and band leader. Turkey and Wills patched things up years after his departure; the first Bob Wills festival was held in 1972, three years before the bandleader's death.

"Bob Wills was a musical revolutionary," the *Country Music Encyclopedia* explains (New York: Times Books, 1994). "Nobody thinks twice about horns, drums, and electric instruments in country music today, but before he demonstrated their potential, they were taboo." Wills classics include "San Antonio Rose," "Faded Love," and "Bubbles in My Beer."

The **Bob Wills Center** houses Turkey's City Hall, senior-citizens center, the justice of the peace, public library, and a three-room **Bob Wills Museum.** The low-key museum has photographs of Wills in trademark white hat and ever-present cigar, with various incarnations of the Texas Playboys in matching suits. There are photos of Wills riding his horse, Punkin (onstage!); a movie poster from *Take Me Back to Tulsa,* in which he starred with Tex Ritter; and cases of mementos, original fiddles, cigar holders, the contents of his wallet, penknives, and spurs and boots. Western Swing plays on a cassette deck in the corner, and a large scrapbook is filled with clippings, telegrams, and letters.

The **Bob Wills Monument** is a tall, octagonal, red marble kiosk on the west side of town with a silver fiddle on top. Panels tell the Bob Wills story: his World War II infantry service, stardom at Tulsa's Cains Ballroom, and the Hollywood years, as well as a list of classic Wills songs, and honors such as induction in the Country Music Hall of Fame. One panel is a map with directions to the Wills farm nearby, between Little Red River and Prairie Dog Town Fork. The monument is free and open all the time.

Although you can see these sites in a few hours, the best way to experience the town is to stay overnight at the **Hotel Turkey** bed-and-breakfast. The 20-room hotel opened in 1927. Two years later, Wills played small evening concerts in the dining room. "There are still eyewitnesses in town who came to the shows," owner Scott Johnson says.

Johnson and his wife, Jane, bought the deteriorating hotel for $25,000 in the late 1980s. "I was tired of selling insurance in Dallas," explains Johnson, whose relatives were from Turkey. The couple restored the hotel to how it was in the 1920s, paying close attention to details: Rooms are equipped with clawfoot bathtubs, overhead fans, lace curtains, and antique writing tables. Guests get Texas sun-dried linens, home-style cooking, and access to a petting barnyard, horseback riding, tennis court, and duck pond. Singers and cowboy poets entertain in the dining room from time to time.

If you can't stay overnight, stop in and take a look around, or stay for a campfire chuckwagon dinner or family-style meal. RV hookups can also be arranged. Room rates start at $35 per night. 3rd and Alexander; (800) 657-7110 or (806) 423-1151.

Thousands of people attend **Bob Wills Day,** on the third Friday and Saturday in April, with a fiddling contest, parade, barbecue, and Western Swing concert. It's impossible to get a room at Hotel Turkey that weekend, but accommodations are available two hours away in Lubbock or Amarillo. There are plenty of campsites at Caprock Canyon State Park west of Turkey, and Palo Duro Canyon State Park south of Amarillo. (*See above.*)

GETTING THERE: Turkey is in the Texas Panhandle, between Lubbock and Amarillo, at Hwys. 86 and 70. The museum is open in the mornings and afternoons on weekdays, or by appointment. Call for times. Allow an hour. 6th and Lyle Sts.; (806) 423-1033 or 423-1490.

Southwest Texas

Brackettville
ALAMO VILLAGE

Alamo Village, built for the John Wayne movie *The Alamo* in 1957, has since served as the location for dozens of Western movies, television shows, and commercials including the *Roy Rogers Show, Lonesome Dove,* and *Streets of Laredo.* The $12 million set includes an exact replica of the original Alamo, with saloons, stores, stables, and many other structures. It's stocked with plenty of authentic props: stagecoaches, wagons, guns, surreys, and live Texas longhorns.

A **John Wayne Museum** and **Johnny Rodriguez Museum** are on the premises. Live gun fights and occasional country shows are presented Memorial Day weekend through Labor Day.

Ninety miles north of Brackettville in Sonora, the **Covered Wagon Dinner Theater** serves a chuckwagon meal accompanied by a musical telling of the area's history. The show is performed in a small natural amphitheater near the Caverns of Sonora, Saturday nights from mid-June through mid-August. Take I-10/Exit 392; (915) 387-3105.

GETTING THERE: Brackettville is 125 miles west of San Antonio. Open daily 9 A.M. to 6 P.M.; closed December 21–26. Admission $6 adults, $3 children. Take Hwy. 90 to Hwy. 674 north; (210) 563-2580.

Wink

ROY ORBISON FESTIVAL

The annual Roy Orbison Festival in the famed singer's hometown of Wink features a "Pretty Woman" contest, headline concert, street dance, flea market, and more in September. Orbison, who died of a heart attack in 1988, formed his first country band in high school here, and called it the Wink Westerners. Wink is on the southwest corner of the Panhandle near the New Mexico border. Take I-20/Exit 66 to Rte. 115 north; (915) 527-3441.

Utah

Vernal

ON THE OUTLAW TRAIL

The hills and mountains around Vernal were a haven for Butch Cassidy and his Wild Bunch around the turn of the century. In Robin Hood style, Butch and his sidekick, the Sundance Kid, robbed from rich train companies, banks, and cattle syndicates, earning the admiration of many small farmers and ranchers, who sheltered and fed them as they marauded along the "Outlaw Trail."

Vernal's **Outlaw Trail Theatre** presents an outdoor Western musical in June and July about these bad guys, and gals. Under starlit skies, their stories are told with original songs, live music, dance, actors on horses, and dramatic scenery. Tickets $5 to $7. Western Park Amphitheater, 302 E. 200 South St.; (801) 789-7396.

In mid-June, local groups sponsor a four-day **Butch Cassidy Outlaw Trail Ride** on Brush Creek Mountain, through areas frequented by Butch and the Wild Bunch; (800) 477-5558 or (801) 789-6932. The musical and trail ride are part of Vernal's Outlaw Trail Festival, celebrated mid-June through July.

In addition to sheltering outlaws, the Vernal area harbored one of the largest concentrations of fossilized dinosaur bones in the world. Dinosaur National Monument, with more than 2,300 fossilized dinosaur bones, is 25 miles to the northeast. The Utah Field House of Natural History in Vernal displays sixteen life-size models of prehistoric animals in its "dinosaur garden."

City attractions include a one-of-a-kind "First Ladies of the White House Doll Exhibit" at Uintah County Library; the Western Heritage Museum; and scenic and historic driving tours.

GETTING THERE: Vernal is in the northeast corner of Utah, at Hwys. 40 and 191. Contact the Dinosaur Land Travel Board; (800) 477-5558.

Vermont

Ben & Jerry's Vermont "One World, One Heart" Festival takes places in conjunction with the funky ice-cream makers' annual stockholders meeting. The free festival, usually the fourth Saturday in June at Sugarbush Valley Ski Resort in Warren, features a headline folk/country act, seven or eight bands, a food court, children's games, and free ice-cream samples for everyone. No alcohol, coolers, or dogs allowed. For current information about festivals sponsored by Ben & Jerry's, call (800) BJ-FESTS.

Ben & Jerry's offers fun 30-minute factory tours with demonstrations of ice-cream making and free samples at its Waterbury headquarters in north-central Vermont. Admission $1. Open daily 9 A.M. to 6 P.M. July and August; 9 A.M. to 5 P.M. the rest of the year. Reservations suggested. Take I-89/Exit 10 to Rte. 100 north; (802) 244-8687 or 244-6957.

Virginia

Chesapeake Bay Area

Alexandria
THE BIRCHMERE

Along with the signature on her photo on the wall at the Birchmere, Mary Chapin Carpenter scrawled, "To the best club in the world." Carpenter lives nearby in Washington, D.C., and cut her teeth as a performer at this intimate, homey joint. Specializing in acoustic country, folk, and bluegrass, the Birchmere is the kind of place where families, couples on dates, and big groups of friends mingle over barbecued chicken sandwiches, Cokes, and pitchers of beer.

The decor is unadorned wood paneling, drab gray carpet, black-and-white-checked tablecloths, and red leatherette chairs. There's no dance floor, just long rows of tables surrounding a smallish stage. In case patrons forget they're here to listen to music, not merely to hang out, smoking isn't permitted near the stage and patrons are reminded several times that talking isn't allowed during the show.

A mainstay of the Washington, D.C.–area country/bluegrass scene for three decades, the Birchmere is a terrific topper for a day touring the national monuments or Mount Vernon. Live music is performed every night. Tickets $15 to $20 per person; up to $35 for a headliner like Merle Haggard.

GETTING THERE: Alexandria is across the Potomac River from Washington, D.C. Take I-395 to Glebe Rd. S., then turn right on Mount Vernon Ave. 3901 Mount Vernon Ave.; (703) 549-5919 for schedule; (703) 573-SEAT for tickets.

Vienna
WOLF TRAP

Located in suburban Virginia, the **Wolf Trap Foundation for the Performing Arts** is America's first and only National Park devoted exclusively to the arts. In 1966, Catherine Filene Shouse donated 100
acres of Virginia farmland to the U.S. government; the park opened
in 1971. Until her death in 1994 at age 98, Mrs. Shouse was a familiar
sight on the grounds.

Wolf Trap is a magical place to see music, with performances year-
round in the outdoor 7,000-seat Filene Center amphitheater as well
as a more intimate indoor 350-seat venue called The Barns. You can
reserve seats or, for less money, spread out a blanket and picnic in
the lawn area. In addition to opera, symphonies, rock and roll, jazz,
and blues, Wolf Trap books a strong country, bluegrass, and folk program. Regular visitors include Mary Chapin Carpenter, Emmylou
Harris, and Vince Gill.

Annual festivals include the Washington Irish Folk Festival in late
May; Louisiana Swamp Romp, with Cajun, zydeco and New Orleans
swing in early June, and Ricky Skaggs's Pickin' Party mid-summer,
featuring top bluegrass performers.

GETTING THERE: Vienna is 10 miles outside Washington, D.C.
Wolf Trap is open year-round. Call for schedules. Ticket prices vary,
but generally cost $22 to $25 for reserved seats, and $10 to $16 for
the lawn. Take I-495 (Beltway)/Exit 12 (Dulles Toll Road). Shuttle
buses run from the West Falls Church metro station. 1624 Trap Rd.;
(703) 255-1900.

Williamsburg
COLONIAL AMERICA AND OLD DOMINION OPRY

Dozens of pioneer villages and living history museums around the
country attempt to show America as it was before the twentieth century, but **Colonial Williamsburg,** on the James River between Richmond and Norfolk, comes closest to the real thing. The 173-acre
museum meticulously restores Williamsburg to pre-Revolutionary

times, when it was Britain's political and cultural center in the New World. There are dozens of historic businesses, homes, stores, and taverns, as well as museums, workshops, and historical exhibits. Actors portray period characters, demonstrate trades and domestic crafts, and march in parades and military drill teams. Open year-round. Prices vary, depending on length of stay and degree of access. Take I-64/Exit 238 to Rte. 132 south; (800) HISTORY or (804) 220-7645.

Numerous tourist attractions surround Williamsburg, including the Busch Gardens amusement park, plantation tours, museums, and shopping. **Colonial National Historic Park** preserves homes and battlefields of Yorktown and Jamestown with living history, films, and exhibit galleries. East and west of Williamsburg, off I-64; (804) 898-3400.

Two miles west of Colonial Williamsburg, *Old Dominion Opry* is a variety show with regional and national talent performing country music and comedy in a 435-seat hall. Open year-round, Monday through Saturday, with fewer shows January through March 15. Admission $15 adults, $7 children. Take Hwy. 60 west. 3012 Richmond Rd.; (800) 2-VA-OPRY or (804) 564-0200.

GETTING THERE: Williamsburg is 50 miles east of Richmond and 45 miles north of Norfolk. Take I-64/Exit 242. Contact Williamsburg Area Visitors' Bureau; (800) 446-9244.

Hudgins
VIRGINIA'S LIL OLE OPRY

Since 1975, fine country music has been performed in Donk's Theater near the Chesapeake Bay. The show, presented every other Saturday night, features fifteen regulars during the first half and a headliner or talent show the second half. "It's like the *Grand Ole Opry,* only better," brags Harriett Farmer. "We don't stop for commercials like they do. It's a tight show." *Virginia's Lil Ole Opry* is run by Farmer; her brother James "Uncle Jimmy" Wickham Smith, the show's emcee and comedian; and her nieces Joanna Mullis and Betsy Ripley, who also perform.

Donk's Theater is a converted 504-seat movie house built in 1947.

It's located in the community of Hudgins in Mathews County, the smallest county in Virginia. Farmer will even pick up boaters docked at Gwynn's Island and drive them to the show.

GETTING THERE: Hudgins is in southeast Virginia on the Chesapeake Bay, across from Gwynn's Island. Opry admission $8 adults, $2 children. Take I-64/Exit 220 to Rte. 33 east, which becomes Rte. 198 into Hudgins; (804) 725-7760.

Blue Ridge Mountains

Winchester
CELEBRATING PATSY CLINE

In 1957, Patsy Cline's career exploded after she won an Arthur Godfrey talent program with "Walkin' After Midnight." She joined the *Grand Ole Opry* and recorded numerous number-one hits with producer Owen Bradley, including the classics "Crazy" and "I Fall to Pieces." Her life was tragically cut short at age 30 by a plane crash in Camden, Tennessee, that also killed manager Randy Hughes, and singers Hawkshaw Hawkins and Cowboy Copas.

While Cline was certainly a star while she was alive, her legend has grown phenomenally since her death. She was inducted into the Country Music Hall of Fame in 1973, and has been the subject of numerous books, plays, documentaries, and a U.S. postage stamp. A greatest-hits collection went triple platinum in 1991.

As her stature grew, squabbling among towns in northwest Virginia over who "gets" Patsy Cline heated up. The city of Winchester, where she attended high school, started her first bands, and was laid to rest, has hosted Patsy Cline festivals since 1987. Meanwhile, residents of Gore, where she was born as Virginia Hensley, have been grumbling that Winchester doesn't deserve Cline because they shunned the singer when she was alive. "We feel left out," a Gore shopkeeper told reporters. Other Virginia towns that have claimed Cline include Elkton, Middletown, and Edinburg.

Officials in Winchester are unfazed. "Up until Patsy was fifteen years old, [her family] moved 19 times," says Judy Kemp of the Winchester Chamber of Commerce. "We have a Patsy Cline subcommittee, and everyone is welcome."

No matter who wins, the fact is that Winchester has the most to offer Patsy Cline fans. The Chamber publishes a brochure with a **Patsy Cline driving tour,** which includes her modest home at 608 South Kent Street, the house in which she married Charlie Dick at 720 South Kent Street, and Handley High School on Valley Avenue. (Cline's mother lives nearby but prefers to maintain her privacy.)

As a teenager, she performed on Jim McCoy's show at **WINC Radio** (520 N. Pleasant Valley Rd.). She also worked as a waitress behind the counter at **Gaunt's Drug Store.** Pharmacist Harold "Doc" Madagan held onto one of the soda fountain's original booths and put up a row of Cline photographs below the prescription counter. S. Loudon St. and Valley Ave.; (540) 662-0383.

While still dreaming of a recording contract, Cline made her first rough recordings at **G&M Music,** which is still in business in Old Town Winchester. 38 W. Boscawen St.; (540) 662-3836.

Kurtz Cultural Center/Old Town Visitors' Center displays a small collection of Cline memorabilia including wedding photos, gold records, and a gray fur stole. Cameron and Boscawen Sts.; (540) 722-6367.

The Chamber planned to open a Patsy Cline museum in 1996. Charlie Dick, Cline's widower, says a major problem the museum faces is "what you're going to put in it. Her career was so short. At that time, you didn't think much about keeping things." Items scheduled to go on display include handmade stage clothing, gold and platinum records, awards, and furniture.

Among the service-club placards on the "Welcome to Winchester" sign at the entrance to town is one that reads "Home of Patsy Cline, Country Music Legend." Several roads have been renamed, including Patsy Cline Boulevard (between Millwood Avenue and Pleasant Valley Road) and Patsy Cline Memorial Highway (Rte. 522 south), the road to **Shenandoah Memorial Park** where she's buried. A bell tower has been erected at the cemetery in her honor, as well as a plaque on the main gate. From the cemetery's North Gate, take the first quick right to a marble bench on the left. Cline's simple marker reads, "Virginia H. Dick [Patsy Cline]. Death Can Not Kill What Never Dies."

Die-hard fans can drive out to the **Rainbow Road Club,** where Cline performed, on Rte. 340 north of Berryville. The **Handley Library** at Braddock and Picadilly Streets maintains Patsy Cline materials in its archives.

Since 1987, fans have gathered in Winchester over Labor Day for the **Celebrating Patsy weekend,** with benefit concerts, fan club meetings, bus tours, and a memorial service. In recent years, the Kountry Krackers, one of Cline's early bands, has performed at the reunion dance.

At one festival, Patsy Cline fans appeared to be a spirited, diverse bunch representing all ages, professions, and walks of life. "She sang like nobody else has ever sang," says James Walker, a Kroger employee who drove in from Lexington, Kentucky. "And she was spunky. She didn't take no crap off nobody!"

Junior O'Quinn, president of the International Hank Williams, Sr., Fan Club, traveled 300 miles to show his solidarity with Patsy Cline fans. "She was the female Hank Williams, as far as I'm concerned," says O'Quinn, a maintenance worker from Watauga, Tennessee. "In my opinion, four people will be remembered as long as there's music: Jimmie Rodgers, Hank Williams, Elvis Presley, and Patsy Cline. I don't think anyone else is in the ball game, let alone the park."

Long before Patsy Cline arrived, Winchester was a picturesque city with a fascinating 250-year history. (During the Civil War, Winchester changed hands 72 times in one day!) Author Willa Cather was born here, and Mary Tyler Moore's great-great-grandfather served as a doctor before the Civil War. Several theaters present live dramas and concerts, and there's plenty of antique shopping, outdoor recreation, and the beautiful Shenandoah Mountains.

Historical attractions include George Washington's Office Museum, from which the general supervised the building of Fort Loudon in 1755 and 1756; Stonewall Jackson's Headquarters Museum, the general's headquarters in 1861 and 1862; and Abram's Delight Museum, a 1754 Quaker meeting house.

The annual **Shenandoah Apple Blossom Festival,** begun more than 60 years ago, attracts more than 100,000 people. The four-day celebration, the first weekend in May, features a parade with national celebrities, food, and numerous special events around town. Sunday is a bluegrass festival with national and regional bands; (540) 662-3863.

(*See also:* Tennessee—Camden)

GETTING THERE: Winchester is in northwest Virginia, 75 miles west of Washington, D.C. Take I-81/Exit 313. Call the Chamber of Commerce; (800) 662-1360 or (540) 662-4135.

Staunton
AMERICA'S STATLER BROTHERS

Since their careers took off with "Flowers on the Wall" in 1965, the Statler Brothers have been the archetype for popular country and gospel-quartet singing. They toured with Johnny Cash through the 1960s, and scored numerous hits in the 1970s with songs like "Do You Remember These?" and "Class of '57." The group won the Country Music Association's Vocal Group of the Year award an incredible nine times between 1972 and 1984, and their TNN variety show is one of the highest-rated shows on cable television.

Based in Staunton, the Statler Brothers consist of Don and Harold Reid, Phil Balsley, and Jimmy Fortune, who replaced Lew DeWitt in 1982. (DeWitt suffered from Crohn's disease and died in 1990.) More than 30 years of memorabilia is displayed at the **Statler Brothers Complex** in the old Beverly Manor School, where the young quartet won their first talent contest. The complex also houses the group's corporate offices and recording studio. (In 1994, the Statler Brothers hosted their twenty-fifth and last "America's Birthday Celebration" on Independence Day.)

One free tour is offered daily at 2 P.M., Monday through Friday. The gift shop is open 10:30 A.M. to 3:30 P.M. weekdays. The complex is closed most major holidays, the week following July 4, and the last two weeks of December. Call for directions. 501 Thornrose; (540) 885-7297.

Attractions in Staunton include Woodrow Wilson's birthplace, historic walking tours, restaurants, antiques, shopping, and the beautiful Blue Ridge Mountains.

GETTING THERE: Staunton is in the heart of the Shenandoah Valley, 30 miles west of Charlottesville at I-81 and I-65. Call the Visitors' Center (800) 332-5219 or (540) 332-3972.

Southwest Virginia Appalachians

Galax
CAPITAL OF OLD-TIME MOUNTAIN MUSIC

In 1935, Galax's new Moose Lodge needed to raise some money. They advertised an **Old Fiddlers' Convention** in the local paper, dedicated to "keeping alive the memories and sentiments of days gone by and making it possible for people of today to hear and enjoy tunes of yesterday."

In their current brochure the sponsors note that "in some measure this purpose has been accomplished." The ongoing success of the four-day festival is testimony to the enduring appeal of old-time mountain music. Tunes considered nostalgic more than sixty years ago are still being played with great pride and skill in Galax.

The Old Fiddlers' Convention, the second full weekend in August, is the country's oldest and largest fiddlers' gathering, with tens of thousands of musicians and onlookers pouring into Galax each year. Contestants vie for $15,000 in prize money in more than a dozen categories, including old-time band, fiddle, autoharp, folk song, and flat-foot dance. There are also stage shows, and plenty of parking-lot picking.

Keep in mind that Galax's reputation as the "Capital of Old-Time Mountain Music" is not limited to the annual convention. Impromptu jam sessions often break out at **Barr's Fiddle Shop** on Main Street in downtown Galax. Just up the street, ***Mountain Music Jamboree*** is presented the second Saturday night of each month (except August), with traditional mountain music and dance. The 7 P.M.

show costs $4, at the Rex Theatre on Grayson St.; (540) 236-4885 or -2184.

About 30 miles east in Floyd, Cockram's General Store hosts a hopping *Friday Night Jamboree* year-round and occasional Saturdays. Floyd is at Hwy. 221 and Rte. 8. 206 Locust St.; (540) 745-4563.

GETTING THERE: Galax is just across the border from North Carolina. Take I-77/Exit 14 to Hwy. 58 west. Contact the Chamber of Commerce; (540) 236-2184.

Hiltons
YOUR CLINCH MOUNTAIN HOME

"My parents were in music," Janette Carter says modestly, explaining why she opened **The Carter Family Fold** with her brother Joe. The Fold honors the original Carter Family, country pioneers who were inducted into the Country Music Hall of Fame in 1970. Among their 300 recorded songs are such standards as "Wildwood Flower," "My Clinch Mountain Home," "Keep on the Sunny Side," and "Will the Circle Be Unbroken."

The Fold is an unusual 1,000-seat shed with a small stage and dance floor enclosed at the foot of Clinch Mountain in Hiltons (Maces Spring), in the southwest corner of Virginia. Bus seats and benches are arranged above the stage in rows, and the side and rear walls can be folded open in good weather.

Joe and Janette Carter open the Saturday night shows at the Carter Family Fold.

Saturday night dances at the Fold are homespun and loose, brimming with fun and laughter, music and dancing, and old-fashioned good fellowship. Janette starts the show by asking guests to call out where they're from. On a typical night, people may have come from Montana, England, Colorado, Georgia, Kentucky, New York, Washington, and California, even Iceland.

Janette and Joe lead off with a few Carter Family songs, she on autoharp, he on guitar. (No electric instruments are allowed here.) Then Janette introduces the headline act, a hip young bluegrass band called the Cluster Pluckers. By the third song, couples are two-stepping alongside tapping buck-dancers and cloggers, while the out-of-towners shuffle around happily. Little kids, teenagers, adults, and old-timers blend together in a beautiful swirl of clapping hands and stomping feet.

During the break, Carter Family recordings and T-shirts are raffled off and fresh popcorn, hot dogs, barbecued beef, and ice-cream sandwiches are sold. This is a good time to walk next door to the **Carter Family Museum,** in A.P. Carter's old store next door.

The one-room museum looks like a cluttered antique shop, until you realize that the dusty piles are actually the Carter Family's treasures, accompanied by hand-lettered explanations. A.P. Carter's Bible is "opened to where he last read before he died" in 1960. Visitors are warned not to play the piano in the corner because "it's very old." A table is stacked with scrapbooks, one labeled "The Joys and Sorrows of the Carter Family."

The original Carter Family consisted of A.P. and Sara (Joe and Janette's parents), and her cousin Maybelle. The group was first recorded in 1927 by Victor's Ralph Peer, nearby in Bristol, Tennessee/Virginia. A.P.'s songs, Sara and Maybelle's lovely harmonizing, along with Maybelle's intricate guitar-picking, made the Carter Family hugely popular in the twenties and thirties and ushered in the modern era of country music.

Despite widespread acclaim, the original group disbanded by 1941. Mother Maybelle started a new Carter Family act with her daughters June, Helen, and Anita. June's marriage to singer Carl Smith produced daughters Rosie and Carlene Carter, now a rockabilly-style singer. June later married Johnny Cash, and continues to perform with her sisters. The museum displays many personal snapshots of this remarkable family, along with Maybelle's handwritten lyrics to "Dixie Darling," a lock of Sara's hair, and A.P.'s work clothes.

After intermission, Joe sings a cornball song about a gal with sweaty feet and gas, then does his hilarious barnyard impressions of randy hound dogs, cat fights, and a sow courting a male hog. "It is a language that only male hogs and country boys can understand," he explains, before breaking into a series of maniacally lusty hog-grunts. "He shoulda never blowed in her ear," he quips. "That was all it took."

Some visiting musicians take the stage for a few songs each, then the Cluster Pluckers return for their second set. The picking and dancing could go on long into the night, but everyone leaves happily when it ends at a reasonable hour.

"Playing here is like taking a step back in history, preserving a way of life and entertainment that's basically gone," the Cluster Pluckers' lead singer, Margaret Bailey, says. "It's very unself-conscious, and a delight."

Another opportunity to spend time at the Fold is the annual **Carter Family Memorial Festival and Crafts Show** the first weekend in August. It features local and regional musicians, food, and crafts. "If you're passing through, make it a point to make a little trip and come to the Fold," Janette Carter says.

The graves of A.P. and Sara Carter can be visited at **Mt. Vernon Methodist Church** nearby. Maybelle Carter is buried in Hendersonville, outside Nashville, Tennessee.

GETTING THERE: Hiltons is abut 15 miles north of Kingsport, Tennessee. Shows begin at 8 P.M. on Saturday nights. The museum opens (Saturday only) at 6 P.M. Tickets $3.50 adults, $1 children. Take I-81/Exit 1 to Hwy. 58/421 west. Go about 17 miles to Rte. 709/614. Follow signs to the Carter Family Fold on Rte. 614 (A.P. Carter Highway); (540) 386-9480 or 386-6054.

Norton
MOUNTAIN MUSIC

In this rural hilly region of Appalachian Virginia, pure traditional music and bluegrass flow as naturally as a mountain stream. Near the Kentucky border in Norton, the well-named *Virginia Kentucky Opry* serves up live bluegrass, gospel, and country music by talented local artists every Saturday night. Radio station WAXM (93.5 FM) in Norton hosts and broadcasts the show, which is done in the style of the *Grand Ole Opry* with a variety of performers and commercial breaks. The fun begins at 7:30 P.M. and costs $5. 724 Park Ave.; (540) 679-1901.

At the **Country Cabin,** Norton's renovated 1937 landmark community center, lively performances of mountain music and clogging are presented on Saturday nights year-round. Hwy. 23; (540) 679-2632.

The **Wayne C. Henderson Music Festival** takes place in mid-June at Grayson Highlands State Park south of Marion. Take I-81 to Rte. 16 south; (540) 579-7092.

When he's not touring with the Clinch Mountain Boys, bluegrass legend Ralph Stanley lives in McClure, northeast of Norton. His four-day **Ralph Stanley Blue Grass Festival** is held Memorial Day weekend on Smith Ridge. From Hwy. 19, take Rte. 63 north to Rte. 643; (540) 395-6318.

The **Doc Boggs Festival** in Wise honors the banjo virtuoso famous for his two-finger, one-thumb picking style, on the second Saturday of September at Wise County Fairgrounds near Norton. Hwy. 23 and Rte. 72; (540) 679-2632.

(*See also:* Tennessee—Bristol; Kentucky—Country Music Highway; North Carolina.)

GETTING THERE: Norton is in the southwest corner of Virginia. From I-81, take I-181 through Kingsport to Hwy. 23 north to Norton. Contact Wise County/Norton Chamber of Commerce; (540) 679-0691.

For area information, call Blue Ridge Mountain Travel Center; (800) 822-9929.

Washington

George
WORLD'S LARGEST CHERRY PIE

Leave it to the folks from George, Washington, to give us the World's Largest Cherry Pie. The eight-foot behemoth is baked and served by the "Georgettes," a local ladies' club, for the town's annual **George Washington Fourth of July Celebration.** (The recipe calls for 150 pounds flour, 72 pounds shortening, 100 gallons cherries, 200 pounds tapioca, 2 cups almond extract, and 1½ cups red food coloring.) The **George Washington Birthday Party** takes place on President's Day in February, with another giant cake, country bands, and children's activities.

George is a small, planned community (pop. 300) established in the 1950s by a developer named Charlie Brown, who decided that there ought to be a town named George in the state of Washington. (After learning about George, folks in Ismay, Montana, whimsically renamed their town "Joe" a few years ago.) The streets of George are all named for varieties of cherries, and the main thoroughfares are planted with cherry, dogwood, and magnolia trees, which George Washington enjoyed at Mount Vernon.

Six miles west of George, the **Gorge Amphitheater** is a 20,000-seat outdoor venue overlooking the spectacular Columbia River Gorge. The summer "In the Gorge by George" concert series features country, rock, and blues headliners. Camping is available on site. Take I-90/Exit 143 or 149 and follow the signs.

Area attractions include parks and outdoor recreation, skiing, hunting, fishing, and several wineries. "The Greatest Dam Tour in the World" is a driving tour of seven hydroelectric power stations on the Columbia River including the Grand Coulee Dam, the largest concrete structure in the world.

GETTING THERE: George is 150 miles east of Seattle and 140 miles west of Spokane. Take I-90/Exit 149 to Rte. 281 south. For concert and festival information, contact the George Visitors' Center; (509) 785-3831 or 785-6955.

West Virginia

Wheeling

JAMBOREE U.S.A. AT CAPITOL MUSIC HALL

West Virginia radio station WWVA made its first broadcast over a home-built 50-watt transmitter in December 1926. In early 1933, the first *WWVA Jamboree* was aired. The show's popularity grew, while the station's signal steadily increased to a powerful 50,000 watts, bringing first-rate country music into homes all over the Northeast on Saturday nights.

The *Jamboree* was based at the Capitol Music Hall from 1933 to 1942. During the forties and fifties, the show's regular cast featured the likes of Grandpa Jones, the Osborne Brothers, Wilma Lee, Stoney Cooper, and Dick Curless. It skipped around various venues in Wheeling before settling back into the Capitol Music Hall in 1969.

Today, *Jamboree U.S.A.* features a regular cast, with a different top-name special guest each week. Tickets $17 to $25, depending on the featured artist. The show is broadcast on country music stations WWVA (1170-AM) and WOVK (98.7-FM). Take I-70 to 1015 Main St. S.; (800) 624-5456 or (304) 234-0050.

Doc Williams and his wife, Chickie, have been a constant in the *Jamboree* cast for nearly 60 years, sticking with traditional country music all the way. When I queried Doc Williams recently, he wrote back, "I've had a very rewarding and satisfying life, and am still *working* at 81 years." The **Legendary Doc Williams Country Store** across the street from the Capitol Music Hall sells Western wear, country recordings, and souvenirs. 1004 Main St.; (304) 233-4771.

Every year, WWVA puts on the **Jamboree in the Hills,** so-called "Super Bowl of Country Music," the third weekend in July. The festival takes place about 15 miles west of Wheeling in St. Clairsville, Ohio, with four days of top country performers in an outdoor amphitheater.

Wheeling, on the banks of the Ohio River, was a thriving frontier port and industrial center for most of its history. The last battle of the American Revolution was fought here in 1782 (news of the peace had not yet reached the city), and the city twice served as West Virginia's capital.

The **Heritage Tour** of Wheeling includes the Wheeling suspension bridge, the longest in the world in 1849. Wheeling National Heritage Area is an ambitious $50 million redevelopment effort of the downtown and waterfront. Wheeling Artisan Center, with crafts, mountain music, and historic reenactments, was expected to open in spring of 1996.

GETTING THERE: Wheeling is in northern West Virginia between Pennsylvania and Ohio, 60 miles west of Pittsburgh on I-70. Contact the Visitors' Bureau; (800) 828-3097.

Oak Hill
HANK WILLIAMS MARKER

Hank Williams was discovered dead in the backseat of his Cadillac on New Year's Day 1953, in the town of Oak Hill about 15 miles north of Beckley. A young man named Charles Carr was driving Williams to a show in Canton, Ohio, when he stopped in front of Burdette's Pure Oil Service station to get directions and found that his passenger was dead. A **marker** on Main Street in front of the public library in Oak Hill commemorates Williams. (*See also:* Alabama—Montgomery, Georgiana.)

GETTING THERE: Oakhill is in southern West Virginia, 40 miles south of Charleston. Take I-79 to Hwy. 19 south. For area information, call (800) VISIT-WVA.

Milton
MOUNTAINEER OPRY HOUSE

October through May, Mountaineer Opry House in Milton presents bluegrass music on Saturday nights (and occasional Fridays) in a 570-seat theater next to the interstate. Two or three bands perform during every show, from national stars to local favorites. "We don't make any money. We just really like bluegrass," says Mary Stevens, who runs the Opry House with her husband, Larry.

Milton is in southern West Virginia, midway between Charleston and Huntington. Shows are at 8 P.M. Tickets $8. Take I-64/Exit 28. The theater is beside the highway, next to an Exxon station; (304) 733-2721.

Wisconsin

The **Wisconsin Dells,** north of Madison, are 15 miles of fantastic sandstone formations carved by the Wisconsin River, to depths of 150 feet. The region offers fishing and outdoor recreation in the summer, as well as hundreds of miles of snowmobile trails, and cross-country and downhill skiing in the winter. Attractions include water and amusement parks, tourist museums, and river cruises on amphibious "duck" boats.

The *Wisconsin Opry* presents local country bands and national artists nightly, Memorial Day weekend through mid-September. Dinner can also be purchased. Take I-90/94/Exit 92 to Hwy. 12 south; (608) 254-7951. Headline acts are booked at the **Crystal Grand Theatre** in downtown Wisconsin Dells. Call for a schedule. Hwy. 23; (800) 696-7999.

GETTING THERE: The town of Wisconsin Dells is 55 miles north of Madison. Take I-90 to I-90/94 north; (800) 22-DELLS or (608) 254-8088.

Wyoming

Cheyenne
FRONTIER DAYS

In 1996, Cheyenne celebrated its 100th Frontier Days, known as "The Daddy of 'Em All." This popular festival, the last full week in July, draws 300,000 people for the world's largest professional rodeo, four parades, free pancake breakfasts, Western art, chuckwagon races, square-dancing, a carnival midway, and an Indian village and pow-wow. There's free live entertainment all day long, and a headline country concert every night. Frontier Park, 8th and Carey Aves.; (800) 227-6336 or (307) 778-7222.

Cheyenne, the state capital, is a classic Western town in the grass-lands of southeast Wyoming with several museums, historic sites, parks, and the Wyoming Game and Fish Visitors' Center. Rodeos take place on Tuesday and Wednesday nights, June through August. The Old Town square comes alive with gunfight reenactments and Wild West activities all summer.

Cheyenne Frontier Days Old West Museum displays one of the best Western wagon collections in the nation, festival memorabilia, and changing art and historic exhibits. Admission $3. Call for hours. Frontier Park at N. Carey Ave.; (307) 778-7290.

GETTING THERE: Cheyenne is in southeast Wyoming at I-25 and I-80. Contact the Cheyenne Visitors' Bureau; (800) 426-5009 or (307) 778-3133.

Wind River Country

The **Wind River Indian Reservation** in central-west Wyoming en-compasses more than 2 million acres in a high, broad valley framed by the Wyoming Rocky Mountains. Home to Shoshoni and Apache Indians, Wind River country is dramatic territory for hiking, trail riding, skiing, fishing, and wildlife viewing, as well as exploring ghost towns and deep wagon ruts on the Oregon Trail. Butch Cassidy roamed Wind River Country in the 1880s and 1890s. Powwows, rodeos, and festivals take place in the spring, summer, and fall in many of the region's towns.

Over Memorial Day weekend, Shoshoni hosts Wyoming's **Old-time Fiddlers' Contest,** with serious competition and a no-holds-barred trick and fancy fiddling contest. The small town's historic Yellowstone Drug Store on Main Street serves memorable milkshakes and malts at an old-fashioned counter. Shoshoni is 120 miles west of Casper, just east of Boysen Reservoir at Hwys. 20 and 26; (307) 876-2515.

Twenty miles southwest of Shoshoni in Riverton, the **1838 Mountain Man Rendezvous** commemorates actual gatherings of fur traders and trappers at the confluence of the Big Wind and Little Wind Rivers in 1830 and 1838. During the first week of July, the original gatherings are reenacted. Wyoming's largest **Cowboy Poetry Round-up** takes place here for two days in mid-October. Take I-25 to Hwy. 26 west; (307) 856-4801.

The **South Pass City Historic Site** is a well-preserved ghost town, a real boom-and-bust mining town circa 1867 to 1875. The women's suffrage movement traces its roots to South Pass City, where in 1869 the town's representative introduced the first successful women's voting bill. (This is how Wyoming got its nickname, "The Equality State.") This attraction includes more than two dozen structures, 30,000 artifacts, living history demonstrations, films, and nature trails. Admission $1. Open daily 9 A.M. to 6 P.M., May 15 to October 15. Take I-80 to Hwy. 191 north to Rte. 28 (35 miles south of Lander); (307) 332-3684.

GETTING THERE: Wind River country is about 100 miles west of Casper and 140 miles north of Rock Springs. Take Hwys. 287, 20, or 26. Contact the Wind River Visitors' Council; (800) 645-6233.

Cody
BUFFALO BILL HISTORICAL CENTER

Founded by Col. William "Buffalo Bill" Cody himself in 1898, Cody is the eastern gateway to Yellowstone National Park. The famed Pony Express rider, Civil War scout, buffalo hunter, and Wild West showman owned a ranch here where he wanted to be buried. (After his death in Denver, Cody was entombed on Colorado's Lookout Mountain, much to the chagrin of Cody residents.)

The small city offers spectacular outdoor recreation and several scenic driving tours; President Theodore Roosevelt called the Wapiti Valley, between Cody and Yellowstone, the "most scenic 52 miles in America." Nightly rodeos take place here June through August, and Western music and entertainment abounds at saloons and lodges around town.

The Buffalo Bill Historical Center in Cody is considered one of the nation's finest Western museums, a vivid and lively documentation of the region's history and culture. The 150,000-square-foot Center is divided into four main museums: The Buffalo Bill Museum displays thousands of pieces of memorabilia; the Plains Indian Museum offers exhibits on the history, culture, and art of nomadic regional tribes; the Whitney Gallery of Western Art displays fine paintings and sculptures; and the Cody Firearms Museum features thousands of guns. Admission $7. Open daily, with varying hours. Closed January through mid-February. Hwy. 14-16-20 at 702 Sheridan St.; (307) 587-4771.

Annual events in Cody include the Buffalo Bill Birthday Celebration at the Historical Center in late February; Cowboy Songs and Range Ballads, with three days of music, humor, and poetry the first weekend in April; and the Cody Stampede, featuring rodeo, parades, and Western entertainment, the first weekend in July.

GETTING THERE: Cody is 50 miles east of Yellowstone National Park in northwest Wyoming, at Hwy. 14 and Rte. 120. Contact Cody Country Visitors' Council; (307) 587-2297.

Jackson

GORGEOUS GATEWAY TO YELLOWSTONE

Located in the Jackson Hole valley, the Old West town of Jackson serves as the southern gateway to Yellowstone National Park. Crowned by the glorious Grand Teton Mountains, the wilderness surrounding Jackson Hole is simply awesome, with dramatic jagged peaks, waterfalls, and canyons.

Area attractions include hiking, fishing, skiing, biking, horseback riding, and float trips on the Snake River; as well as the fine National Wildlife Art Museum, performing arts, galleries—and gondola rides up steep mountain slopes.

Rodeos take place on Wednesday and Saturday nights, Memorial Day weekend through Labor Day, and Wild West gunfights are staged on the town square nightly. Saloons in town play live country music, with plenty of room for two-stepping and Western Swing dancing.

Several **chuckwagon** outfits offer cowboy-style dining accompanied by live Western music and comedy during the summer season. These shows cost around $13 including the meal, and several begin with wagon rides to an outdoor ranch site. Reservations required. Call for details.

- A-OK Corral Covered Wagon Cook-out and Western Show (*breakfast and dinner*); (307) 733-6556.
- Bar J Chuckwagon Supper and Original Western Show (*dinner*); (307) 733-3370.
- Bar T-5 Covered Wagon Cook-out and Wild West Show (*dinner*); (307) 733-5386.
- Grand Teton Covered Wagon Cook-outs (*breakfast and dinner*); (800) 729-1410.

Over Memorial Day weekend, **Old West Days** is four days of parades, rodeos, and street dancing in Jackson, with a cowboy poetry gathering, dance contest, and mountain-man rendezvous.

The **Cowboy Ski Challenge** at Jackson Hole Resort features cowboys and their steeds in hilarious competition on snowy slopes of the Grand Tetons. The three-day festival is held in late February, with a Friday-night headline country-western concert; (307) 733-3316.

At Grand Targhee Resort, 42 miles northwest of Jackson near the Idaho border, a four-day **Bluegrass Music Festival** takes place in mid-

August with music, crafts, and food. Take Rte. 22/33 north to Driggs; (800) TARGHEE.

GETTING THERE: Jackson is 50 miles south of Yellowstone National Park and 15 miles south of Grand Teton National Park, at Hwy. 89 and Rte. 33. Contact the Jackson Hole Visitors' Center; (800) 782-0011 or (307) 733-4005.

Canada

Nova Scotia
CANADA'S COUNTRY LEGENDS

Three of Canada's biggest country music stars were raised in Nova Scotia, a province composed of several large islands east of Maine. Attractions featuring Hank Snow, Anne Murray, and Rita MacNeil can anchor for a tour of these rugged, beautiful islands.

Hank Snow, an early protégé of Jimmie Rodgers's, was already a star in Canada before he achieved success in America with songs like "Movin' On" and "I've Been Everywhere." The Yodeling Ranger recorded more than 100 albums, with 35 Top Ten hits; he joined the *Grand Ole Opry* in 1950, and was inducted into the Country Music Hall of Fame in 1979.

Snow was born in 1914 in Brooklyn, on the south shore of Nova Scotia, and used to walk several miles along train tracks to attend school in Liverpool. The railroad depot at the end of those tracks is now home to the **Hank Snow Country Music Centre.** The museum was expected to officially open in spring of 1996.

Michael Anthony of the Friends of Hank Snow Society says the museum displays a large collection of Snow memorabilia, including the yellow 1947 Cadillac that transported the singer and his family to Chicago, Hollywood, and then Texas. A 30-foot-long mural depicts Snow and his Nashville friends.

The History of Country Music Room features vintage instruments, photographs, videos, and exhibits on important Canadian country artists such as Carroll Baker, Wilf Carter, and Ronnie Prophet. The Centre also houses a music library and archives. Open May to October, and by appointment. Call for hours. Admission $4. Allow an hour. Take Hwy. TC 103/Exit 19 to Bristol Avenue; (902) 354-4675.

The Society hosts the **Hank Snow Birthday Concert and Celebration** in Liverpool on the weekend closest to May 9, and a three-day **Hank Snow Tribute** at Queens County Fair Grounds in Caledonia in mid-August. The festival features concerts, a "Sounds Like Hank" contest, and barbecue.

"From Springhill to the World" is the motto of the **Anne Murray Centre,** located in the popular singer's hometown in northern Nova Scotia. While working as a physical-education teacher, Murray sang in the chorus of the *Singalong Jubilee,* a popular folk-music showcase on CBC Halifax. In 1970, *Snowbird* was released in the United States, instantly catapulting her to stardom. Murray has since sold 20 million records, won three Country Music Association awards and four Grammys, and toured the world.

Built jointly by Canada's federal and provincial governments, the $1.5 million Anne Murray Centre has succeeded in drawing tourists to Springhill since it opened in 1989. A series of award-winning exhibits and audiovisual displays feature Murray's awards, memorabilia, and career highlights. Another attraction nearby, the **Springhill Miners Museum,** takes visitors on a guided tour of the town's last working coal mine, 300 feet below the surface.

Both attractions are open daily 9 A.M. to 5 P.M., mid-May through early October, and by appointment and by chance in the off season. Tickets $5 (museum). Allow one hour. Take Hwy. 104/Exit 5 to Rte. 142. Turn left on Rte. 2, then right on Main St.; (902) 597-8614.

Rita MacNeil was born in Big Pond, a hamlet on the coast of Nova Scotia's Cape Breton Island. Although relatively unknown in the United States, MacNeil has released twelve albums, received many Canadian awards, and was appointed to the prestigious Order of Canada in 1992. Her ballad, "Working Man," is a moving tribute to the region's coal miners.

This homegrown, fedora-wearing singer/songwriter, who describes her craft as "the music of Rita, songs of love and friendship," has put Big Pond on the map. In 1989, she converted a tiny 1938 schoolhouse into the charming **Rita MacNeil Tea Room.** Staffed by local residents, the Tea Room serves fresh-baked goods and sandwiches and displays MacNeil's awards, photographs, and gifts from fans. Open daily 9 A.M. to 7 P.M., June through mid-October. Take TC Hwy. 104 to Rte. 4; (902) 828-2667.

GETTING THERE: Nova Scotia is a province in eastern Canada. Take I-95 to TC Hwy. 2 east. Contact the Visitors' Bureau; (800) 341-6096.

Saskatchewan
CANADA'S COUNTRY MUSIC HALL OF FAME

The Canadian Country Music Hall of Fame, run by Canadian singer/songwriter Gary Buck, pays tribute to Hank Snow, Myrna Lorrie, Wilf Carter, and other national legends in Swift Current, a city in southwest Saskatchewan.

The 4,800-square-foot museum displays a collection of stage costumes, gold records, and memorabilia such as Johnny Horton's Canadian-crafted guitar and Ian Tyson's saddle. Inductees are honored with original portraits by Canadian artist Ken Danby. Free live entertainment is presented from time to time.

GETTING THERE: Swift Current is 150 miles west of Regina. The museum is open daily 9 A.M. to 9 P.M., late May through October; 9 A.M. to 5 P.M. Monday through Friday, and 1 to 7 P.M. Saturday and Sunday, the rest of year. Allow an hour. Admission $4. Take TC Hwy. 1. 1100 5th Ave. N.E.; (519) 886-8500.

Index